The City in the Third World

The City in the Third World

EDITED BY
D. J. DWYER

BARNES & NOBLE
BOOKS
10 East 53d St., New York 10022
(a division of Harper & Row Publishers, Inc.)

Selection, editorial matter, translations and introduction
© D. J. Dwyer 1974

First published in the United Kingdom 1974 by
The Macmillan Press Ltd

Published in the U.S.A. 1974 by
Harper & Row Publishers, Inc.
Barnes & Noble Import Division

ISBN 06–491860–2

Printed in Great Britain

Contents

Acknowledgements

THE editor and publisher wish to thank the following for permission to publish articles and extracts:

William H. Bartsch, 'Unemployment in Less Developed Countries: A Case Study of a Poor District of Tehran' from *International Development Review*, **13** (1971), reprinted by permission of Society for International Development; Gerald H. Blake, 'Urbanisation in North Africa'; Jennifer M. Bray, 'The Craft Structure of a Traditional Yoruba Town' from *Transactions of the Institute of British Geographers*, No. 46, by permission of the Institute of British Geographers; John E. Brush, 'Spatial Patterns of Population in Indian Cities' reprinted by permission from the *Geographical Review*, **58** (1968), copyrighted by the American Geographical Society; Kingsley Davis, 'Colonial Expansion and Urban Diffusion in the Americas' reprinted by permission from *International Journal of Comparative Sociology*, **1** (1960); D. J. Dwyer, 'Attitudes Towards Spontaneous Settlement in Third World Cities' from *The City As A Centre of Change in Asia* (ed. D. J. Dwyer, 1972) reprinted by permission of Hong Kong University Press; Bert F. Hoselitz, 'The Role of Urbanization in Economic Development: Some International Comparisons' from *India's Urban Future* (ed. Roy Turner, 1961), originally published by the University of California Press, reprinted by permission of the Regents of the University of California; B. S. Hoyle, 'The Economic Expansion of Jinja, Uganda' reprinted by permission from the *Geographical Review*, **53** (1963), copyrighted by the American Geographical Society; Barrington Kaye, 'Some Residents of Upper Nankin Street, Singapore' from *Upper Nankin Street, Singapore* reprinted by permission of the University of Malaya Press Ltd; A. L. Mabogunje, 'The Pre-Colonial Development of Yoruba Towns', from *Yoruba Towns* reprinted by permission of Ibadan University Press; Rhoads Murphey, 'The City as A Centre of Change: Western Europe and China' reproduced by permission from *Annals of the Association of American Geographers*, **44** (1954); Ronald Ng, 'A Study of Recent Internal Migration In Thailand' reprinted by permission from *The*

8 *Acknowledgements*

Journal of Tropical Geography, **31** (1970); Nan Pendrell, 'Squatter Life in Salvador'; Dr L. Sternstein, 'Planning the Future of Bangkok' from *The City As A Centre of Change in Asia*, (ed. D. J. Dwyer, 1972), reprinted by permission of Hong Kong University Press; Alan Turner and Jonathan Smulian, 'New Cities in Venezuela' from *Town Planning Review*, **42** (1971), reprinted by permission of Liverpool University Press.

Introduction

D. J. DWYER

Towns and cities are rapidly expanding in both the industrialised and the developing countries and this unprecedented urban growth is bringing with it a host of problems. It is probably true to say that urban problems today are reaching such dimensions on a world scale as to place them third in importance only to those of the threat to civilisation from nuclear warfare and the continued existence of hunger among large sections of the world's population. Yet what is not yet widely enough appreciated is the fact that more than half of the world's urban population now lives in the developing countries rather than in the industrialised countries. This proportion will increase significantly before the end of the present century. It is the purpose of this book to outline the major dimensions of the urbanisation process in the developing countries and also to examine both the more pressing urban problems which have arisen and the directions of current thinking towards the solution of those problems.

Though precise statistical information on urbanisation is very incomplete at a world scale—for example, reliable data on the size of urban populations is still lacking for more than half the population of the Third World—it is thought that between 1800 and 1970 the population of the world living in towns of 5000 inhabitants or more increased from 81 millions to 1399 millions, or by 17 times (Table 1). Total world population grew much more slowly, in fact by a little less than 3 times over the same period. The last one hundred and fifty years or so have therefore seen a revolutionary shift in the location of the world population and in the relative importance of city and countryside. Nevertheless, the earth as a whole is not yet very highly urbanised (Table 2). The transition to a fully urbanised world—that is, one as urbanised as the United States or Britain today—is proceeding so rapidly, however, that it may be completed within less than a century.

Much of the future development towards a fully urbanised world will concern the Third World, though historically the process has

For References to the Introduction, see page 25.

Table 1   Growth of the World's Urban and Rural Populations

Year	Total population ($\times 10^{-6}$)	Rural ($\times 10^{-6}$)	Urban* ($\times 10^{-6}$)
1850	1262	1181	81
1900	1650	1426	224
1950	2520	1796	706
1970†	3628	2229	1399

* Population in places of 5000 and more.
† Projection based upon data available in December 1968.
Source: Based on Kingsley Davis. The Role of Urbanisation in the Development Process. Unpublished paper presented at the Sixth Rehovot Conference, Israel, August 1971, p. 12, Table 5.

been led by the today's industrialised countries. The urban process is by no means new; there were cities over five thousand years ago, but before the Industrial Revolution they were relatively few. The acceleration in the urbanisation process which occurred during the early nineteenth century was associated with industrialisation and it affected first the countries of Western Europe and the U.S.A. The new industries in these countries made such demands that, as Hoselitz has stated, '. . . in the long run the period of European

Table 2   Historical Change in World Urban and City Proportions

Year	Proportion urban*	Proportion in cities of 100 000+
	(Percentage of world population)	
1800	3·0	1·7
1850	6·4	2·3
1900	13·6	5·5
1950	28·2	16·2
1970†	38·6	23·8

* Population in places of 5000 or more.
† Projection based upon data available in December 1968.
Source: As for Table 1; p. 10, Table 2.

industrialisation and urbanisation must be regarded as one characterised by shortage of labour'[1]; but health conditions in the cities were so poor that at certain periods comparatively little of their population growth occurred through natural increase. Their expansion was in varying measures due to their power to attract rural migrants. Concurrently, the rationalisation and technical development of agriculture allowed declining rural populations to participate in rising living standards resulting from accelerated national economic growth.

Today, there are two distinct facets within the general urbanisation trend. The industrialised countries are showing declining rates, but because they include only one quarter of the world's population this has not been sufficient to retard the general trend. The huge populations of the Third World, in contrast, are playing a major part in an urbanisation more massive than any before.

Unlike the early industrial cities, contemporary cities in the Third World are not death-traps; in fact in many cases their health records are almost as good as today's cities in industrialised countries, and they are far better than those of the Third World's rural areas. The Third World city has benefited disproportionately from the conquest of death that has taken place in the tropics, but at the same time the fertility of its inhabitants has remained very high both by the contemporary standards and by the historical standards of the cities of the industrialised countries. As Davis reports, city-dwelling Moslem couples interviewed in Lebanon in 1957 had a fertility that would yield 6·6 children to each wife if she lived through the reproductive period. In Accra, Ghana, the figure in 1960 was 6 children. In Bangalore, India, the average woman aged 45 or over had borne 5·3 children[2].

This combination of 'pre-industrial fertility and post-industrial mortality', to quote Davis[3], has given the contemporary Third World city the greatest rate of natural increase ever found in cities. Yet rural–urban migration is also proceeding apace. The Third World today is the scene of the greatest movements of people in history, and though the waves of political refugees from war-torn areas usually make the headlines, it is a quieter, spontaneous movement of people from the countryside to the cities which constitutes the mainstream. Paradoxically, the rate of urbanisation and the current size of the major cities throughout the developing world seem to be more expressions of lack of national economic development than the results of it. Conditions in the cities, poor though they may be, nevertheless seem to be becoming increasingly preferred by the rural masses, and it can only be concluded that this largely reflects the abysmal lack of development in the countryside.

The result is a swelling tide of rural–urban migration. To take the case of metropolitan Manila as an illustration, the projected 1977 population of the city based upon a rate of natural increase of 3·2 per cent (the projected national average rate of population growth for the period 1955–77) would be 3·7 millions. But the lowest United Nations' estimate of actual population for the city in 1977, based upon current rates of growth, is 5·1 millions, indicating the addition of almost one and a half million in-migrants and their children during the decades of the sixties and the seventies[4]. The United Nations' 'high estimate' for the 1977 population of Metropolitan Manila is 6·2 millions. What makes such figures even more disturbing is that so far urban growth in the developing countries, significant though it has been in recent decades, has made little impression upon the vast reservoirs of population in the countryside. Figures for Venezuela show that while the number of people living in urban areas (in this case towns and cities of 5000 or more inhabitants) increased massively from 0·74 to 4·3 millions during the period 1936–61, the nation's non-urban population also grew, from 2·6 to 3·2 millions[5].

As a result of these trends, the balance of urban populations between the industrialised countries and the Third World is in process of most significant change. Urban populations in the developing countries are now growing twice as fast as those in the industrialised countries. They are also growing in numbers greatly exceeding those of the industrialised countries, even during the periods of most rapid growth of the latter.

In consequence, whereas the number of people in settlements of 20 000 inhabitants or more in the industrialised countries grew from 198 millions in 1920 to 450 millions in 1960, or more than doubled, this increase was dwarfed by a quadrupling of similar populations in the Third World, from 69 to 310 millions[6]. The growth of populations in settlements of 20 000 inhabitants or more in the industrialised countries is expected to amount to 211 millions during the period 1960 to 1980 and to 240 millions during the period 1980 to 2000. However, in the Third World an additional

383 and 743 millions respectively is expected for each period, and by the year 2000 the Third World should account for 1436 millions of the expected world total of 2337 millions living in settlements of 20 000 or more. By the end of the present century the balance of world urban population will have clearly tipped towards the Third World; indeed at present we are just over the point of equilibrium in urban population distribution between the industrialised and the developing countries. In all probability we have reached the end of an era of association of urbanisation with Western-style industrial-isation and socio-economic characteristics. The magnitudes alone of some of the urban increments expected in the Third World are such that it will probably become increasingly debatable to what extent this urbanisation can be related to very much that is meaning-ful in past Western urban experience.

There are, of course, significant differences both in rates of urban-isation in the distribution of urban populations within the Third World itself. Africa is the least urbanised of the major regions but also the one which is now urbanising the most rapidly. There is a marked difference within Africa itself, however, between the countries north of the Sahara, which already have reached a level of urbanisation comparable to that of Southern Europe, and those to the south which, with the exception of South Africa, as a group are the least urbanised on earth outside of Oceania (Table 3).

A similar dichotomy is apparent in Latin America—which in general is by far the most highly urbanised major region of the Third World—between Venezuela, Chile, the River Plate countries and the remainder. The urban problems of Africa and Latin America, severe as they may be, are nevertheless dwarfed by those of Asia which, largely because of the vastness of its total population, is already an urban colossus even in comparison with the industrial-ised countries. It has been estimated that in 1960 Asia contained between 36 and 39 per cent of the total world population in towns of 20 000 inhabitants or more, depending upon how China's urban population was estimated[7]. This compares with 5 per cent for Africa and 9–10 per cent for Latin America, with 23–24 per cent for Europe (excluding the U.S.S.R.) and with 12–13 per cent for North America. In terms of bald statistics Asia's probable urban future is indeed frightening, for it is expected that by the year 2000 its urban population, even defined at the relatively high cut-off point of 20 000 persons, will have increased to 993 millions[8]. This compares

Introduction

Table 3   World Urbanisation, 1950 and 1960

Regions	Level of urbanisation (percent of total population)*		Percent of increase 1950–60
	1950	1960	
World total	21	25	17
More developed regions	37	41	10
North America	43	46	6
Europe (excluding U.S.S.R.)	37	40	8
Northwestern	52	54	3
Central	37	40	9
Southern	23	27	16
U.S.S.R.	31	36	17
Australia and New Zealand	58	65	12
Less developed regions	14	18	28
Africa	10	13	37
North	21	26	23
South, West, and East	6	9	50
Asia	14	18	26
[excluding China (Mainland)]	17	19	15
China (Mainland)	10	15	50
Latin America	25	32	28
Argentina, Chile, Uruguay	47	56	19
Remainder of Latin America	21	28	33

* In places with 20 000 or more inhabitants.
Source: Glen T. Trewartha. *A Geography of Population: World Patterns.*
New York, 1969, p. 152.

with a 1960 level of 265 millions, when already in terms of their physical facilities many of Asia's cities were being described as in a state of crisis. Clearly, it is in Asia that the core of most Third World urbanisation problems lies.

There will be about 6×10^9 people on Earth by the end of the present century and one half of them may be urban. How long, it may be asked, will the level of world urbanisation continue to rise, and how fast. According to Kingsley Davis, who is perhaps the foremost student of the statistical dimensions of world urbanisation, this is hard to say with any degree of finality at the present time, but during the two decades between 1950 and 1970 the possibility of a gradual slackening in the rate of urbanisation has become more likely while the prospect of much acceleration has become correspondingly more remote. At some time not far off, Davis predicts, the rate of urbanisation must begin to taper off, for if the 1950–70 rate was to continue, 100 per cent of the human population would be living in urban places by the year 2031[9]. At present, therefore, we may be living during the peak period of urban formation in world history. As we have seen already, however, it is precisely this most crucial period which largely concerns the developing rather than the industrialised countries.

THE READINGS

Problems of urbanisation in the developing countries cannot be considered in isolation from the current preoccupation of those countries with the search for modernisation and rates of economic growth adequate enough not only to sustain their rapidly growing populations but also to leave sufficient over to make significant improvements in general living standards. One dimension that is often neglected in current development studies is the historical and therefore it is worth emphasising, not only that the events of the colonial period were of fundamental importance in helping to shape present patterns of urban growth and urbanisation, but also that the roots of urban growth in the developing countries extend back to earlier periods than the colonial one. The paper by Mabogunje with which the Readings begin illustrates clearly the very vigorous traditions of urbanism that were present in the Yoruba country long before the first colonial powers penetrated West Africa. In the New World, the Spanish *conquistadores*, whose urban progress is described by Davis in the second paper, discovered magnificent indigenous cities which all too often they obliterated prior to imposing an urban mesh of their own creation upon the countryside[10]. In Asia too, pre-colonial urban traditions were strong, for example, in South-East Asia both important trading towns like Malacca and major cult centres such as Angkor may clearly be distinguished.

Although the imprint of pre-colonial urbanisation is still apparent in many cases, and remains significant, within the present-day urban mosaic, a very large number of the most important contemporary cities in the developing countries were colonial creations. Arab colonisation resulted in the creation of many new towns in the

Middle East at a time when Europe was passing through the Dark Ages[11]. In South-East Asia at a later period, to take a second example, all of the largest cities except Bangkok were developed as the seats of colonial powers, and though Bangkok was nominally the capital of an independent state, like the other cities of South-East Asia its growth was closely linked to the economic penetration by the West which was a major motif of colonial rule.

Most of the larger towns in the developing countries grew during the colonial period through being locations from which the development of natural resources could be directed[12]. Characteristically, they grew at points from which large productive areas could be commanded, and especially wherever access to the sea coincided with this requirement. A recurrent theme in their urban history is that indigenous settlements upon the site were small before foreign entrepreneurs and government officials created the towns as essential points for military control, trade funnels, service points and administrative centres. The locations chosen were usually those at which exportable products could most conveniently be assembled; the same access worked equally well in reverse for imports and, of course, for the needs of colonial administration. Major traditional lines of movement often focussed on the site choices of the colonial powers. Later, modern transport services were introduced to supplement them. The new cities became the seats of government. Hence they rapidly developed into the largest settlements in their respective countries.

The colonial imprint on the developing countries was by no means even either in the areal extent of the patterns of resource development it introduced or in terms of the development of regular hierarchies of towns and cities. Frequently one major city assumed primate status at a size many times greater than its nearest rival. Sometimes the new colonial towns eclipsed older, traditional urban centres. In other important cases, notably that of China, viewed at a national scale there was little urbanisation that could be related to the kinds of economic change that characterised the colonial period.

In the paper that forms the third of the Readings, Murphey discusses the important Chinese case. He shows that '... while the peasant and the countryside were in some respects like the West, the city's role was fundamentally different'[13]. Before the Communist revolution, Chinese cities were essentially administrative centres; this function was dominant with few exceptions whatever their trade or manufacturing components. As their remarkably consistent physical plans reveal, they exhibited a high degree of common administrative creation. Little urban independence or urban-based revolutionary change appeared, except in the Western-dominated treaty ports, even in the exceptional cases in which trade or manufacturing dominated the city's functions. Neither were the cities decisive centres of economic change. Their business was the official administration of the vast Chinese countryside. They tended to decay markedly, whatever their manufacturing or trade, if the emphasis in administration was shifted in favour of a rival. It was not possible for the merchants to win independence from this system because agriculture was so predominant in the economy, thus maintaining the bureaucracy in an unassailable position of command. The merchants never occupied proportionately as large a place in the economy as in Europe. The universities were urban but they stimulated little dissent: their function was to train imperial administrators. The cities thus remained '. . . centres of the unitary national state and of the traditional order rather than its attackers, epitomes of the status quo'[14].

Turning to the present situation in the developing countries, the paper by Blake gives an overview of the dimensions of recent urban change within the context of one important regional example, North Africa. Here we find first that as in most other parts of the Third World there are considerable statistical difficulties even in establishing such fundamental facts as the present level of urbanisation. There is no common definition of what is 'urban' and published international figures are therefore not directly comparable. In Morocco, as Blake points out, some settlements with fewer than 5000 persons are regarded as urban, whereas in Algeria several centres with 10 000 to 12 000 inhabitants are officially excluded from this definition. The Libyan census of 1964 even went so far as to omit all classification of urban agglomerations, merely giving statistics for large administrative divisions which included both urban and rural populations.

In his survey, Blake takes an arbitrary figure of 10 000 inhabitants as qualifying a settlement for urban status. On this basis, the figures reveal that today one person in three lives in an urban place in the Maghreb and Libya compared with approximately one in ten at the beginning of the present century. Seventy years ago North African towns were not only much smaller but also far fewer than today.

None had more than 100 000 inhabitants. For much of the nineteenth century surprisingly high proportions of their populations were non-Moslem traders, principally from Spain, Italy and Malta, plus significant Jewish communities; later, with French, Spanish and Italian colonial penetration of the area, European city-based populations became highly important. During the last twenty years this urban picture has changed very significantly. The rate of urbanisation of the Moslem population of North Africa has increased spectacularly, whilst there has been a general exodus of non-Moslem populations. As Blake points out, less than 2 per cent of the urban population of present-day Algeria is non-Moslem. Throughout the area rural–urban migration is now proceeding apace; traditional ethnic groupings in the towns and cities (as typified, for instance, by the formerly distinctive Jewish or European quarters) have largely been replaced by groupings on other bases, often socio-economic; squatter shanty towns are expanding rapidly whilst the classic signs of unemployment and underemployment have become much more obvious, especially in the large-scale emergence of patterns of petty employment in the tertiary sector.

These fundamental changes can be paralleled in many other parts of the Third World and for this reason Blake's paper is an excellent case study of the workings within a particular geographical region of more widespread processes associated with urbanisation in the developing countries. In the second section of his paper, Blake calls attention to a consideration which for long has been significant within the general field of urban geography: the evolution of rank-size hierarchies of towns and cities. Urban primacy is not, in fact, as evident in the Maghreb and Libya as might be expected. It is most marked in Tunisia, where Tunis is showing an increasing tendency to outstrip its nearest rival in size. Libya, however, is characterised by duality rather than primacy at the topmost level of its urban structure, while Algeria has a markedly low level of primacy for a developing country. In terms of balanced regional development a high degree of primacy in an urban structure is, of course, a serious disadvantage. North Africa, except perhaps for Libya, is relatively fortunate in the development of smaller towns, often market centres established in areas of European colonisation, but nevertheless there are, as elsewhere in the Third World, severe problems of regional population concentration centred on the major cities.

Consideration of rank-size hierarchies leads naturally into that of population distribution within Third World cities. This field of enquiry is represented by an outstanding paper by Brush on spatial patterns of population in Indian cities. In this paper Brush analyses published population data for a wide variety of cities in order to test existing models of urban structure particularly with regard to the negative exponential rule on urban population density that has been accepted by Berry and others[15] (that is, that population density decreases from the greatest concentration in or near the city centre towards the urban periphery) and with regard to differential changes in intra-urban population density through time, a topic upon which there has been some theoretical dispute.

Brush finds that in the case of cities centred upon an indigenous bazaar, such as Ahmedabad and Poona, there has been a tendency towards progressive intra-urban concentration concurrently with growth in the total number of inhabitants. In the great port-cities founded during the colonial period, such as Bombay, Calcutta and Madras, concentration in the central wards is increasing but population is also building up on the periphery. Bombay Island has unusually long and continuous population records for India and these show that during the forty years 1881 to 1921 the increase in the city's population from 773 000 to 1·17 millions was absorbed by expansion in both the central and the northern parts of the city. Between 1921 and 1961 the population of the Island increased to 2·77 millions and by the latter year population densities throughout the city had risen to new high levels, even though large areas for urban development had been opened up on nearby Salsette Island since the late 1940s. Today, Bombay as a whole represents the apex of India's urban population concentration. The 1961 census recorded a gross density of 3760 per hectare in one of the central divisions of the city, Bhuleshwar, which covers 17 hectares. This compares with a maximum gross density of 750 persons per acre in central Calcutta census divisions at the same date and with maximum figures of less than 1200 persons per hectare in Madras.

Only in cities characterised by very marked dualism between the indigenous centre and a later colonial centre and with relatively low overall population densities—such as Hyderabad-Secunderabad and Bangalore—and in the planned new towns such as Jamshedpur and Chandigarh is little increase in inner area population densities observable. 'It is clear', states Brush, 'that a large share of population growth in Indian cities has been absorbed into existing urban areas, resulting in progressive congestion in the previously occupied tracts'[16]. In Poona the maximum gross density reaches 1900 persons an hectare in the old town but immediately outside density falls to below 240 persons per hectare. These are the inner suburbs. They have not yet received much spillover from the crowded central city and they remain occupied by housing for the relatively affluent. Beyond this belt, however, density starts to rise sharply again as newer areas of close, unplanned settlements occupied by low-paid workers are reached. Most of these are squatter settlements.

From these findings, the negative relationship of distance from the city centre to population density which has been observed so widely by urban geographers in cities in the industrialised countries clearly can by no means be taken for granted in the contemporary Third World, nor can the inverse relationship between population density and growth rates that has been previously postulated by some[17]. The city in the United States and other economically advanced countries may be in process of being turned inside-out through the increasing affluence of urban populations, the decay of functions at the centre, the growth of suburban commercial and shopping nodes, the residential flight to the suburbs and the developemt of commuting on a scale undreamt of by previous generations. But in the Third World the situation is very different in several important respects. Because of their general poverty, few urban dwellers can afford to pay for much transport and what accounts for many peripheral squatter settlements such as those noted by Brush in Poona is not the emptying of the inner areas but rather the reverse: the development of residential conditions near the city centre to levels approaching absolute human saturation in terms of the possibilities of further subdividing residential living space in the local socio-economic and cultural context.

The paper by Ng expands upon a topic touched upon by both Blake and Brush: the process of internal migration and its contribution to Third World urban growth. A very marked acceleration in rates of in-migration has been a feature of the urban experience of developing countries during the present century and, in general, it is true to say in very approximate terms that one-half of the growth of urban populations in the developing countries is currently due in-migration and the subsequent birth of families to first-generation migrants in the cities. Ng's study of Thailand illustrates very well how complex the actual migration processes are and how difficult it is to identify and evaluate them.

In a context of general underdevelopment, the extremely uneven population distribution that characterises most Third World countries makes inevitable internal spatial mobility of considerable magnitude, both rural and urban, and to this general circumstance must be added the attractions of the urban areas, both actual and imagined, to the relatively unsophisticated rural populations which predominate to such a great extent in almost every developing country. The Thais live in two main areas, the first being around Bangkok itself—which in relation to Thailand's other urban centres is the ultimate in primate cities—and the alluvial plain that runs 300 miles northward from the city, and the second a northeast basin centred on Roi-et. Population densities in the countryside of these areas are three or four times higher than in other parts of Thailand. In order to identify population mobility to and between the various parts of Thailand and to overcome deficiencies in the official data, Ng constructs a series of ten migration regions and analyses the patterns in the migration streams between them. As might be expected from the classic laws of migration, movement within the migration regions is the dominant mode of internal migration in Thailand but movement towards the metropolis across the boundaries of the migration regions is also important. There is thus a dual trend towards both inter-rural redistribution of population and rural-urban metropolitanisation though, again as might be expected from the laws of migration, rates of participation in the metropolitanisation trend seem to be governed by physical distance.

From internal migration the focus in the Readings now shifts to the relationship between urbanisation and industrialisation in the Third World. This important theme is central to the papers by Hoyle, Bray, Bartsch and Hoselitz. Greater rates of industrialisation are being assiduously sought in every Third World country, yet in relation to population growth the results so far have been somewhat disappointing. Many towns and cities, like Jinja in Uganda which is described by Hoyle, now have some modern industries, often existing behind a protective national barrier of rigid restrictions upon competing imports. Yet very few Third World towns and cities qualify for the description 'industrial' in the modern sense. On the other hand, a good deal of employment is characteristically provided by small-scale units of production such as the traditional weaving industries of Iseyin in Nigeria which are analysed in the Readings by Bray; and within the modern industrial sector small-scale, mechanised units of production using up-to-date methods are sometimes important, as in Hong Kong[18]. In addition to the employment provided by such small units, everywhere the tertiary sectors of the urban economies are grossly inflated.

Given the rapid growth of urban centres in the developing countries and the present size of the largest cities, these circumstances raise important conceptual considerations which lead inescapably to the conclusion that the previous urban experience of the industrialised nations of the present day, especially during the period of their so-called Industrial Revolution, is by no means being completely imitated in the contemporary Third World.

This can be explored in many dimensions but space permits the examination of only two of these in the Readings. The first, emphasised in Bartsch's paper, concerns the concept of unemployment in the developing countries. Bartsch questions the fact that, given the general assumption of a widening gap between the growth of urban populations and the creation of new employment opportunities, surveys conducted in recent years do not in general indicate levels of unemployment very much higher than those found in many industrialised countries. He submits that the problem lies in faulty conceptualisation of the employment situation in the Third World's urban areas and, as a consequence, in the type of methodology used to measure unemployment. As evidence Bartsch cites a case study of a poor district in Tehran.

The low-income people who form the vast majority of urban populations in the Third World are all too often reduced to creating work for themselves in casual and petty occupations which will provide little more than a bare subsistence income. Such irregular employment is, however, quite rare in the industrialised countries and consequently few employment surveys that are based on Western models are able adequately to take account of it. Bartsch's case study showed that in the poor district he studied labour force participation rates were considerably higher than for Tehran as a whole, especially in the case of females. This is not surprising of course in the face of dire poverty. However, the incidence of self-employment was also considerably higher than for the city as a whole, presumably because of inability to obtain regular wage employment; but the nature of the self-employment was such that, in a sense, it could be looked upon as disguised unemployment. In all, through refining previously accepted Western-oriented concepts of employment and unemployment, it could be shown that just over 70 per cent of the community's economically active population was either in open or disguised unemployment or else was only intermittently employed.

An even more fundamental issue is raised in the paper by Hoselitz, who compares the degree of urbanisation in India with that of certain European countries during the nineteenth century and relates this comparison to progress in industrialisation. In 1951, Hoselitz points out, according to the national census of India 11·9 per cent of the population lived in settlements of over 20 000 population. Austria was at this stage of urbanisation in 1890 as, broadly, were Norway and Switzerland. France had attained it somewhat earlier. But generally when these European countries had reached this stage of urbanisation, the proportion of the labour force engaged in manufacturing industry was considerably greater than that in India in 1951. In Austria, for example, 30 per cent of the labour force was in manufacturing in 1890, compared with 11 per cent in India in 1951. One vital difference between the historical experience of today's industrialised countries compared with that in the contemporary Third World would therefore seem to lie in the relationship between urbanisation and industrial growth.

The remaining papers in the Readings form a group concerned with living conditions in the towns and cities of the developing countries. The conditions under which the mass of the people live are graphically indicated in the contributions by Kaye and Pendrell, though in fairness it must be added that since Kaye wrote so brilliantly about Upper Nankin Street, Singapore, massive re-housing programmes have been instituted in that country. For most of the countries of the Third World, the future, as expressed in their development plans, simply refuses to be born. As a result, in their cities the industrial estates, the steel mills, the prestige public buildings symbolising nationalism triumphant, the opulent new housing of the tiny minority of the rich and the tall commercial symbols of the central business districts stand like islands which today seem about to be submerged in a sea of urban problems typified by the rapid spread of squatter shantytowns and the development of environmental problems to horrendous proportions.

In many respects housing is the most intractable of all the problems of physical provision now facing Third World cities. The dimensions of the problem as far as urban squatters are concerned are sketched in the paper in the Readings by the present Editor. Contrasting minimal standard high-rise and self-help solutions are examined, with special reference to the experience of Hong Kong in the former (where over 40 per cent of the total population have been re-housed since the early 1950s) and to Peru in particular in the latter. Clearly, in many cases a mixture of the two approaches is called for, probably with the greater emphasis on self-help, but before existing experience can become transferable fundamental changes in official attitudes towards housing the urban poor will have to take place in many Third World countries.

This latter consideration leads into an examination of physical planning processes, as exemplified by Sternstein's case study of Bangkok. The planning record he sets down is by no means a good one either in terms of its internal organisation or in terms of the appropriateness of the end product to local situations. Something of the flavour of Bartsch's paper on employment runs through Sternstein's work. All too often, he complains, physical planning in the developing countries is directed towards the production of static land-use exercises, heavily biased towards the urban experience of the industrialised countries and often contracted out in large part to Western consultants who possess but the most brief acquaintance with the communities whose futures the plans so vitally concern.

To redress the balance somewhat, however, the paper on new towns in Venezuela by Turner and Smulian, which concludes the volume, outlines realistic approaches to planning for basically poor people in a rapidly urbanising situation which have been evolved through the combination of local expertise with overseas advice. In particular, the approach to housing provision outlined in this paper is worthy of wide attention elsewhere in the Third World, for all too often in other cases which could be mentioned, both in respect of housing and with regard to other pressing urban problems, the politicians and the planners alike have tended in the past to look forward to the millennium without specifying in operational detail the individual rungs on the ladder to urban heaven for the developing countries. It is as a small and indirect contribution towards the solution of the many pressing problems of life in the towns and cities of the Third World that the present book is intended.

REFERENCES

1. B. F. HOSELITZ. The Role of Urbanisation in Economic Development: Some International Comparisons, in Roy Turner (ed.), *India's Urban Future*, Berkeley and Los Angeles (1962), pp. 157–81; reference p. 168.
2. KINGSLEY DAVIS. The Role of Urbanisation in the Development Process. Unpublished paper presented at the Sixth Rehovot Conference, Israel, August 1971, p. 8.
3. Ibid., p. 9.
4. UNITED NATIONS, DEPARTMENT OF ECONOMIC AND SOCIAL AFFAIRS. *Population Growth and Manpower in the Philippines*, New York (1960), pp. 14–15.
5. JOHN FRIEDMANN. *Regional Development Policy: A Case Study of Venezuela*, Cambridge, Mass. (1966). p. 132.
6. UNITED NATIONS, DEPARTMENT OF ECONOMIC AND SOCIAL AFFAIRS. Growth of the World's Urban and Rural Population 1920–2000. *Ekistics*, **29** (1970), 467–76.
7. GLEN T. TREWARTHA. *A Geography of Population: World Patterns*, New York (1969), p. 147.
8. UNITED NATIONS. (1970). Op. cit., p. 473.
9. KINGSLEY DAVIS. *World Urbanization* 1950–70, *Volume II*, Berkeley (1972), pp. 52–3.
10. See for example RENÉ MILLON. Teotihuacan. *Scientific American*, **216** (1967), 30–48.
11. G. HAMDAN. The Pattern of medieval urbanism in the Arab World. *Geography*, **57** (1962), 121–34.
12. See for example D. J. DWYER. The city in the developing world and the example of South-East Asia. *Geography*, **53** (1968), 353–64.
13. RHOADS MURPHEY. The city as a centre of change: Western Europe and China. *Ann. Ass. Am. Geogr.*, **44** (1954), 349–62; in particular p. 353.
14. Ibid., p. 356.
15. BRIAN J. L. BERRY, JAMES W. SIMMONS and ROBERT J. TENNANT. Urban population densities: structure and change. *Geogr. Rev.*, **53** (1963), 389–405.
16. JOHN E. BRUSH. Spatial patterns of population in Indian cities. *Geogr. Rev.*, **58** (1968), 362–91; in particular p. 380.
17. See for example BRUCE E. NEWLING. Urban growth and spatial structure: mathematical models and empirical evidence. *Geogr. Rev.*, **56** (1956), 213–25.
18. D. J. DWYER. Problems of the small industrial unit. In D. J. DWYER (ed.). *Asian Urbanisation: A Hong Kong Casebook*. Hong Kong University Press (1971), pp. 123–36.

1 The Pre-colonial Development of Yoruba Towns

A. L. MABOGUNJE

IN spite of their size, many Yoruba settlements fail to meet the criteria of urban status as defined in the more developed countries of the world. Dickinson defines a town in Western Europe and North America as 'a compact settlement engaged primarily in non-agricultural occupations'[1]. To this definition other writers have added such criteria as specialisation of economic activities, division of labour and factory-centred production. Very few large centres of population in Nigeria conform to these criteria. Most of them are compact settlements but a sizeable proportion of their population is still engaged in agricultural occupation. Moreover, the level of economic specialisation and division of labour in them is low and factory-centred production is at best very rudimentary.

Nonetheless, these settlements are towns in a very real sense. The problem here is largely one of definition, for towns are the products of their time and culture and must be seen and appreciated within that context. This fact is forcibly underlined by the differences of definition which one encounters all over the world. In Britain, a town is a place with a minimum population of 3500. In the United States, the figure is 2500; in France 2000; and in the U.S.S.R. 1000. On the other hand in Asia, one finds that an urban centre is in South Korea any incorporated city of 40 000 or more inhabitants; in India any place of 5000 or more inhabitants, possessing definite urban characteristics; in Communist China it is an area having a resident population of 2000 or more, of which 50 per cent or more is non-agricultural; while in Burma, it is any place so designated either statutorily or by executive decree. In fact, in the latter country some normal-size villages are classified as urban, if the local population regard them as urbanised!

It must be added that it is not the mere statistical number that is important but the fact that it involves, however crudely, a recog-

For References to this chapter, see page 33. The text here is a slightly shortened version of the original article.

nition that somewhere around the chosen figure and within the cultural context of the particular country a town becomes generally distinguishable from a village.

What then are the criteria, apart from size, for defining an urban centre in Yorubaland? First, there is the greater complexity of economic activities found in towns. Although a majority of their population is made up of farmers, there is a sizeable proportion which depends for its livelihood on non-agricultural employments, notably administration, trading and craft. In fact, before the present century all weaving, sewing and dyeing were carried out only in towns, much as was the case in mediaeval Europe. Similarly, all wood and leatherwork, blacksmithing, silver and brass-working, and numerous other crafts were almost exclusively town-oriented[2]. Some of these crafts, notably calabash-decorating and leather-working, have recently received a new lease of life in response to tourist demands. Secondly, there is the greater intensity of trading activities in towns. This is shown by the presence not only of a periodic market held at four to eight days' interval and involving exchange with people from neighbouring towns and villages, but also of daily morning and night markets which serve only the town's population. Thirdly, there is the more elaborate system of administration. This is based in many instances on the institution of divine kingship ruling through a hierarchy of chiefs who derive their status through their lineages or by personal distinction. These criteria are fulfilled by many settlements of over 5000 population today.

Thus, within their culture context these settlements must be regarded as towns. At this juncture, it is also important to stress two features which differentiate Yoruba from Western European type of urbanisation. The first is that whereas the present level of the Western European type of urbanisation has been largely generated by industrialisation, Yoruba urbanisation is due largely to non-industrial factors and all their towns, with the possible exception of Lagos, are even now still pre-industrial. Secondly, whereas Western European type urbanisation was carried out with considerable social dislocation and disorganisation, Yoruba urbanisation has been based firmly on social cohesion as expressed by the importance of the lineage system in the social, political and economic life of the town. Even today, with greater mobility both in the physical and socio-economic sense, the lineage system, though undergoing considerable modifications, remains as vigorous as ever. And it is a measure of its continued strength that many individuals who have emigrated and have become very prosperous and socially successful in their new abodes still strive to keep up their connection with their home town. This form of social attachment I shall henceforth refer to as 'identification'.

Having made my definition of Yoruba town, I can now pose the question—what are the problems of Yoruba urbanisation? In a general way, these problems are related to the nature of the evolution of Yoruba towns and are, therefore, best considered chronologically. First, there are those problems relating to the pre-colonial history of these towns; secondly, there are those originating from the manner of operation of the colonial regime; and thirdly, there are those due to recent political developments, notably the acceptance of a democratic system of government in the Western European sense.

It must be emphasised that although I shall concentrate on the problems it raises at present, Yoruba urbanisation has been a great asset both socially and economically. In no small measure, it has helped the rapid diffusion of culture and sophistication throughout Yorubaland and has facilitated the rise in standard of living and of expectations among the people. Equally vital has been its contribution to economic development. Economics of scale resulting from the high market potential of large, compact agglomerations of people have always made it easier to expand commercial intercourse and stimulate greater productivity. It can hardly be denied that one reason for the relatively higher per capita income of people in Yorubaland compared with others elsewhere in the Federation is related to this fact.

THE PRE-COLONIAL DEVELOPMENT OF YORUBA TOWNS

All Yoruba towns trace their origin to Ile-Ife. According to Biobaku, Ile-Ife itself was founded probably between the seventh and tenth century A.D. in the early days of the Yoruba migration into this part of West Africa[3]. Soon after this, a number of princes and notables moved out to carve out other kingdoms for themselves and to organise some of the indigenous inhabitants of their new kingdoms into towns along lines similar to Ile-Ife. At a later date, other secondary towns were founded by dissatisfied princes or simply grew up on sites with favourable locational characteristics.

A second wave of the incoming migration of Yoruba is suggested for the founding of Old Oyo[4]. From here, a similar movement to that from Ile-Ife gave rise to still more towns being founded, and led eventually to the creation of an extensive empire based on Old Oyo which, in its heyday, included most of Western Nigeria, nearly half of Dahomey and parts of Northern Nigeria.

There is a growing body of evidence to show that the founders of these new towns reproduced not only the social and political institutions of their parent towns but also their physical plan[5]. Samuel Johnson in *The History of the Yorubas* made specific reference to the fact that the town of Ilesha was laid out consciously on the same plan as that of Old Oyo[6]. He mentioned also that at the time he was writing, which was about 1891, most of the towns in eastern Yorubaland, notably those in the kingdoms of Ile-Ife, Ilesha and Ekiti, still retained their planned forms. This was in sharp contrast to towns in the Oyo-Egba kingdoms where, owing to the vicissitudes of war, the art of town-planning was hardly observed[7].

The Yoruba Town Plan

What the Yoruba town plan is like can be easily appreciated by a view of the lay-out of Ile-Ife shown in Figure 1.1. Since it is the presence of an Oba that gives town status to any settlement it is understandable that the Oba's palace is centrally placed within the lay-out. The palace ground usually occupies an extensive area of land and is often walled round. Clapperton in 1825 described the palace at Old Oyo as occupying 'about a square mile ... having two large parks, one in front and another facing the north'[8]. And Leo Frobenius indicated in 1911 that the most impressive sight in Ile-Ife was the massive walls of the palace which could be seen from whatever quarter one approached the town. 'Its front,' he went on to say, 'especially with the fine open square on which it stands, makes an imposing effect in spite of all its ruin ... The walls are mighty, over a yard at the base and some eighteen feet high'[9].

Usually in front of the palace is the most important market of the town. Both the palace and the market form the hub from which roads radiate to neighbouring towns. These roads are usually wide thoroughfares, sometimes 10 metres wide and important also for taking large groups of dancers in procession to the market-place or the palace. Elsewhere in the town, streets are laid out on a rectilinear pattern, the average width being about 5 metres. In the past, each street sometimes formed a 'quarter' consisting of a number of compounds housing members of one or more extended families. The compound is the traditional unit of settlement. It is an enclosed space, generally in the form of a square, bounded by a mud wall about 2 metres high. There is only a single entrance to it but, inside, it is divided into numerous rooms housing a number of related families. Until the early twentieth century, most of these compounds were roofed with thatch but since then this has been replaced almost

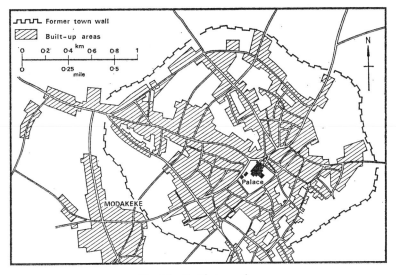

Fig. 1.1   Ile-Ife town plan.

everywhere by corrugated iron sheets. The smallest compound may cover about 0·2 hectare of land; the compounds of chiefs cover several acres. The town is surrounded by a wall and ditch. Some towns, such as Ilesha, have more than one wall and ditch. Along the walls of most towns are at least four gates where the toll-collectors sit.

What the sanitary arrangements were is not clear although they could hardly have been anything but primitive. The general up-keep of the town was undertaken on the basis of each quarter looking after its own portion of the town. Very often the work of cleansing the town and the compound fell on the domestic slaves as well as on the women and children.

Such then is the picture of the planned Yoruba town. It is very probable that such towns were distributed almost uniformly over most of Yorubaland, except perhaps in the south-east which was and still is largely under forest. A basic distinction was between the 'metropolitan' and the 'outlying' towns. In the former resided the most important Oba of the kingdom, to whom the Obas of the outlying towns were related either by blood or by office. The relationship was not as between vassals and king but as between senior and junior leaders of communities accepting a common historical origin or association. The situation, however, was quite fluid and a metropolitan town could attain under one Oba a position of virtual dominance whilst, under another, the Obas of the outlying towns could re-assert their independence. Before the nineteenth century, it is doubtful if any of the metropolitan towns had more than 30 000 people and their outlying towns more than 5000.

The Nineteenth-Century Wars and the Growth of Large Cities

At any rate, from about 1817 began the series of wars which were to alter the face of the country and to create the problem of very large, amorphous and squalid towns. In that year the town of Owu, some 50 km east of Ibadan, was attacked by neighbouring towns. About the same time, the Fulani, who had successfully carried out their 'jihad' against the Hausa kingdoms, were already devastating vast areas in the grassland region of Northern Yorubaland. The displaced population from towns in this region moved further south to swell the populations of towns favourably placed for defence in the border country between grassland and forest[10]. Some of the more adventurous joined the attacking armies at Owu and together they razed that town to the ground about 1824. They then turned their attention to the Egba towns nearby which supported Owu and in a series of attacks destroyed them one by one.

One of the Egba towns which escaped total destruction, although it was deserted, was Ibadan. This became the seat of operations of the victorious army and has grown in size and importance since then. Another town that grew out of these troubled circumstances is Abeokuta which was founded in 1830 by the remnants of the Egba people after all their towns had been destroyed. Other towns which became very large as a result of the large influx of refugees are Ogbomosho, Oshogbo, Iwo and Ile-Ife. In the case of Ile-Ife, the refugees were housed outside the town in a district still known today as Modakeke meaning, 'I remain quiet in this corner'. Figure 1.2 shows the distribution of Yoruba towns and emphasises the location of these very large cities in the transitional zone between grassland and forest.

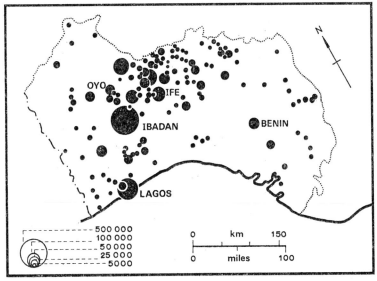

Fig. 1.2   Western Nigeria settlements of over 5000 people.

Refugees cause confusion

In most of these large towns, the sudden influx of refugees made any planning difficult. Land was taken up in blocks by chiefs, and dependants simply built their compounds hastily anywhere within the block. Moreover, the newly discovered strength in numbers meant for these large towns the emergence of a large body of young men, organised loosely as a standing army. They were shared out among the various war-chiefs to whom they looked for sustenance. Not only the new large towns but metropolitan centres of kingdoms which were not yet attacked had to organise an army of sorts for defence. The presence of such armies intensified economic activities in some directions. For instance, it created a demand for more blacksmiths to produce implements of war and stimulated greater production of food by slave labour to feed the war-boys. Nonetheless, the emergence of such military groups had a generally depressing effect on the towns. It created a body of unemployed people who interpreted their civic duties only in terms of a readiness to go to war for booty. In many towns, the Civil Authorities became less important than the Military Authorities and as was to be expected many towns became dirty, squalid and very unwholesome. Stream beds through the town were fouled, public places were neglected and even the town walls were not always in a good condition of repair.

THE COLONIAL REGIME

By the time of the effective occupation of Yorubaland by Britain after 1893, most towns were only gradually recovering from the decades of confusion and were trying to adjust to a new pattern of trade and political organisation. Some metropolitan towns had disappeared and new ones had arisen. In the Egba country, there were no longer any outlying towns. Abeokuta, with its population variously estimated at between 60 000 and 100 000 around 1861, was surrounded now only by small hamlets. It had 'vassal' towns in Otta, Ibara, Ishagga and other Egbado towns which it had actually conquered in war. Ibadan showed much the same pattern—a single, large town surrounded by thousands of small hamlets. Only in the northeast in the kingdoms of Ekiti, Ile-Ife and Ilesha, in parts of the Old Oyo empire, and in the Ijebu country to the south, was anything left of the old pattern. Even in these places considerable modifications and sometimes re-grouping had taken place . . .

SOURCE: A. L. Mabogunje, *Yoruba Towns*, Ibadan University Press, Ibadan (1962), pp. 3–10.

REFERENCES

1. R. E. DICKINSON. *City Region and Regionalism*, London (1947), p. 25.
2. P. C. LLOYD. Craft organisation in Yoruba towns, *Africa*, **23** (Jan. 1953), 32.
3. S. O. BIOBAKU. *The Origin of the Yoruba*, Federal Information Service, Lagos (1955), p. 21.
4. Ibid., p. 22.
5. At present, I am engaged in a study of the morphology of Yoruba towns. Already, a good number of the towns so far studied show distinctive similarities in their lay-out.
6. SAMUEL JOHNSON. *The History of the Yorubas*, London (1921), p. 22.
7. Ibid., p. 93.
8. HUGH CLAPPERTON. *Journal of a Second Expedition into the Interior of Africa*, London (1829), p. 58.
9. LEO FROBENIUS, *The Voice of Africa*, London (1913), p. 276.
10. The Fulani military power was based on cavalry which can operate best only in open grassland country, hence wooded country was better protected against their onslaught.

2 Colonial Expansion and Urban Diffusion in the Americas

KINGSLEY DAVIS

B y virtue of European penetration and domination, the entire world became after 1500 an increasingly interrelated system. The process of expansion took time, but by 1800 there was hardly an inhabited corner of the earth that had not felt, directly or indirectly, the impact of the European. Urbanisation, like all other basic modifications in human life, could not fail to be affected by this world development.

The nature of European penetration, however, was not everywhere the same. It differed according to the type of overseas area and the kind of Europeans involved, as well as with the particular time and circumstances of contact. Any account of urban diffusion in colonial areas must therefore give attention to the contrasting factors affecting different regions.

LATIN AMERICA

The Portuguese and Spaniards found the New World so sparsely inhabited and so weakly defended by natives that European colonisation was entirely feasible. The main purpose of the invaders, however, was not colonisation as such, but ready exploitation. This is indicated by the fact that they gave prime attention to the tropical regions. These warm regions were not only the points of initial contact in the New World but also the most promising sources of immediate wealth and the most abundantly supplied with native labour. Yet tropical areas are normally resistant to European settlement; although the conquerors did settle in significant numbers, it is noticeable that, as with the English and French later, the racial composition of the tropical colonies seldom remained predominantly European. In any event, the planting of permanent nations abroad which would be economically self-sustaining was not the main Iberian goal. The Portuguese and Spaniards thought rather of

For References to this chapter, see page 47; the references in the original article have been reorganised, and certain notes incorporated in the main text.

extracting wealth as quickly as possible, and their complex colonial policy was bent to that end.

TOWNS AS INSTRUMENTS OF POLICY

One of the elements in the Spanish colonial policy was the deliberate founding and maintenance of towns. (This was not true of the Portuguese, except for the clergy. We shall deal in what follows with the Spanish colonies, making only occasional reference to the Portuguese territories). In some cases this simply meant taking over the cities of the aborigines. Tenochtitlan (Mexico City), for instance, was rebuilt after 1522 as the metropolitan centre for New Spain; and Cuzco, the erstwhile Inca capital in Peru, was retained as an important centre. The native cities, however, were too few in number and too far from the coast to serve all the urban needs of Spanish policy. The conquerors therefore set out with remarkable speed to create what was for that time and under those frontier conditions a large number of new towns. In Mexico, as soon as Cortes landed on the coast he founded Vera Cruz (1519), and only a few years later 'all authorities engaged in a steady, unsystematic, and prolific campaign of urban creation'[1]. In Peru there was not at first such a wholesale policy of town-founding, yet in 1535 Lima was started near the coast as the seat of the Viceroy of a huge region, and Potosí and La Paz followed within ten years. In 1538, in what is now Colombia, Bogotá was 'laid out from scratch on a vacant site'[2]. Far to the South, in Chile where the indigenous people had no towns at all, Valdivia founded Santiago, and on the other side of the continent Buenos Aires was started in 1570. In Brazil, in the meantime, the Portuguese had founded Bahia, Rio de Janeiro, and Sao Paulo. Thus within a century after the discovery of America, when the European population in the new territories was still extremely small and the native population severely decimated, the conquerors had already established a surprising number of towns, many of which are great cities today.

The motives for this emphasis on towns and cities were several, all of which were connected with the central features of the Spanish (and, to a lesser extent, the Portuguese) colonial system. First of all, the Spaniards, confronted with the most advanced natives of the Americas and still influenced by their long war at home against another non-Christian people (the Moors), had their minds bent on military action. They thus pursued the invariable policy of establishing towns 'as bases from which to carry on the work of military conquest'[3]. Having no intention of developing a balanced and durable economy with a large transplanted European population, but rather of making the quickest gains for the government and the elite at home, they needed towns in America both to protect and to control their own people—to protect them from the more numerous natives, and to regulate their economic and political life. It was thus recognised that a highly centralised colonial administration could be made effective only through a few powerful urban centres and a network of secondary towns. Since the Spaniards did not engage mainly in agriculture or industry but rather in mining, the production of hides, and the appropriation of native products, they could congregate in towns with little hindrance to their economic gain. As collecting points or mining centres, inland towns thus had an economic function, as did the seaport cities for shipping goods out and receiving supplies in return. In addition, the towns played a role in the control and utilisation of the Indians, who were of most value as labourers and most easily governed as subjects when they were assembled in particular spots. In this regard the church and its mendicant orders formed an effective instrument of imperial policy, shepherding the Indians together in compounds and settlements for purposes of religious indoctrination and thus helping to subjugate them*. The church, moreover, being highly centralised like the government, located its headquarters in towns and cities[4].

Given the motives and circumstances that made towns of strategic value in the colonial system, it is not surprising that the Spaniards adopted in the sixteenth century a deliberate and carefully developed pro-urban policy. The Laws of the Indies, first written in 1523 and revised many times, established consistent standards of design regulating the 'size and form of the main plaza, width of streets, orientation of gates and walls, location of public buildings, and subdivision of land into lots'. As a result, according to Violich, such widely separated cities as Bogotá and Concepcion, 'and practically every city between, have exactly the same size of block, the same width of street, the same general urban pattern'[5]. Not only

---

* Towns founded for missionary purposes often remained small and backward, but they were numerous. Sao Paulo, for instance, inaugurated in 1555 chiefly for the purpose of Christianising the natives, had no immediate basis of wealth and remained an unimportant town for more than two centuries.

the physical layout but also the principles of town government were standardised. 'The Spanish municipality in the New World was governed in accordance with the *Ordenanzas de cabildos*', drawn up in 1574[6] and setting forth the nature of the town officials and the mode of their selection.

Not all cities conformed to the specifications. Some, like Potosí, arose too quickly and feverishly to conform to a deliberate plan[7]. The Portuguese towns were allowed to grow haphazardly, and the Spanish theory of the proper municipal government was thwarted by Spain herself and by colonial conditions. Nevertheless, it is interesting how, in this thinly peopled and far-away wilderness and in response to a deliberate policy, Spanish colonial life was organised from the very beginning to centre in cities.

URBAN INNOVATIONS AND CONTINUITIES

As a result of this pro-urban policy, one might expect the towns of South and Central America to have had much the same character as those on the Iberian peninsula at the time. This, however, was only partially true. It should be recalled that in sixteenth-century Europe centralised nations were newer than towns. Most of the towns had their origin in the Middle Ages and were in no sense the product of national policy. The Spanish idea of utilising a definite urban policy in handling the vast possessions of the New World was therefore a major innovation, more characteristic of the Romans than of the mediaeval monarchs and princes. In making this innovation, the Spaniards had to adopt new precedents to suit their national goals.

In the matter of physical layout, for example, the planned cities of America had new features. The idea of a central rectangular plaza, located at the intersection of the main streets, framed by public buildings, and constituting a monumental town centre, was not embodied in the mediaeval towns of Europe. ('In the Middle Ages, such open spaces grew as markets, near the junction of old and new city quarters, or as gradual excrescences upon traffic arteries, ultimately culminating, but rarely beginning as the specialized square'[8]). Furthermore, the absence of walls around most of the New World towns was in striking contrast to those of Europe. Mexico City never had a wall, nor did Lima until 1683. The tendency, instead, was to fortify the central buildings, usually the church. (For example, the nucleus of Buenos Aires was a fort, a means of defence and a place of refuge for the inhabitants[9].) The colonists apparently felt it safe to forgo the expense of walling entire towns, being satisfied merely to have a place of refuge in the town's centre. Such urban walls as were erected were found mainly in the port towns. Both Lima and its port, Callao, for instance, were eventually walled. In such cases the purpose was protection against other Europeans rather than against natives. The same motive led to the construction of massive stone ramparts and cannon emplacements overlooking important harbours, as was the case at San Juan in Porto Rico and at Cartagena. Bitter experience showed that port towns were likely to be sacked unless strongly protected.

Apart from novel physical requirements, the colonial towns were faced with a circumstance having no exact parallel in Europe—the Indian problem. Chronically short of European labour, they were under the constant necessity of somehow utilising the Indians. One practice, already mentioned, was to herd them into towns and compounds—a measure which multiplied urban problems. Native compounds could not all be located at a distance from the European towns (even when desired by the mendicant orders). If native labour was to be utilised, a substantial portion of the Indians had to reside *close* to the Europeans; yet, unless living in as servants, they were too distinct in language and customs, and too poor, to occupy exactly the same parts of the town as the Europeans. The result was that the natives generally lived either in the colonial towns but *segregated* in certain parts, or in towns of their own but near by the Spanish centres. In Lima 'the Indians were put into special settlements called Las Reducciones, consisting of smaller blocks and narrower streets than those of the Spanish settlement, and amounting to little better than concentration camps'[10]. In Mexico City, they were assigned to the western and northern edges forbidden to whites, and some dwelt in neighbouring villages where they were available for labour in the city. In some towns different Indian tribes occupied separate quarters[11].

The urban agglomeration of Indians had several important consequences. One was that it subjected the natives to frightful mortality by heavily exposing them to European diseases against which they lacked immunity. As the losses occurred, still more natives were brought into towns, to be decimated in turn. (The population of Mexico declined from about 11 million in 1520 to approximately 2·5 million in 1650[12].) The reduction of the native population was so enormous that it greatly aggravated the labour shortage and encouraged the importation of slaves from Africa.

The class structure of the New World towns was unlike that found in any European city. Not only were there large numbers of Indians, but there were Negro slaves, *peninsulares*, and creoles—all added to the ordinary occupational and nobility distinctions of European communities. The creoles had a lower status than persons born in Spain (they were excluded, for example, from high political offices) because the crown feared that the creoles would be more loyal to the colony than to Spain herself. Further, although it was not made in any sense a deliberate policy, it did fit the purpose of Spain to have the creoles interbreed with Indians and Negroes; because this, by creating half-breed groups, fragmented the caste structure below the *peninsulares*, thus increasing the divisiveness among the lesser strata and minimising the danger of popular revolt. ('The creole hated the Spaniard, but he did not rise against him, as he would have needed the assistance of the lower classes, who hated him and whom he loftily despised'[13]). The result, though effective from the standpoint of retaining political control, was less satisfactory in terms of economic development. The *peninsulares*, a small aristocracy dependent on political ascendancy, were not required to survive by economic ingenuity. They thus exemplified and reinforced, at the highest level, the typical Spanish prejudice against labour, industry, and retail trade—a prejudice imitated by the creoles. Productive work, whether in the mines at Potosí, on ranches in Mexico, or in handicraft shops in Peru, was done by the subordinate races. These people, whose rise in the social scale was blocked by caste barriers, had no incentive or opportunity to advance the economy.

If in these respects the New World cities were different from those on the Peninsula, there were of course other respects in which they were similar. For instance, the Spaniards in the colonies, like those in Europe, tended to prefer the central part of town for their residences. These were customarily on the second and third floors, with shops on the first floor, a pattern that still persists. Also, the tendency to regulate prices on a municipal basis, the persistence of guilds, the indifference to sanitary conditions and public convenience, all were reminiscent of sixteenth-century towns at home. Even in the matter of local government, the structure required by the colonial authorities was, at least in the early years, much like that in Spain, though important differences soon arose. In general it can be said that there was a transfer of urban institutions to the New World, but that the mode of transfer and the impact of new conditions altered not only the role of towns but also their physical and social structure.

DECADENCE OF TOWN GOVERNMENT

The towns and cities of Europe gradually lost their autonomy. In Spanish America they never had much autonomy, and they tended soon to lose even that. In origin they were supposed to follow the old form. The founding citizens signed an act of organisation and swore to support it. A municipal council, or *cabildo*, was to be elected annually by the sworn citizens from among their number, and they were to appoint the town officers (one or two *alcaldes* and other officials if needed). The *cabildo* and officers were to have wide local powers, judicial as well as executive and legislative[14]. However, this system never functioned generally in the New World, and as time went on it functioned less and less. The crown's anxiety to control the colonies was too great to allow such local self-government.

Whereas the towns of the Peninsula possessed ancient charters of municipal liberties, these liberties were not granted to the New World towns. Soon, in addition, it became clear that the provincial governors in America, *peninsulares* to a man and representing the crown and the viceroy, would reduce the power of the elected town officials, who were mostly creoles. The governor received the right to preside over the *cabildo* of his capital city and generally to appoint a deputy to preside in the *cabildo* of every town in his province[15]. Controlling the militia, he could be highhanded if need be, sometimes imprisoning the members of a refractory *cabildo*. Acquiring the right to confirm the appointment of city officials, he might insist on appointing them himself, or the crown might do so directly[16]. Finally, the taxing and spending power of the city officials was severely and increasingly limited by the prior claims of crown officials.

A further factor in the decay of town government was a development that was also affecting the cities in Spain—namely, the practice of selling municipal offices. This procedure, adopted by Philip II for revenue purposes, grew steadily worse. Since not much money could be realised from the sale of an office for a year, appointments were sold for life or for a series of lives[17]. Small wonder that town government became scandalous. For example, 'in all the cities (of New Spain) municipal finances were in a state of incredible disorder and confusion. In many towns no books at all were kept of simplest receipts and expenditures. Corruption in public administration was universal'[18].

Reform characteristically took the path of reducing still further the vestiges of municipal authority. In Mexico a general accounting office was set up to which all municipalities had to send their ledgers for audit and from which prior approval had to be obtained for *any* expenditure of municipal funds. Toward the end of the eighteenth century a new territorial administration was instituted which cut up the entire American empire into smaller jurisdictions. The rulers of these territories, *intendentes* and their subordinates, 'took over virtually complete control of municipal affairs—budgeting of town funds, street cleaning, water supply, regulation of hospitals and jails, markets, and bakeries, etc.', and often the administration of municipal justice. The towns were improved, but at the cost of virtually complete subjection to higher authority[19]. Thus in Spanish America the last vestiges of the once proud autonomy of the mediaeval city were lost, never to be regained; the city was merely an instrument and a subject of the all-inclusive state.

CAPITAL CITIES IN THE SPANISH COLONIES

Spain's centralised administration operating through a network of urban strong-points where population was deliberately concentrated, led naturally to an emphasis on colonial capitals—an emphasis even stronger than the similar tendency in Europe. Royal courts (*audiencias*) and royal officials (viceroys, or *virreyes*) were established in America directly under the jurisdiction of the Council of the Indies in Madrid. The territory administered by each of these authorities was huge. In the whole of the Americas there were only ten *audiencias* in the sixteenth century, with only one added in the seventeenth and two in the eighteenth. Only two viceroyalties were created at first (Mexico and Peru) which divided between them the entire colonial area until the eighteenth century when two more were inaugurated (Bogotá in 1718 and Buenos Aires in 1776). Under the viceroys were the captains-general, who ruled subordinate but still large territories. Each authority was located in a city, and the higher the jurisdiction and the wider its territory, the more important was the capital. Thus Mexico City and Lima became and remained the two most important cities in the Spanish colonies.

The church similarly centralised its government, concentrating its wealth, its clergy, and its control in the capital cities[20]. When it is added that the universities, when founded, were located in these centres, together with all the machinery of economic and military control; that it was in the capitals that the dominant *peninsulares* lived; and that it was here that funds were lavishly expended for governmental and ecclesiastical buildings, monuments, and such civic improvement as occurred, one can see that the capital city idea had taken firm hold. Lima, for example, 'acquired many of the features of an old-world capital. All persons wishing to achieve social distinction, and all persons who had achieved such distinction, found it desirable to live in Lima. The presence of the highest officers of the government and the dignitaries of the Church made it the social centre of South America'[21].

The Spanish colonial capitals looked to Europe rather than to the native and alien hinterland for their cultural stimulation and economic orientation. A great gulf therefore came to separate them from the vast, crude domain over which they ruled. This concentration of all major functions in the dominant cities, this gulf between the city and the hinterland, has characterised Latin American urbanisation to this day. Curiously, it is one of the factors that has retarded economic advancement and, as a consequence, urbanisation itself.*

OBSTACLES TO URBANISATION

Oddly enough, the Spanish colonial policy of encouraging town-dwelling for all races was not accompanied by economic measures

* Portuguese America was less urban-oriented than Spanish America, partly because of the self-sustaining and isolated plantation economy that arose in northern Brazil. An aristocracy of wealthy land-owners living on their latifundia served as a counterweight to the officials and merchants living in the towns. Nevertheless, Rio de Janeiro was unquestionably the capital city. When the royal government was transferred there from Lisbon in 1807, it acquired more of the accoutrements of a Latin capital. Naval and military academies, a royal printing press, a school of commerce, a national library and museum were established in Rio de Janeiro shortly after that event. By the time the royal household returned to Portugal in 1820, the city was more the centre of Brazil than it had been before. It can be seen, however, that this development came late in the colonial period.

that would stimulate steadily increasing urbanisation. Any economic advance that did not immediately redound to the mother country's profit was regarded with suspicion and was subject to repression. For instance, Spain's desire to monopolise colonial trade led her not only to prohibit the colonies from trading with other European nations but also to deny them, until 1778, the privilege of trading with one another except by special permission. In order to enforce these restrictions, the crown closed certain ports to all international trade. One such closed port was Buenos Aires. The non-use of this strategic harbour had the fantastic consequence of forcing the trade of the whole Plata region to go by way of Peru and Panama at such enormous cost that the rich pampa region of Argentina was left for two centuries in a primitive and undeveloped condition, the growth of Buenos Aires being far less than it could have been. (Two hundred years after it was founded, Buenos Aires still had only 25 000 inhabitants, whereas New York City, the same length of time after its founding by the Dutch, had approximately 150 000. The speed with which Buenos Aires, once its shackles were removed, surpassed Lima also indicates the depressing effects of the early restrictions on the Argentine city.) 'In general, throughout the colonial period the Spanish restrictive trade policy resulted in shortages of goods, exorbitant prices, depressed living standards, universal smuggling, and wholesale bribery from one end of Spanish America to the other'[22].

Some measures were taken to promote agriculture—the dispatch of seeds, plants, and breeding animals to America; the encouragement of native crops such as Indian corn and vanilla; and the facilitation of farm-labour migration from the Canaries. But, on the other hand, crops that competed with those in Spain—grapes, olives, silk—were discouraged and forbidden, and processing plants were often disapproved[23]. Furthermore, the colonists themselves avoided agriculture, disdaining the labour involved and preferring quicker avenues to wealth. They liked to own land, to be sure, but they left the work to be done by the subordinate races. 'Partly because of this individual dislike of farming, and partly because of primogeniture which kept large holdings intact, vast plantations became a characteristic feature of Spanish America. Both the favored Church and the heavily rewarded conquistadores soon built up huge landed estates which they worked with servile labor and with primitive methods . . . , actually cultivating only a small portion. This wasteful form of farming prevailed throughout the colonial age . . .'[24]

With respect to industry, the obstacles were overwhelming. The fact that 'the Laws of the Indies forbade the colonies to have any form of manufacturing which might compete with the same industry in Spain'[25] would not alone have been of much consequence, because Spain did not have much industry. But, since Spanish merchants were the middlemen in the trade of goods from other European countries to the colonies, almost any kind of manufacturing in the colonies would endanger an important source of profit. The colonial industrialist, if permitted to exist, could have at best only a local market, since he was hampered by monopolistic middlemen in the trade with Europe and by prohibitions against intercolonial trade in the American markets. Owing, however, to poverty and depopulation, the local market was thin. Finally, the inappropriateness of the Spanish institutional order for industrial development was even more of a retarding factor in America than it was in Spain herself. 'Spaniards in the colonies, most of whom were of the real or quasi nobility, felt the normal aversion of their class for the mechanical industries. Even the artisans who came from Spain refused to work at their trade in the Americas, affecting to despise it. . . .'[26] None of the government officials, ecclesiastics, and soldiers who dominated the colonial regime had a knowledge of industry, and few realised its importance in the creation of wealth. Like agriculture, it was too slow an avenue to riches for the impatient Spaniards; the latter had come to the colonies to fight, plunder, and rule, not to work. The elite of colonial society, the *peninsulares*, were by definition temporary; if they held office they were required by law to return to the mother country, and if they did not return, their sons born in America of course lost their status as *peninsulares*. The next class, the creoles, although permanent, were parasitic on Indians and slaves. As a labouring class, however, the Indians and slaves were by no means the equals, in skill or motivation, of the artisans of Holland, England, Germany, or even Spain. They were not only untutored and resentful, but also so frequently riddled by disease and death that they could scarcely acquire industrial skills. Such a labour supply was ill suited to industrial development; in fact, no industrial society has ever been built by labour of that sort.*

* For rather similar reasons, Portugal gave little encouragement to colonial industry. When gold and diamonds were discovered in Minas Geraes and Matto Grosso, it was ordered that in those territories 'all factories or other establish-

Economic progress in the Iberian colonies was also discouraged by the predominance of the church. Not only vast rural holdings fell into ecclesiastical hands, but also much urban real estate[27]. In addition, despite papal admonition, the church engaged in business and finance, often charging exorbitant interest rates. The disadvantage of ecclesiastical dominance was that, whereas its means were economic, its goals were not. The wealth of the church was inalienable and non-taxable. The entire weight of supporting the government and community development fell upon laymen, whose position became progressively weaker *vis-a-vis* the church. The church used its increasing wealth, not to capitalise economic enterprise, but to multiply its own edifices and increase its power. In Mexico, for example, fewer civil buildings were constructed than churches; 'religious architecture was the dominant mode, and secular buildings rarely assumed durable and monumental forms'[28].

As a consequence of these factors in the colonial situation, the lack of economic advance during three centuries was extreme. As late as the end of the eighteenth century there were still few roads suitable for wheeled vehicles. No road was opened across the Isthmus of Panama until 1846. Transport was still chiefly on the backs of animals. Chronic unemployment and poverty prevailed despite the enormous resources and the sparsity of population. Spain restricted immigration in an effort to keep foreigners and non-Catholics out of the colonies. The lack of foreign ideas, the Inquisition, the prevailing illiteracy all gave the colonists a xenophobic and ultra-conservative frame of mind. The colonists reacted to their economic problems by general corruption. Smuggling and bribery were essential parts of colonial life, along with piety and ignorance. Efforts the colonists might make to get together to discuss their common problems were effectively discouraged. Early in the sixteenth century, for example, some municipalities, thinking of co-operation, appointed delegates to meet together. 'Disapproval came promptly from Spain, Charles V in 1530 despatching the specific order: "Without our command it is not our intention or will that the cities or the towns of the Indies meet in convocation" '[29].

---

ments not essential to the extraction of gold or diamonds should be closed'. Joao Pandiá, CALOGERAS. *A History of Brazil*. Chapel Hill, 1939, p. 39. The purpose was to divert labour to mining and thus to obtain government revenue (diamonds were a royal monopoly). The crown hardly governed the colony at all except in those areas where quick mineral wealth was obtainable.

As a result of the failure to develop industry, to create a stable and skilled labour force, to evolve a diversified and progressive agriculture, or to integrate the cities culturally and economically with the hinterland, the early promise of urbanisation in Latin America was not fulfilled. The crown's encouragement and interest in town-building was not accompanied by a policy of laying an economic and social basis for continued development. The creoles long remained an exploiting class, gaining their living through the use of subordinate labour in mining, ranching, and agriculture, while the *peninsulares* dominated government and commerce. Both groups were looking always for a quick profit, wasting resources, and, with the help of the clergy, keeping the bulk of the population in a state of ignorance and poverty.

It is not strange that urbanisation showed little progress during the colonial period. The speculative character of the economy reflected itself in the ups-and-downs of mining towns, such as Potosí and Villa Rica.* Even the more permanent places gained little headway. They 'remained small colonial towns completely under the domination of Europe[30]'. Lima, capital of a huge viceroyalty, housed only some 87 000 people by 1810; Mexico City, about 135 000 by 1820; Rio de Janeiro about 130 000 by 1807; Buenos Aires about 45 000 in 1806; and Santiago de Chile, about 30 000 in 1790. During the eighteenth century the total population was probably growing. The cities were growing too, but not much faster than the rural areas. As a result, the Iberian part of the New World was not very urbanised by the end of the colonial period—far less than France or England at the time. Even the largest cities were diminutive compared to Paris, London, Naples, Berlin, and Madrid. Since no basis was laid during the colonial era for industrialisation,

---

* Two years after silver was discovered on a bare Andean mountain in 1545, Potosí reportedly had 2500 houses and 14 000 inhabitants. It sprang up fast and haphazardly, 'so that the streets were winding and narrow and ran in every direction.' Cobb, p. 51: see Note 7 below. Since no produce could be grown near by, supplies had to be hauled by llama and mule over tortuous routes. Fantastic inflation resulted, and the government of the town was corrupt and violent. Yet the population grew to something like 160 000 by 1650, and, according to a census taken about 25 years later when the silver mines had started giving out, it was still 120 000. In 1650 Potosí was probably the largest city in the hemisphere, but by 1825 it had only 8000 inhabitants. Chapman, p. 149.

In Brazil the mining towns had similar histories. Villa Rica (now Ourô Preto), in the gold region, rose to a reputed 100 000 population, but later sank to a bare 8000. Tijuco (now Diamantina) reached 40 000 at the peak of the diamond rush, but later declined to 10 000. Pandia Calogeras, *Op cit.*, p. 44.

the Latin American countries lagged behind Anglo-America in urbanisation from about 1840 on, despite their head start. . .

SOURCE: *International Journal of Comparative Sociology*, 1 (1960), pp. 43–55.

REFERENCES

1. GEO. KUBLER. *Mexican Architecture of the Sixteenth Century*, New Haven, (1948), p. 68.
2. FRANCIS VIOLICH. *Cities of Latin America*, Reinhold, New York (1944), p. 29.
3. VERA BROWN HOLMES. *A History of the Americas*, Ronald, New York (1950), p. 129.
4. 'The great majority (of both regular and secular clergy) were to be found in the cities.' CHARLES EDWARD CHAPMAN. *Colonial Hispanic America*, Macmillan, New York (1933), p. 191.
5. VIOLICH. *Op. cit.*, p. 28.
6. RAFAEL ALTAMIRA. *A History of Spain*, trans. by Muna Lee, Van Nostrand, New York (1949), p. 405.
7. See GWENDOLIN B. COBB. Potosí, a South American Mining Frontier. *Greater America*, University of California Press, Berkeley (1945), pp. 39–58.
8. KUBLER. *Op. cit.*, pp. 97–8.
9. *Ibid.*, pp. 94–5.
10. VIOLICH. *Op. cit.*, p. 29.
11. KUBLER. *Op. cit.*, pp. 82–3, 148.
12. SHERBURNE F. COOK and LESLEY B. SIMPSON. *The Population of Central Mexico in the Sixteenth Century*. University of California Press, Berkeley (1948), pp. 38, 47.
13. CHAPMAN. *Op. cit.*, p. 118.
14. BERNARD MOSES. *South America on the Eve of Emancipation*, Putnam's, New York (1908), pp. 77–9.
15. C. H. HARING. *The Spanish Empire in America*, Oxford University Press, New York (1947), p. 163.
16. 'It can easily be established that in most of the important cities of America the appointment of *regidores* was from earliest times entirely in the king's hands or in those of his colonial representatives, and that any privilege of election that might be granted to the *cabildo* was a concession from the crown.' HARING. *Op. cit.*, p. 165.
17. By 1606, 'all vendable offices were granted in perpetuity, with a right of resale or bequest within the holder's lifetime on condition of paying, the first time a half, and thereafter a third part of their value into the royal exchequer . . . Municipal office thus became to all intents and purposes a piece of private property which passed freely by sale from one person to another, or between members of the same family, . . . A vacancy might even be purchased for a minor, the post being held by the father or other suitable substitute until the coming-of-age.' HARING. *Op. cit.*, p. 166.
18. *Ibid.*, p. 176.
19. *Ibid.*, pp. 176–7.
20. 'About one-sixth of all the churchmen in New Spain were in Mexico City alone. In Lima in 1778, according to Antonio de Ulloa, . . . there were 40 convents, and those of the nuns were so crowded that, as he put it, they

could populate a city.' CHAPMAN. *Op. cit.*, p. 191. The seat of the Inquisition in South America was located in Lima.

21. MOSES. *Op. cit.*, p. 2.
22. HOLMES. *Op. cit.*, p. 184.
23. From 1618 to 1794 the construction of sugar mills was prohibited in Peru, as was the making of brandy. Grape cultivation was frequently, though not always successfully, suppressed, and Peruvian wine could generally not be sold in other parts of the Americas. For a while coca plantations were forbidden, the ostensible reason being the protection of the Indians who were thus permitted (or forced) to work (or die) in the mines from which the Spanish government took one-fifth of the gain. MOSES. *Op. cit.*, pp. 300–9.
24. MOSES. *Op. cit.*, p. 186.
25. CHAPMAN. *Op. cit.*, p. 147.
26. *Ibid.*, pp. 146–7.
27. In Chile, for example, the Jesuits came to own about 70 rural estates, 'some of them as large as a modern province.' MOSES. *Op. cit.*, p. 239. In the cities of America, soon after the Conquest, 'a large part of the choicest municipal property had passed into the hands of ecclesiastical corporations.' The Mexico City *cabildo*, in 1578, complained that the Dominicans and Augustinians possessed the largest and best part of the property in the city . . . In 1748, it was reported of Lima by special royal investigators that, of a total of 2806 buildings in the city, 1135 belonged to religious communities. HOLMES. *Op. cit.*, p. 327.
28. KUBLER. *Op. cit.*, p. 187.
29. HOLMES. *Op. cit.*, p. 168.
30. VIOLICH. *Op. cit.*, p. 31.

3 The City as a Centre of Change: Western Europe and China

RHOADS MURPHEY

EVERY sedentary society has built cities, for even in a subsistence economy essential functions of exchange and of organisation (both functions dealing with minds and ideas as much as with goods or with institutions) are most conveniently performed in a central location on behalf of a wider countryside. The industrial revolution has emphasised the economic advantages of concentration and centrality. But is it true to say that change, revolutionary change, has found an advantage in urbanisation; in concentration and in numbers? The city has instigated or led most of the great changes in Western society, and has been the centre of its violent and non-violent revolutions. In western Europe the city has been the base of an independent entrepreneur group which has successfully challenged and broken the authority of the traditional order. In China, while cities with the same universal economic functions arose, they tended until recently to have the opposite effect on the pattern of change. China has consistently reasserted itself as a single political unit, but it is otherwise the appropriate qualitative and quantitative counterpart of Europe, and provides a reasonable basis for comparison. China and Europe have been the two great poles of world civilisation, and an examination of the different roles which their cities played may help to elucidate other differences between them.

The following generalised and capsulised discussion aims only to suggest this difference, as an example of what might be made of an approach to the study of society through an analysis of the city's role in the process of change[1]. By cutting a familiar pie in another way we may arrive at useful insights. In doing so in the short space of an article the writer realises that he must raise or beg more questions than he answers, and may in particular be guilty of over-simplification or distortion. But the virtue of such an attempt may

For References to this chapter, see page 65. Certain of the Notes in the original article are here incorporated in the main text.

lie in its disturbing or even irritating nature; it aims less to prove than to provoke. To quote from Karl Marx with this in mind, '... the whole economical history of society is summed up in the movement of this ... separation between town and country'[2]. In distinguishing between European and Chinese civilisation, we must of course assume a complex multiplicity of causes, many of which may elude us, and many of which may have little or nothing to do with geography. The distinctions and the arguments which follow do not imply that this basic fact is disregarded, but they pursue the matter from a point of view which has frequently been neglected and which may be suggestive of important factors.

The cities of western Europe have been, at least since the high middle ages, centres of intellectual ferment; of economic change; and thus, in time, of opposition to the central authority. They became rebels in nearly every aspect of their institutional life. It was trade (and to a somewhat lesser extent specialised manufacturing) which made them strong enough to maintain their challenge to the established order. Their spirit of ferment was the spirit of a new group, urban merchant-manufacturers, which could operate from a base large and rich enough to establish increasingly its own rules. This setting tended to ensure that the universities, which grew up in cities originally for convenience and centrality, would frequently nourish scepticism, heresy, and freedom of enquiry. Even where they did not overtly do so, the concentration of literacy and learning in the cities was a stimulus to dissent. (Oxford and Cambridge, as rural universities, help to enforce this point. They were proverbially conservative, their most important job the training of students for the ministry. Spain's distinction from western Europe on this and nearly every other point raised is merely a reminder of the old aphorism 'Africa begins at the Pyrenees'.)

Most of the cities which rose out of the cultural and social chaos following the destruction of Roman unity and preceding the development of a new national unity grew in answer to new conditions, for northwest Europe was ideally situated for trade. Most of them were in their origins much older than this, and had begun as administrative, military, or ecclesiastical centres. But a score of major rivers, navigable and free from floods, silting, or ice throughout the year in this mild maritime climate, led across the great European plain to the open sea; the peninsular, indented nature of the coast critically heightened mobility. The invitation which this presented to inter-European trade furthered the ascendancy of the commercial function. The shift of commerce and associated urbanism from the Mediterranean to northwest Europe seems to have begun before the Age of the Discoveries, notably in the Hansa towns and in Flanders. This may be in part a reflection of the mobility inherent in the lands around the Baltic and North Seas, once they had learned from the Mediterranean the lessons of commerce and absorbed the civilising influences of this earlier developed area. In any case, these northern cities came to be dominated by trader-manufacturers. Trade was a heady diet, and enabled urban merchants to command cities which had originally been administrative creations. While the cities did not alone destroy feudalism, they owed much of their prosperity and independence to its decline: freer trade, wider exchange, and failing power of the landed mobility. And their very growth as rival power bases accelerated the collapse of the old feudal order.

As the growth of national unity progressed, under the institutional and emotional leadership of monarchy, an alliance of convenience between king and city arose which met the crown's demands for funds and the city's demand for representation. Urban merchants had the money to support the king in his foreign wars and in his struggle with the divisive domestic ambitions of the nobility and the church. In return the city received an increasing voice in the affairs of state, through representation in parliaments, and indirectly through the making of policy in which the throne was obliged to follow. But while this alliance of revenue in exchange for concessions was one of mutual interest, its ultimate result was the strengthening of the urban commercial sector until it overthrew or emasculated the monarchy, and with it the traditional order as a whole. Having helped the king to power over the nobility, the city achieved a *modus vivendi* with him which left it in control of the affairs vital to it. As a current reminder of the development of urban independence, 'the city' of London retains its originally hard-won privilege of excluding the reigning monarch, who is also excluded from the House of Commons, in part the city's creation and in part its weapon. To a certain extent the king, and even the nobility, were willing to go along with the process of economic change instigated by the city since they profited from it as the principal source of wealth in which they were often investors as well as tax collectors. But the new values which the city emphasised, and their institutional expression, were in direct conflict with the traditional society based

on land; the city repeatedly bred overt revolutionary movements
designed to establish its new order as the national way of life.

As centres of trade, the cities were free of the land and of its social
and political limitations embodied in the institutions of post-Roman
society. They developed their own law which was in differing degrees
independent of the traditional, rural law. Their institutions were
self-made, and they were not beholden to the traditional system
which they challenged. The companies and corporations which the
merchants organised went far beyond the scope of guilds in their
successful attempt to order most of the social and economic fabric
(instead of being limited to a trade-union function, as the guilds of
China predominantly were). Traditional guilds were overlaid with
new merchant organisations, or were clothed with new functions
and powers, although some of the older guilds remained as conservative or retarding influences. The economic institutions which
arose concurrently were also new-made sources of strength: banking,
letters of credit, private property, interest, speculation and investment, representing needs and ideas which were almost wholly
foreign to the traditional society of the countryside, and which were
the accompaniment of an ever-widening trade. For the invitation
to commercial expansion overseas was as strong in Europe's
geography as the earlier invitation to trade among the lands surrounding the Baltic, Mediterranean, and North Seas. A leading
agent of this process was necessarily the city, where trade flowed
through break-in-bulk points such as the mouths of the Rhine or
the English ports facing the Channel. Merchant corporations for
overseas trade became the strongest and most progressive, or revolutionary, of the city's agents. Interestingly, the original charter of
the British East India Company stated that 'gentlemen' (by which
was meant the landed gentry) 'shall be excluded' from membership.

The city was the natural centre of political change as it had been
of economic change. The growth of modern Europe may be regarded as the steady progress of a new class of urban traders and
manufacturers toward a position of control in a society and
economy which their own enterprise had largely created. It was they
who had realised the potential of Europe's location for world trade,
and they who had developed and applied the technological and
economic tools which made Europe the centre of the world. The
destruction of the old pattern was implicit in this process, and also
implicit was the revolutionary expression, by the cities, of their

claim to political power. City–country alliances were formed, and the dissident groups from the country often bore the brunt of the effort, since they were the more numerous, as well as sharing in the spoils. But the city was in the van, and even diverted or perverted rural dissent and rural force to its own ends; leadership and money were frequently more decisive than numbers. It is of course true that at least in England this city–country alliance left and perhaps still leaves the landed gentry with prestige and thus with considerable power, while it left wealth with the urbanites. Characteristically this wealth was used to acquire land and gentry status. This balance of advantage was particularly pertinent in the matter of parliamentary representation.

Revolutionary changes are nearly always the work of an alliance of groups, but the history of modern Europe is suggestive of the city's key role, despite the recurrent blurring of city–country distinctions. The first great modern revolution, in seventeenth-century England, was the work of a city–country alliance, but London was mainly Puritan, and the outcome might be regarded as the victory of urban merchants and their country confreres over the traditional authoritarian alliance of cavalier and peasant based on the land[3]. Two centuries later Manchester and Birmingham had joined London in the final stages of the contest between urban 'radicalism' and country 'conservatism', epitomised in the struggle over the Corn Laws, the Reform Bills, free trade, and the Manchester School. By this time cotton textiles had well supplanted woollen textiles as the chief manufacturing industry; since it came relatively late it was not greatly hampered by guild restrictions, as wool had been; it established itself in Manchester, which as a then unincorporated town lacked formalised controls. It may irritate many readers as a loose generalisation, but still seems worth stating for argument, that representative government and the industrial revolution, perhaps modern Europe's two most significant products, were created by the city. The Low Countries provide as good an illustration of this as does England.

In France the picture was less clear since urban merchant-manufacturers were less prominent in the national economy. Even so, it was Paris which created and carried the revolution. Paris used peasant distress and rebellion, but was never dethroned by it. One may say that Paris later destroyed Charles X and Louis Philippe. By this time, however, the Napoleonic land reform had given the

peasant a stake in the status quo and helped to keep him a conservative counter-influence to the city, after his revolutionary ardour
of the 1790's had served its purpose and cooled. Thus, in part, is
derived the country's role in the destruction of the Second Republic
and the Paris Commune, 'radical city movements'. Across the Rhine
these distinctions become increasingly blurred, as for example in the
Peasant War in early Reformation Swabia and Franconia. In eastern
Europe it is difficult to draw distinctions between city and country,
or to find an independent urban-based group living on trade and
challenging the existing order. Nevertheless even in twentieth-
century Russia, while the Soviet revolution was in part carried by
peasant groups, leadership remained in the urban intellectual group
which had instigated the change.

In northwest Europe, which is our concern here, the city has been
a consistent seat of radicalism. This is not to overlook the recurrent
Jacqueries which in every society have been the desperate recourse
of an oppressed peasantry. But in the West these have often been
closer to reaction than to revolution—the peasants were demanding
the restoration of the status quo ante, not the establishment of a
new order. Where they did attack the old order it was characteristically on specific points, such as Wat Tyler's demand in fourteenth-
century England for the disendowment of the church. The same
pattern is apparent in rural opposition in America, in uprisings like
the Whiskey Rebellion or in political parties like the Populists.
The removal of abuses does not necessarily mean revolutionary
change, despite the violence or the 'levelling' sentiments which
usually characterised rural dissidence.

In China, while the peasant and the countryside were in some
respects like the West, the city's role was fundamentally different.
Chinese cities were administrative centres. With few exceptions this
function dominated their lives whatever their other bases in trade
or manufacturing. Their remarkably consistent, uniform plan,
square or rectangular walls surrounding a great cross with gates at
each of the four arms, suggests their common administrative creation
and their continued expression of this function. Local defensive
terrain, such as at Chungking, occasionally made this common
plan unsuitable, but the stamp of governmental uniformity is nonetheless apparent. This was true for cities which had originally risen
as trade centres, or which became more important commercially
than they were administratively. It is possible to find a clear

separation in many provinces between administrative and commercial cities, where the capital is not the most important commercial base: Chungking and Chengtu in Szechuan, Chengchow and Kaifeng in Honan, Hankow and Wuchang in Hupeh, Hsiangtan and Changsha in Hunan, Soochow and Nanking in Kiangsu, Wuhu and Anking in Anhwei, Tientsin and Peking in Hopeh, and other less clear cases. (Compare for instance the original development of London as two cities separated by open country, Westminster as the administrative centre, and 'the city' as the centre of business.) But despite this degree of functional specificity, little urban independence or urban-based revolutionary change appeared until the traditional fabric was rent by the growth of Western-inspired treaty-ports. Even in the exceptional cases where trade or manufacturing was the sole or predominant basis of the city: Chingtechen, the site of the Imperial Potteries, or Canton, the consistent focus of foreign trade, there never developed a merchant-controlled urban base free in any significant sense of the traditional state order.

A case in point is Shanghai. Long before the city became a treaty-port under foreign domination, it was the leading commercial hub of the Yangtze Valley and may even have exceeded Canton in the volume of its trade. A British visitor in 1832 maintained that it did, and his count of junk traffic suggests that Shanghai was then among the leading ports of the world[4]. It nevertheless remained well down on the list of delta cities by size despite its lion's share of the trade. Another British visitor in 1843, the year in which Shanghai was opened to foreign trade as a treaty-port, estimated its population at 270 000, Hangchow at one million, Soochow, Ningpo, and Nanking at half a million each, and six other delta cities at figures equal to or greater than Shanghai's[5]. Shanghai has never performed any administrative functions outside its own metropolitan limits, and it may be for this reason that it did not dominate the delta until Western entrepreneurs largely took over its development. In bureaucratic China, trade alone could not rival administration as an urban foundation. Outstanding locations for trade, such as Hankow (or Shanghai), as advantageous as Amsterdam or London, were frequently not put to full use until European traders built major cities there. Wuchang, opposite the mouth of the Han, was an almost exclusively administrative city before 1850, while Hankow itself was only a moderate sized town.

Large cities seem to have been proportionately more numerous in China than in Europe until the nineteenth century, and until the eighteenth century urbanism may have been higher. Perhaps a quarter or more of the population lived in towns and cities of more than 2500 population, and perhaps 10 or 15 per cent in cities over 10 000. The big cities of the East as a whole were huge by European standards; this was a consistent feature of what has been called 'Oriental society'[6]. In China most cities or towns of 5000 or more had well-defined commercial or manufacturing districts, and special areas for each important enterprise: banking, metal goods, food markets, textiles, woodwork, and so on. This pattern remains in most contemporary Chinese cities. But the cities were not decisive centres of change in a commercialised economy. They served as imperial or provincial capitals, seats for garrison troops, and residences for governors, viceroys, and the ubiquitous cloud of officials and quasi-officials with their 'service-providers'. Their business was administration, and exploitation, of the countryside. Marco Polo, in describing the magnificence of Peking, accounts for it as follows:

> ... and this happens because everyone from everywhere brings there for the lord who lives there and for his court and for the city which is so great and for the ladies and barons and knights of whom there are so many and for the great abundance of the multitude of the people of the armies of the lord, which stay round about as well for the court as for the city, and of other people who come there by reason of the court which the great lord holds there, and for one and for another ... and because the city is in too good a position and in the middle of many provinces[7].

Here is a clear picture of a city based on administration from a central location, where trade flows in largely in response to the existing structure of officials, troops, court, hangers-on, and the host of people necessary to support them, from secretaries and servants to bakers and dancers. Six hundred years later at the end of the nineteenth-century European travellers in China reported the same phenomenon, on a smaller regional scale: large cities whose sole function appeared to be administration, or important trading cities at key locations which were nevertheless dominated by officials and the magistrate's *yamen* (office). Thus Archibald Little, describing the city of Kweichowfu in Szechuan where the manufacture of salt brine and coal dust balls, and trade on the Yangtze River, were the apparent sources of its prosperity, writes that the city was a main station for the collection of *likin* (internal customs tax) and 'the town is studded with the numerous mansions of the wealthy officials and their dependents'[8]. With the opening of Chungking as a treaty-port, *likin* was collected at Kweichowfu only on local hauls and the city rapidly decayed despite its apparently strong economic base in manufacturing and trade.

The trade process appears to have lacked the dynamic quality by means of which Europe's cities rose to power. Pre-eighteenth-century China had a trade as great as or greater than pre-eighteenth-century Europe, but Europe's subsequent commercial expansion left China far behind. Why this happened, and why China never produced the revolutionary economic and political changes which re-made Europe into an arbiter for the rest of the world is a vital question. An analysis of the city's role may help to suggest some relevant factors. Why was the Chinese city not a European-style centre of change?

China is geographically isolated by a formidable assemblage of barriers. To landward lies the greatest mountain mass in the world, with its extensions from the Pamir Knot, reinforced on the south by rainforests and spectacular river gorges, on the north by the barren wastes of Siberia, and on the west and northwest by a vast sweep of desert. Seaward a coast deficient in harbours faces a huge and until recently commercially underdeveloped ocean, by European standards. Chinese trade with Japan was at several periods considerable, and with southeast Asia even larger, but it did not approach eighteenth- or nineteenth-century European levels. It tended to be characterised by luxury goods, strategic goods (such as copper for coinage), or specialties such as Chinese porcelain. With these exceptions, especially the highly developed and diversified trade between southeast coastal China,* and southeast Asia, China did not greatly extend herself commercially, and was for the most part content to send specialised goods, like silk, to the rest of the world through middlemen intermediaries: the Arabs by sea and the Turkish peoples of central Asia by land. Significantly, the largest

---

* Southeast China has many fine harbours and overseas trade has been prominent there for centuries. But it is effectively isolated from the main body of China by mountains, including those which help to make its harbours, and trade there has thus made much less impact on the rest of the country. The distinctiveness of the southeast is also clear in its many regional ethnic and linguistic elements.

concerted Chinese attempt in foreign trade was an imperial government project (the famous Ming expeditions of the fifteenth century), which lasted only some 30 years and apparently found no
solid base in the Chinese economy or in its merchant group.

Internally, trade moved largely on the great river systems, running
fortunately east and west, but there was no such close interconnection
between these river basins as in Europe, by sea or across plains.
Physically China is built on a grander scale, but the landscape
presents no such invitation to exchange as has sparked the development of Europe. Europe is multi-peninsular, each peninsula
tending towards economic distinctiveness and political independence,
but joined by cheap sea and river routes. This plethora of comple-
mentary areas and their transport links magnified the basis and the
means of exchange. Although its early trade development was not
larger than China's, by the middle of the eighteenth century commercial expansion overseas had joined and accelerated commercialisation at home, and Europe stood in a class by itself. The cities of
western Europe were both the creators and inheritors of this development. But in China the cities remained centres of the unitary
national state and of the traditional order rather than its attackers,
epitomes of the status quo. As direct links in the official hierarchy,
they were the props of the empire. The universities were urban, for
convenience as in Europe, but they stimulated no dissent. Their
accepted function was to train scholars who could staff the imperial
civil service, and they fed their graduates into the imperial examination system. This, and the better economic and social position of
scholars generally in China than in Europe, encouraged the universities and the literati to support the status quo; European intellectuals
may have taken a vow of poverty, but they remained a dissident or
discontented group.

Physically, China lacked Europe's outstanding advantages for
trade, and on the other hand presented a base for highly productive
agriculture, through irrigation. Wittvogel's revealing work on the
organic connection between the need for mass organised water
control and the growth of a monolithic bureaucratic state in China
lends insight into the origins and pattern of the institutional structure[9]. With China's environmental advantages, water control made
agriculture the massive core of the economy, and at the same time
left the bureaucracy in a position of ramified command. It was not
possible for urban merchants to win independence from this system.

They had less economic leverage than the rising European merchants because, with the preponderant position of agriculture, they never occupied proportionately as large a place in the economy.

The state of course did its part to prevent the development of a rival group, and by taxation, requisition, and monopoly ensured that the merchants would be kept relatively impotent. This was a job which European states and monarchs, though equally determined, failed to accomplish; their merchants were in a stronger position, and the state was weaker: it was merely *primus inter pares.* Land hunger in China, as a reflection of a population too large for the available arable land (increasingly serious during the past 200 years, but even in Han times worse than in most other parts of the world, including Europe), also acted to restrict commercial development, since it meant high land rents. Capital could almost always be invested with greater profit and safety in land, or in rural loans, than in productive or capital-generating enterprises outside the agrarian sphere.

Where extra-agricultural opportunites for investment did exist, the individual entrepreneur was at the mercy of the bureaucratic state. Many of the major trade goods were government monopolies. Elsewhere the essentially Western concepts of private property and due process of law, in a word, of the entrepreneur, were lacking in a society dominated by agriculture and officials. Extortion, forced levies, confiscation, and simple financial failure as the result of arbitrary government policies were the daily risk of the merchant. Some individuals did indeed become very rich, for example the famous *hong* merchants of Canton, but their wealth came necessarily through official connection: by possession of gentry status, by office holding or official favour, or by trading as part of a government monopoly (such as foreign trade under the Canton system and at most other periods was). Even so their gains were never secure. The greatest and richest of the *hong* merchants died in poverty, having lost official favour. While this also happened to many of the pre-eighteenth-century European capitalists, it did not prevent the survival and growth of individual capitalist families or firms or of a moneyed group. The famous Ch'ing dynasty billionaire Ho Shen, said to have been worth the equivalent of nearly a billion and a half U.S. dollars, was not a merchant at all, but a favourite minister of the emperor Ch'ien Lung, which demonstrates the real source of wealth in traditional China. Yet he too died in poverty and disgrace (by suicide in place of a suspended death sentence in 1799) at the hands of Ch'ien Lung's successor.

In China merchant-capitalists did not use their money to establish their independence, as did the merchants of London or Antwerp, or to stimulate the growth of a new economic pattern. Unfortunately for the Chinese merchants, the imperial revenue was at most periods derived largely from the land tax and from the government trade monopolies. Agriculture was proportionately more productive than in Europe, and revenue from trade less necessary. Peking thus did not need the merchants as the king had needed them in Europe to finance the ascendancy of the national state, to pay for its wars with rival states, or to meet its normal bills. No concessions were necessary; the merchants could be squeezed dry, and were, with no harm to the state. The commanding position of the bureaucracy, and the fact of the bureaucratic state, are perhaps explainable by a similar process of default. Merchants were necessary or useful to perform essential (and, to the state, profitable) commercial functions; they were tolerated, but kept under strict control, and this was simpler and cheaper than for the state to manage all commercial dealings itself. (K. A. Wittvogel, in his *Oriental Society and Oriental Despotism* speaks of this arrangement as based on 'the law of diminishing administrative returns'.)

But the merchants were also identified with the state as well as being stifled by it. Their numbers were recruited largely from the gentry class, who had the capital and the official connections essential to commercial success. Gentry merchants worked willingly with gentry officials in the management of the state monopolies, including foreign trade. Outside the monopolies, the same partnership operated, as a matter of mutual interest. In addition, most gentry members, whether or not they were engaged in trade, also performed other semi-official functions, comparable in some degree to the British landed gentry. These 'services' represented a considerable part of their income; they were not likely to attack the system which nourished them. In a more general sense, the tradition of revolt in this hierarchical society did not include the re-ordering of social or economic groups, but concentrated on the removal of bad government. Individual or group improvement was not to be won by destroying the fabric, but by making optimum use of one's position within it.

Finally, China had maintained since Han times and with few

breaks a remarkable degree of unity* and a central power which no single European state achieved until quite late in its modern development. In China even towns of the *chen* (market town) rank (population c.3000–5000) were seats of garrison troops, whatever their prominence in trade. In Europe in the course of the crown's contest with the nobles, and of the international rivalries which also developed among the plethora of separate national states, urban merchants found an opportunity which contrasted sharply with the rooted monolithic nature of the Chinese state.

The cities of China were consequently microcosms of the empire, not deviants. They were not backwaters, for necessarily learning, art, and the trappings of cosmopolis were concentrated in them. Yet, each was a symbol of the imperial system, operating not only under the direct thumb of Peking, but according to its precepts. Obvious considerations of convenience made them central places, market towns, transport termini or break-in-bulk points, and exchange centres of varying degrees of sophistication. But these universal urban functions do not automatically bring with them the character of rebellion or innovation which we have rightly come to associate with cities in the West. The main distinction of the Chinese city was concentration, as the node of the traditional society and as its power base. Imperial authority filtered down more slowly into the countryside, becoming more dilute with every level. Every government with ambitions of central power attempted to control the peasant. In a largely pre-commercial and pre-industrial society of a basically molecular character, this could never be perfect control. China lacked not only the tools of control for its huge area, such as communications and literacy, but the bond of common interest and attitude which as completely commercialised economy tends to create, often by sublimating or suppressing conflicting interests. In the absence of such tools or conditions to implement rural control in China, the importance of the city as a centre of political and military power on the side of authority was magnified.

Change in China, as elsewhere, has been the work of a city-country alliance, with the leadership coming usually from the gentry based in cities or towns. But the origins of dissent and the main force of attacks on the status quo have been far less urban in China

---

* The persistent unity of China despite wide regional diversity is something of a puzzle, but may be related to China's dramatic isolation and to the unitary rather than peninsular nature of her continental base.

than in the West. While the rebellions were in many cases closer to the usually unsuccessful Jacqueries of the West than to the really revolutionary changes generated in Western cities, they were the predominant agents of what change did take place. They were successful where their Western analogues failed because there was no more potent agent of change, no other group (if we except the several nomadic invasions and conquests) and no other economic base by which change might even superficially be forced. The similarity with the Jacqueries lies in the fact that Chinese rebellions rarely challenged the basic nature of the existing order, but only its administration. The new dynasty which resulted might mean new blood, but seldom new institutions.

Given a largely closed, agrarian system, it is understandable that each dynasty, as it lost its momentum, lacked the means of maintaining a high productivity and effective distribution as population increased, and that it eventually declined into corruption. This was especially so in the rural sphere, easy prey to tax and rent manipulation (and the source of most of the national revenue and income), but marginal enough to be sensitive to oppression. At the same time, the lack of large extra-agricultural economic bases for an independent group prevented the growth of new ideas or new institutions to challenge the old, even while the old lay in ruins. The city–country alliance which in Europe meant revolution made only a change of administration in China. The city was too dependent on the traditional order to attempt its destruction.

The accelerated impact of the West on China during the nineteenth century has by the twentieth century set in train profound changes, and it is natural to find that these are reflected also in the city's role. The Kuo Min Tang was a largely urban-based movement, and though its revolutionary aspects became less and less prominent under the more compelling problems of security against Communists and Japanese, it was far more than a change of administration. It was in fact the political vehicle of a new group, nurtured not only in Western thought, but in the essentially Western milieu of the treaty-ports. Negatively also the cities have made a new impression. The present Communist regime had prominent rural roots, and came to power with an announced resentment and distrust of cities, calling them the centres of reaction (and also of degeneracy, softness, and vice), though its venom was directed particularly against the foreign-created treaty-ports.

It was basically the impact of the West, including the Soviet Union, which ensured that this latest of rebellions would for the first time successfully destroy the existing fabric. In the treaty-ports themselves development had been too brief, and too much limited by the inertia of the agrarian economy, to produce an effective base for change to rival Communism in its originally rural base. Nevertheless these urban centres, many of them new as large cities dependent on trade, played much the same role as the cities of late mediaeval Europe. They were rebels against the traditional order because for the first time in the history of China they provided opportunity for the merchant. Money could not only be made, but invested, in trade or manufacturing, with safety, profit, and prestige. Private property, and all of the values of R. H. Tawney's 'Acquisitive Society' had been enthroned in the treaty-ports by the West, and to the Chinese businessman Shanghai or Tientsin were all that traditional China was not. He was prepared to work for the establishment of a government and society which would make a respectable place for a commercial industrial bourgeoisie, based, as the term implies, in cities.

This new group, shaped by the West, largely created the Kuo Min Tang. They formed an alliance with some of the landed gentry, for example, Chiang Kai-shek, who was both landed and bourgeois, but they were never in any sense a peasant party, and their ties with the land were feeble. While they answered, or promised to answer, many of the needs of the new class of treaty-port Chinese, and kept peace with the gentry, they did not seriously attempt to answer the questions and strivings of the Peking intellectuals, nor the more compelling needs of the peasants. Communism ultimately rode to power in part as a crusade against the 'merchant capitalists' of Shanghai on the one hand and the Western-inspired intellectuals of Peking on the other.*

* As the capital and as the seat of the largest Western-founded universities, Peking was a centre of intellectual ferment by the end of the nineteenth century since intellectual contact with the West was easiest there. Traditional, imperial China had by then lost enough prestige that dissension flourished in Peking itself. While many of the intellectuals rejected China's traditional civilisation in whole or in part, their struggles in this scholar's community made little impact on the nation as a whole. The Chinese Communist Party was founded in Peking in 1921, but largely deserted it for a rural base. Student and intellectual ferment in Peking was revolutionary in thought, but ineffective in action. Both the treaty-ports and the countryside proved in the end to be much more effective bases for change or for rebellion.

To be sure, the Chinese Communist Party and its leaders are urban-trained Marxists operating intellectually and practically in an urban framework, and dedicated to an industrialisation programme which necessarily centres in the cities. Their political control also depends substantially on their control of city populations and city enterprises. Insofar as they thus push the city toward the middle of the stage as a recognised base at least for economic and technological change, they continue the about-face in the city's role which the Western impact began in the treaty-ports. In any case, active urban agency for change is a recent phenomenon in China, perhaps one may say a direct transmittal from the West.

This analysis, in attempting to particularise the city's role in the two great centres of world civilisation, has necessarily dealt with institutions as much as with place. The urban differences were expressions of distinct societies. It was broadly speaking the bureaucratic state in China which stifled the growth of European-type cities despite the volume of trade or the regional specialisation of commerce and manufacturing which existed. In Europe, too, wherever bureaucratic and/or persistently authoritarian governments ruled, commercialisation and industrialisation were late and/or little, and the urban-based entrepreneur usually exerted small influence. Some other common ground may exist between these bureaucracies, and the suggestion that physical conditions required or invited central control, and that geographic factors helped to minimise the opportunity of the merchant, are perhaps as applicable to eastern Europe, or to Spain, as to China. The imprint of Roman Law and of Mediterranean urban traditions may also help to account for the east-west distinction in Europe. In any case, maritime western Europe followed a course whose urban direction lay at the root of its wealth, its power, and its distinctiveness.

Sir George Sansom, in a characteristic series of lectures given at Tokyo University in 1950 and published in 1951 under the title *Japan in World History*, typifies the modern European attitude and contrasts it with the Tokugawa Japanese by quoting as follows from Alexander Pope's 'Windsor Forest', written about 1712:

> The time shall come when free as seas or wind
> Unbounded Thames shall flow for all mankind,
> Whole nations enter with each flowing tide
> And seas but join the regions they divide.

This is so revealingly and typically English, and so untypically Chinese, because it shows the world through the eyes of the London merchant. Ironically, merchant towns of a European type had begun to develop in Japan by the sixteenth century around the Inland Sea (perhaps an oriental Mediterranean?), including self-governing Sakai, living on the trade with China and southeast Asia. Sakai, with its own army and its council of merchants, was so close to the European pattern that contemporary Jesuit observers compared it with Venice. This promising development was crushed, despite its apparently strong economic base, by the feudal revival of the Togukawa and its superior armies reacting to the political threat which they felt was posed by the existence of even quasi-independent merchant cities. Here we may perhaps see an expression of Japan's insularity and strategic commercial location, and perhaps *inter alia* of the weight of influence from China. The latter was earlier expressed in the great period of Japanese borrowing from T'ang China when Nara, Japan's first real city, was built on the Yamato plain as a smaller scale copy of Ch'ang An, the T'ang capital. Nara omitted Ch'ang An's massive walls, and walled towns as such have never existed in Japan at any period, one reflection of a basically different set of geographic and social conditions.

But our purpose here has been only to suggest. The city has been a centre of change in western Europe, while it has been the reverse in traditional China, despite the broad similarity in urban economic functions in both areas. Urban character and urban roles may be useful indicators of the nature and dynamics of the diverse entities of society.

SOURCE: *Annals of The Association of American Geographers*, **44** (1954), pp. 349–62.

REFERENCES

1. This is not a new idea. Other and older applications of it would include Giovanni Botero. *A Treatise Concerning the Causes of the Magnificance and Greatness of Cities*. Transl. ROBERT PETERSON. (London 1606); GEORG SIMMEL. *Die Grosstadt und das Geistesleben* (1900); THEODORE PETERMAN (ed.), *Die Grosstadt* (1903); N. S. B. GRAS. 'The Development of the Metropolitan Economy in Europe and America,' *American Historical Review*, **27** (1921–22); MICHAEL ROSTOVTZEFF. 'Cities in the Ancient World,' in *Urban Land Economics*, ed., RICHARD ELY (1922). E. W. BURGESS, et al. *The City* (1925); HENRI PIRENNE. *Medieval Cities: Their Origins and the Revival of Trade*

(1925); Max Weber. *Wirtschaft und Gesellschaft* (1925), Part I, Chap. 8; Louis Wirth. 'Urbanism as a Way of Life,' *American Journal of Sociology*, **44** (1938); A. M. Schlesinger. 'The City in American History.' *Mississippi Valley Historical Review*, **27** (1940); William Diamond. 'On the Dangers of an Urban Interpretation of History,' Chap. 4 in *Historiography and Urbanization*, ed. E. F. Goldman (1941). Sylvia Thrupp. *The Merchant Class of Medieval London* (1948); Pierre George. *La Ville: le fait urbain à travers le monde* (1952).

2. Karl Marx. *Capital*, edition of 1903, Chicago: Vol. I, p. 387.

3. Generalisation on matters such as this is particularly hazardous. A serious doubt has been cast on these commonly accepted alignments: see D. H. Pennington and Douglas Brunton. *Members of the Long Parliament*, London (1953).

4. Rhoads Murphey. *Shanghai: Key to Modern China*, Cambridge, Mass., (1953,) p. 59.

5. Robert Fortune. *A Journey to the Tea Countries of China and India*. London, (1852) Vol. I, pp. 97–8.

6. K. A. Wittvogel. *Oriental Society and Oriental Despotism*. For example, ancient Alexandria had a population of about 1 million in a country (Egypt) with a total population of only 7 million.

7. A. C. Moule and Paul Pelliot. *Marco Polo, the Description of the World*. London (1939), Vol. I, pp. 236–37.

8. Archibald Little. *Through the Yangtze Gorges*. London (1898), pp. 87 ff.

9. K. A. Wittvogel. Foundations and stages of Chinese economic history. *Zeitschrift für Socialforschung*, **4** (1935), 26–58. *ibid.*, Die Theorie der Orientalischen Gesellschaft, *loc. cit.*, **7** (1938), 90–123. (This article clearly states the administrative basis of the Chinese city, and discusses the reasons and implications.) *ibid.*, *Wirtschaft und Gesellschaft Chinas*, Leipzig (1931). *ibid.*, *Oriental Society and Oriental Despotism*.

4 Urbanisation in North Africa: Its Nature and Consequences

GERALD H. BLAKE

IT IS not possible to say with certainty what proportion of the populations of the Maghreb countries and Libya were urban dwellers before 1900, but one tenth may be a fair estimate. Figures of 8–9 per cent have been suggested for Morocco (1900) and Tunisia (1880) and 16 per cent for Algeria (1886), while urban life was probably least developed in Libya[1].

In spite of the availability of census data for all four countries, attempts to establish present levels of urbanisation raise certain problems. To begin with, there is no common definition of 'urban', and published international figures are therefore not directly comparable. Morocco includes 117 declared urban centres, some of which have fewer than 5000 inhabitants yet fulfilling urban functions. These include mining settlements and tourist resorts. Algeria regards only the 55 most important communes having local self-government as genuinely 'urban', thus excluding several centres with 10 000–12 000 inhabitants. Tunisia uses a similar definition. The latest Libyan census of 1964, however, is unique in failing to recognise urban agglomerations at all, giving statistics for large administrative divisions only, which usually comprise rural and urban populations. The Ministry of Planning and Development has, however, subsequently published separate figures for most settlements with more than 2000 inhabitants[2]. It is possible of course to disregard national definitions and adopt a numerical basis, but this also introduces many anomalies. In preparing the accompanying statistical tables and diagrams any settlements with more than 10 000 inhabitants were regarded as having 'urban' status. Among those which thus qualify by size but clearly do not qualify by function are the remarkable rural agglomerations of the Sahel region of Eastern Tunisia, while a number of smaller centres with entirely non-agricultural activities are excluded. The oil towns of Hassi

For References to this chapter, see page 79.

Messauoud in Algeria or Marsa Brega in Libya are obvious examples. Using 10 000 as a suitable threshold for urban populations, Table 4.2 indicates that at the latest census the level of urbanisation was highest in Algeria (36·2 per cent) and Libya (34·8 per cent) and lowest in Tunisia (30·2 per cent) and Morocco (26·9 per cent). Using national census definitions of 'urban population', the gap between Morocco and Algeria is however decreased. Another shortcoming of these figures is that they refer to different census dates over a six year period, which undoubtedly has the effect of making the level of urbanisation in Morocco appear relatively low. Nevertheless, the figures reveal the basic fact that today one person in three lives in an urban place in the Maghreb and Libya compared with approximately one in ten at the turn of the century. The degree of urbanisation is thus lower than in the rest of the Arab world and the Middle East, but higher than in tropical Africa and South Asia.

Before 1900 North African towns were not only smaller but fewer in number than today. Table 4.3 indicates 191 centres with more than 10 000 inhabitants in the 1960s whereas in 1900 there may have been only half as many, the majority in the 15 000–50 000 range, though with one or two exceptions such as Marrakech (90 000 inhabitants). None had more than 100 000 inhabitants and Casablanca, Algiers and Tripoli were still moderate size towns of 20 000–30 000 inhabitants. The majority were of ancient origin[3]. On the coast, most were on or adjacent to Carthaginian or Roman town sites, while inland a number of cities founded during the golden age of Arab civilisation (8th–13th centuries) continued to flourish. Along the Atlantic coast of Morocco some small Portuguese foundations remained, but very small towns with genuine urban status were rare. One may not entirely agree with Despois and Raynal[4] that without a mosque, a permanent market, public baths and ramparts, no centre could be regarded as a town, but the idea illustrates the much clearer distinction between urban and non-urban agglomerations in form and function compared with today.

More remarkable than the actual level of urbanisation in the Maghreb and Libya is the rate of urban growth which has shown almost unchecked acceleration through the twentieth century. During the period as a whole Libya shows the most rapid rate of expansion largely as a result of exceptional increases in urban populations during the last decade. Morocco has achieved similar rates in spite of the exodus of many thousands of Europeans and Jews mainly from the towns since 1956. Estimates of annual percentage increases vary, but the following figures illustrate the trend in Morocco[5]:

Table 4.1   Percent Annual Increase of Urban Population

1900–36	3·3
1936–52	4·0
1952–60	4·8
1960–67	5·1

Although Algeria remains the most highly urbanised country of the four, the rate of increase has been slower than in Libya and Morocco, partly as a result of losing between 800 000 and 900 000 non-Moslem town dwellers through emigration since 1954. The present annual growth rate of Algeria's urban population has fallen since the early 1960s to around 4·5 per cent. Tunisia, with ancient traditions of town life, shows the least rapid growth rate, in spite of the marked expansion of Tunis; the present rate may be as low as 3·2 per cent per annum[6].

The rate of urbanisation of the Moslem population of North Africa has been almost spectacular during the post-independence period. Even in the first half of the nineteenth century a surprisingly high proportion of town dwellers were non-Moslems. Many of the largest towns were ports trading with the Mediterranean world, and most had Spanish, Italian and Maltese communities. In addition, almost every town including many small ones, possessed Jewish communities which sometimes made up a significant proportion of the population. For example one third of the population of Tripoli were Jews. The latter half of the nineteenth century witnessed the influx of Europeans in increasing numbers. The French gained effective control of Algeria in 1857 and Tunisia in 1881 and before the end of the century well over half the inhabitants of most large towns in these countries were Europeans or Jews. France and Spain partitioned Morocco in 1912, and Italy conquered Libya in the 1920s and in these regions too, urban growth was stimulated by the commencement of European colonial rule. On the eve of the war of independence in 1959, 80 per cent of Algeria's urban population was European or Jewish. Between 1962 and 1964 some 600 000 Europeans left Algerian towns, while during the same short period 800 000 Algerians moved in from the countryside, 'regroupment' centres, and

Table 4.2 Percentage of Population by Locality size

	Latest Census	Total population (thousands)	100 000– 999 999		50 000– 99 000		20 000– 49 999		10 000– 19 999		Urban population
			%	cum.%	%	cum.%	%	cum.%	%	cum.%	%
Morocco	1960	11 626	18·9	18·9	2·1	21·0	3·2	24·2	2·7	26·9	29·3
Algeria	1966	11 833	21·1	21·1	4·7	25·8	7·5	33·3	2·9	36·2	33·3
Tunisia	1966	4 457	10·3	10·3	4·0	14·3	9·2	23·5	6·7	30·2	?
Libya	1964	1 564	25·5	25·5	—	25·5	1·6	27·1	7·7	34·8	?

Source: CLARKE, J. I. Urban population growth in the Middle East and North Africa. Unpublished paper submitted to Institute of British Geographers Population Study Group Symposium, Keele, September 1969.

Table 4.3   Number of Towns and Cities with over 10 000 Inhabitants

	100 000–999 999	50 000–99 999	20 000–49 999	10 000–19 999	Total
Morocco (1960)	8	5*	12	22	47
Algeria (1966)	4	13	52	24	93
Tunisia (1966)	1	3	14	22	40
Libya (1964)	2		1	8	11
Total:	15	21	79	76	191

(* including the Spanish towns of Melilla and Ceuta)

refugee camps in Morocco and Tunisia. Less than 2 per cent of the urban population of Algeria is now non-Moslem. In Morocco, as recently as 1952, only 16 per cent of the urban population were Moslems, the remaining 84 per cent being largely French, Spanish and Jewish. The departure of Europeans and Jews from Morocco has been more gradual since independence in 1956, but by 1964 once again less than 2 per cent of the urban population were non-Moslems, and the proportion has since fallen further. When Tunisia became independent in 1956 only 11 per cent of the population of towns with over 20 000 inhabitants were Moslems, the rest being French, Italians and Jews[7]. By 1964 following the exodus of 200 000 Europeans the proportion had increased to 92 per cent. The 'Moslemisation' of urban life has been less complete in Libya. More than 100 000 Italians and Jews have departed, many before 1951, but non-Moslems still constitute about one tenth of the urban population.

The transformation of the cultural and ethnic composition of North African towns in the course of a few years has had far-reaching consequences, particularly in Algeria—less so in Libya. In physical terms, traditional ethnic groupings (notably the Jewish 'hara' or 'mellah' and the European quarters) have been largely re-placed by socio-economic groupings. Frequently, incoming tenants have been unable to maintain property at a suitable standard, and decay has set in, as in parts of Algiers—a process known locally as 'gourbisation'[8]. Economically, the movement has served to exac-erbate many of the problems familiarly associated with rural–urban migrations, with observable signs of unemployment and underemployment, and the emergence of a massive tertiary sector. It might also be argued that the large towns have now become less effective instruments of change and development. A recent paper by Professor H. Bowen-Jones is of particular interest in this context[9]. In it, he hypothesises that in the Middle East centuries of complex commercial and financial activity have bred a special type of hybrid urbanism superficially similar to Western urbanism, in which socio-economic values persist which are not conducive to rapid economic development. These include non-contractual as opposed to con-tractual relationships, 'caste' consciousness and kinship bonds as opposed to class consciousness and individualism. The hypothesis cannot be easily proved, but if it is valid for Middle Eastern towns, it seems a reasonable proposition that the Moslem dominated cities of North Africa may now embrace these economic values to a greater extent than prior to independence.

Discussions of the causes of rapid urban growth in the Maghreb and Libya have frequently undervalued the high rate of natural increase, which in the majority of towns is more significant than the migration component. In the early years of this century the annual rate of natural increase was about 1·8 per cent, whereas today the figure for North Africa as a whole has risen to 2·7 per cent, the highest in Africa. The highest rates are those of Morocco (2·9 per cent), and Libya (2·8 per cent but the subject of some debate)[10] with Algeria (2·5 per cent) and Tunisia (1·6 per cent) growing less rapidly[11]. There is, however, ample evidence to suggest that natural increase is very much higher in the towns on account of better medical facilities, sanitation, and housing conditions, and increases of 3 to 4 per cent may be common. When compared with the previously mentioned annual urban growth rates, the significance of these figures is obvious. It should be remembered, however, that in Algeria during the 1954–1966 intercensal period massive migration occurred to the towns during the fighting and immediately after independence, and more than half the towns in the country grew more rapidly from migration than natural increase. Some of the most notable increases were in the medium-sized towns, which lost few French but gained many Algerians. Average annual rates of increase of 50 per cent were not unknown in one or two towns. Algiers (8·2 per cent per annum) and Constantine (9·2 per cent per annum) grew in spite of the departure of many Europeans[12]. Since 1964 the rate of urban growth and the scale of migration to the towns in Algeria has declined. In Morocco on the other hand it is difficult to find more than a dozen towns whose rate of expansion unquestionably owes more to migration than natural increase. Casablanca increased at 5·2 per cent per annum between 1952 and 1960, a rate exceeded only by two out of the twelve largest towns in Morocco[13]. In Tunisia only Tunis shows a persistently strong migration component, while in Libya, Tripoli and Benghazi are also growing rapidly primarily as a result of a high rate of in-migration.

The causes of rural–urban migration lie beyond the scope of this paper: they are of infinite complexity, varying from country to country and locally from region to region. At a superficial level, however, migration displays certain similarities in all four countries. Three features which may provide interesting comparisons with the process in other developing regions are worth mentioning:

1. Migration occurs primarily to the large cities, but in Morocco and Algeria many small towns also attract rural migrants, usually from their immediate hinterlands. Indeed, the smaller the town the stronger its regional influence seems to be. These small towns include those sustaining vigorous economic growth (mining centres, ports, etc.) and others in which the economic incentives appear quite weak (small market towns, regional centres, etc.). There is some evidence at least in Morocco that such towns are used in a process of stepped migration to the large towns.

2. Most movements are permanent and involve the family at an early stage of the migration process. Thus the degree of masculinity in North African towns is not exceptionally high. A further result of family migrations is that links with home areas are weak. At the same time there is some tendency for tribal and kinship groupings to persist in the towns.

3. Most migration occurs without the prospect of employment or accommodation[14]. As a result many towns experience the accretion of 'bidonvilles'—unsightly shanty developments in peripheral locations in which unemployment is high and social problems of every kind manifest. Following independence in Algeria successful attempts were made to replace the worst bidonvilles utilising large numbers of unemployed to construct proper housing. But in Morocco between one tenth and one third of the populations of several large towns are still accommodated in bidonvilles in spite of rehousing programmes. The phenomenon exists in Tunisia and Libya but is largely confined to the major cities of Tunis, Tripoli and Benghazi.

THE RANK–SIZE HIERARCHY

The rank–size hierarchy reveals a number of interesting features. (See Tables 4.2 and 4.3, and Fig. 4.1.) Urban primacy, for example, is not as evident in the Maghreb and Libya as might be expected. It is most marked in Tunisia where Tunis, the political and economic capital of the country, shows an increasing tendency to outstrip the nearest rival in size. In Libya on the other hand duality rather than primacy can be observed with a relatively small difference in size between the two largest towns followed by an enormous drop to the third largest town. Morocco is notable for having one large city with a population now well over a million and seven other cities with more than 100 000 inhabitants. Thus although Casablanca

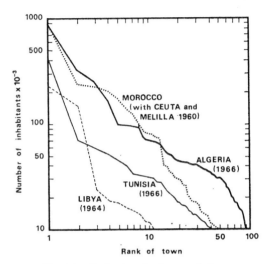

Fig. 4.1   Rank–size of urban populations.

is a great deal larger than Marrakech (244 000 in 1960) it does not contain an excessively large share of Morocco's urban population. Similarly in Algeria, in spite of the size of Algiers (898 000 in 1966) the presence of two other large cities in Oran and Constantine together with several medium-size towns reduces primacy to a relatively low level for a developing country. The situation is well summarised in Table 4.4 (after J. I. Clarke)[15].

Table 4.4   Percentage Total Population

	In the largest city	In two largest cities
Morocco (1960)	8·3	10·4
Algeria (1966)	8·0	10·5
Tunisia (1966)	10·3	11·9
Libya (1964)	14·9	24·6

A second feature is the small number of medium-size towns in the 50 000–100 000 range, and the large number of small towns. Some of those counted in the 10 000–20 000 range are not proper towns, but there are nevertheless over 150 centres in the 10 000–50 000 range, the great majority of which may be regarded as having predominantly non-agricultural functions. Libya again provides the exception in that urbanisation has not been accompanied by settlement multiplication as in the Maghreb. The small towns of the Maghreb nearly all came into being during the French occupation to fulfil a variety of functions. Few were directly associated with mining, though Khouribga in Morocco owes its existence to phosphates and other towns in Morocco and Algeria owe much of their growth to coal mining. Other towns developed initially as small ports associated with mining or lately oil exports (Beni Saf, Kenitra, Bejaia, etc.), and a few were founded as coastal and even ski resorts. A large number of towns, particularly in Algeria, were originally garrison towns with administrative functions (for example, Batna, Sétif, Sidi-Bel-Abbès, etc,). By far the largest category, however, were the village and market centres established mainly in regions of European colonisation. Such towns sprang up widely in Morocco and Algeria and most survive today. Souk-Ahras, Boufarik, Le Sig, and Saida are examples in Algeria, Kasba-Tadla, Khemisset and Souk-El-Arba in Morocco. Deliberately located as the foci of discrete geographical and agricultural regions many of them are now lively social and economic centres for the surrounding countryside in areas far removed from the large towns.

It has already been suggested that primacy is not an acute problem in the Maghreb and Libya, though it is evident in Tunisia. The regional concentration of population in several towns, reinforced by the surrounding rural population is, however, more prevalent, and the process is accelerating. Morocco provides the supreme example, where a zone no more than one hundred miles long and thirty miles wide extending from Casablanca to Kenitra embraces nearly a quarter of the population of the country. Fifty years ago the population of this small area was insignificant compared with the inland lowland regions, but it now appears to be destined for even more rapid growth in response to impressive geographical advantages—centrality, accessibility by land and sea, a rich hinterland, and political and commercial ascendancy. Similarly in Tunisia, Tunis it is true, may be considered a primate city, but it is also the heart of a strongly urbanised region extending to a radius of some fifty miles including nearly half the towns with more than 25 000 inhabitants in Tunisia. The trend is less marked in Algeria, but increasing. Within a radius of eighty miles of Algiers a dozen or so urban centres grew at very high rates between 1954 and 1966 and the region now contains about half Algeria's urban population. In contrast several towns in Western Algeria are growing no faster than the rate of natural increase. Indeed it is characteristic of these emerging core regions that they provide a major attraction for

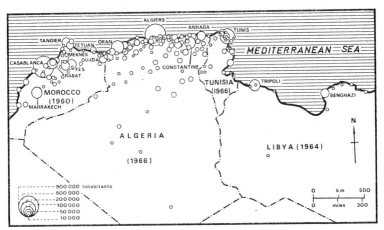

Fig. 4.2   Towns with over 10 000 inhabitants at latest census.

migrants at the expense of other regions. Moreover, nearest neighbour distances appear to be rather shorter than the national average.

The overconcentration of population regionally is undesirable for the same reasons that conventional urban primacy is undesirable, particularly from the point of view of improving the quality of life in rural areas. There is an urgent need to decentralise investment and encourage the growth of medium-sized regional centres from which social change might radiate and which could offer 'intervening opportunities' for the rural migrant[16]. To be successful such towns would need some of the industrial units, the social and economic services and professional personnel now accumulating in the metropolitan regions.

The distribution pattern shown in Fig. 4.2 is remarkable for the concentration of towns within 240 kilometres of the coast. Most rapidly expanding towns are less than 80 kilometres from the sea, and the only large inland centres (Constantine, Fes, Meknes and Marrakech) are old foundations whose importance as regional centres on great trade routes has been largely superseded by trade focused on the ports. In broad terms this pattern coincides with the distribution of the sedentary rural population which is largely confined to the lowlands and river basins north and north-west of the Atlas mountains where mean annual rainfall of over 250 millimetres can be expected. Outside this zone are a number of oasis towns, mining centres, and small market towns associated with nomadism. The great distance between these towns affects only a fraction of the total population and tends to present problems of access to social services (schools, hospitals, cinemas, etc.) rather than economic services (markets, garages, shops, etc.) because of the essential nature of economic activity in semi-arid regions. Within the closely settled zone, access to centres with 10 000 inhabitants or more would rarely necessitate a journey of more than 65 kilometres. In Algeria, particularly in areas once densely settled by Europeans the distance is often nearer 25–30 kilometres while in contrast the densely populated plains of Doukkala and Rehamna in Morocco have no towns of this size. It is, however, misleading to gauge access to services in North Africa in this way for two reasons. First, towns as small as 10 000 inhabitants cannot support adequate services, though they may well be flourishing market centres. Secondly, throughout the Maghreb markets are commonly located in villages and other small towns so close to one another that an elaborate arrangement of 'staggered' market days has evolved. Thus in areas of traditional farming, outlets for both agricultural and pastoral produce are numerous, while in regions of modern farming, centres have been planned and located in colonial times to cater for a different pattern of marketing. Both types of market centre provide an obvious framework for the provision of social facilities at a local level, and most country dwellers have reasonable access to a mosque, a clinic, and a primary school. Services at a higher level, however, may involve journeys of up to 160 km and the *prima facie* case for intermediate centres seems strong.

CONCLUSION

Two distinct challenges are presented by the nature of urbanisation in North Africa today. First, the task of development and renewal within towns. Because of their dual inheritance of a Moslem–Arab and colonial past the largest towns frequently present the problem of integrating an old closely-knit 'Medina' with a modern European-style town usually grafted awkwardly on to the original core. The chaotic and generally unplanned development of the early years of independence, including the bidonvilles, has vastly complicated the planning problem. In recent years, however, a start has been made towards rationalisation and planned development particularly in the large cities where the lessons of western urban development can be of value if adopted with extreme caution.

The second problem concerns national and regional planning. The present urban network is adequate in terms of nearest neighbour distances, but the scarcity of medium-sized towns is a great weakness. The selection of certain small towns as growth points is therefore of fundamental importance but it is becoming increasingly clear that the small towns bear least comparison with towns of comparable size in the western world. Work in Libya[17] and Algeria[18], for example, has revealed unexpected relationships between town and region in terms of marketing, land ownership and other aspects. When these relationships are more fully understood it may well be possible to revitalise town and region together.

SOURCE: Based on a paper presented to the Conference on Urbanisation and Regional Change, organised in Oxford, 1970, by The Regional Studies Association.

REFERENCES

1. S. AMIN. *L'économie du Maghreb*, 1965–1966, Paris (1966). pp. 21–35.
2. MINISTRY OF PLANNING AND DEVELOPMENT, LIBYA. *Inventory Reports of Planning Consultants*, Tripoli (1966).
3. G. HAMDAN. The pattern of mediaeval urbanism in the Arab world. *Geography* (April 1962), 121–34.
4. J. DESPOIS, and R. RAYNAL, *Géographie de L'Afrique du Nord-Ouest*, Paris (1967), p. 65.
5. D. NOIN. L'urbanisation du Maroc. *Inf. géogr.*, **32** (1968), 2, 69–81.
6. K. DAVIS. *World urbanisation 1950–70, Vol. 1. Basic data for cities, countries and regions.* Population Monograph Series No. 4. University of California (1969), Table D.
7. S. AMIN. *Op. cit.*
8. H. ISNARD. *Le Maghreb.* Paris (1966), p. 83.
9. H. BOWEN-JONES. *Urbanisation and economic development.* Paper given at Fourth Annual International Seminar in the Social Sciences, University of Edinburgh (1968).

10. R. G. Hartley. *Recent population changes in Libya: economic relationships and geographical patterns:* Ph.D. Thesis, University of Durham (1968).
11. K. Davis. *Op. cit.*
12. Fiche documentaire in *Annales Algériennes de Géographie*, No. 4 (July/December 1967).
13. H. Awad. Morocco's expanding towns. *Geogr. J.*, **130** (March 1964), 49–64.
14. J. Buy. Bidonville et ensemble moderne. *Bulletin Economique et Social du Maroc.* (September 1966), 71–122.
15. J. I. Clarke. Urban population growth in the Middle East and North Africa: Paper submitted to Institute of British Geographers Population Study Group Symposium, Keele (September 1969) (Unpublished).
16. J. L. Abu-Lughod. Urbanisation in Egypt: present state and future prospects. *Economic Development and Cultural Change.* No. 11 (1963), 313–43.
17. G. H. Blake. *A market town in Tripolitania.* University of Durham Research Paper Series in Geography No. 9 (1968).
18. M. Prenant. La propriété foncière des citadins dans les régions de Tlemcen et Sidi-Bel-Abbès, *Annales Algérienne de Géographie* (1967), 2–94.

5 A Study of Recent Internal Migration in Thailand

RONALD NG

THE statistical data published in the 1960 Population Census Report of Thailand is the most important single document on the demographic patterns of that country. The Census tabulates data for the whole Kingdom and by individual *changwads* (provinces). It has been evaluated to be the most accurate and informative of all enumerations to date[1], but reservations have been expressed regarding certain aspects[2]. Nevertheless, the report provides for the first time detailed information on inter-*changwad* changes of residence for the quinquennium prior to the Census date, 25 April 1960. (Data on changes of residence are published as Table 6: Migration of population 5 years of age and over, in *Thailand Population Census, 1960, Whole Kingdom* and *Changwad Series*.) It is the purpose of this study to introduce a method of analysing this type of population movement data and to present some preliminary conclusions on the spatial pattern of internal redistribution in Thailand.

POPULATION MOBILITY IN THAILAND

Several aspects of the demographic changes and economic development in Thailand have been responsible for the high rate of internal spatial mobility in the country in recent years. Throughout the post-war years, Thailand has been experiencing a country-wide 'population explosion'. The present rate of natural increase of 3 per cent per annum[3], if unchecked, would lead to the doubling of the population in three decades. There is evidence that this pace is increasing as a result of the ever widening gap between the relatively high birth rate and the declining death rate. However, Sternstein's study of growth trends leads him to conclude that the rapid upward surge of population has not yet strained local carrying capacities unduly, but he warns of several areas being on the verge of serious difficulty (see Ref. 1, p. 22).

For References to this chapter, see page 103.

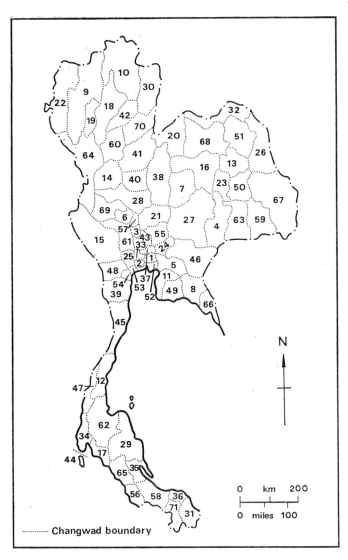

Fig. 5.1 *The 71 changwads of Thailand. (The changwads are listed by name and 1960 population in Table 5.1).*

Table 5.1   Changwads of Thailand with 1960 Population Totals
(*in thousands*)

1.	Phra Nakorn	1577	37.	Pathumthani	190
2.	Thonburi	559	38.	Petchbun	320
3.	Angtong	198	39.	Phetburi	238
4.	Buriram	584	40.	Phichit	389
5.	Chachoengsao	323	41.	Phisanuloke	352
6.	Chainat	245	42.	Phrae	299
7.	Chaiyaphun	486	43.	P. Sri Ayuthia	479
8.	Chanthaburi	158	44.	Phuket	76
9.	Chiengmai	798	45.	Prachaupkirikhan	152
10.	Chiengrai	812	46.	Prachinburi	335
11.	Chonburi	392	47.	Ranong	38
12.	Chumphun	175	48.	Ratburi	411
13.	Kalasin	427	49.	Rayong	148
14.	Kamphangphet	173	50.	Roi-et	668
15.	Kanachanaburi	233	51.	Sakornakorn	427
16.	Kornkean	844	52.	Samut Prakan	235
17.	Krabi	94	53.	Samut Sakorn	166
18.	Lampang	472	54.	Samut Songkhram	162
19.	Lamphun	250	55.	Saraburi	304
20.	Loei	211	56.	Satun	70
21.	Lopburi	336	57.	Singhburi	154
22.	Maehongsong	81	58.	Songkla	500
23.	Mahasarakarm	499	59.	Srisaket	601
24.	Nakornnayoke	154	60.	Sukhothai	316
25.	Nakorn Pathom	370	61.	Suphanburi	491
26.	Nakorn Phanom	436	62.	Surathani	325
27.	Nakornratchsima	730	63.	Surin	582
28.	Nakornsawan	648	64.	Tak	168
29.	N. Sri Thammarat	730	65.	Trang	240
30.	Nan	240	66.	Trat	66
31.	Narathiwas	266	67.	Ubolratchthani	1131
32.	Nongkai	257	68.	Udornthani	744
33.	Nonthaburi	196	69.	Uthaithani	146
34.	Pang-nga	93	70.	Uttaradit	260
35.	Patalung	234	71.	Yala	149
36.	Patani	282			

Note: Ordinal numbers refer to Fig. 5.1.

When the problem is set against the background of an extremely uneven population distribution, internal spatial mobility of a considerable magnitude seems inevitable and imminent. The vast majority of the Thais live in two main areas: (1) on a long stretch of alluvial plain running almost 300 miles northward from Bangkok narrowing from about 100 miles in width in the south to no more than 50 miles in the north and becoming at the same time less densely settled; and (2) in a circular area in the northeast basin centred approximately on Roi-et and averaging about 125 miles in radius[4]. The population densities of the *changwads* in these areas in 1960 were at least three to four times higher than those in other parts of the country. However, in a predominantly agricultural country such as Thailand where three-quarters of the people reside in agricultural households,* it is more realistic to consider not the overall but the *physiological density* in bringing out the spatial variations in the man–land ratio. Thus, it may indeed be true that the *changwads* on the Lower Chao Phrya Plain have a physiological density that is much higher than the national average, but it is the riverine settlements of the northernmost *changwads* which carry the largest number of inhabitants on a unit area of cultivated land.

The *changwad* physiological densities vary considerably and cluster at the two extreme ends of the continuum rather than around the national average of 206 rural inhabitants to the cultivated square kilometre. In fact, the ten most congested *changwads* had densities of over 450 in 1960, while at the other end of the scale, eleven *changwads* had no more than 150. The distribution of the administrative units with regard to their degree of congestion presents a highly complicated pattern and the only generalisation that can be made is that the ten northern *changwads* had an average physiological density of 494 persons per square kilometre of farm land whereas some 600 miles south in Peninsular Thailand the corresponding figure was 171. Elsewhere, contrasting *changwad* densities occur in close proximity. Consideration of the patterns of population distribution and density variations suggests that a high level of internal mobility is to be expected.

Although reliable statistical data on *changwad* population totals

---

* An agricultural household is defined by the Census as 'one which operated two or more rai (0·16 hectare), had sold agricultural products valued at 2400 baht or more, or had livestock valued at 2400 baht or more'. *Thailand Population Census, 1960, Whole Kingdom*, p. IV. (50 baht equal approximately £1 sterling).

and cultivated acreages for the various periods leading up to the 1960s are difficult to obtain, there is reason to believe that a real disparity in physiological density is a fairly permanent feature of the demographic scene. However, the period 1955–60 saw the introduction of a new economic policy which aimed at improving trade conditions, making more use of the market mechanism and creating new public works. Because of their attendant effects on population mobility, three aspects of economic development between 1955 and 1960 were particularly noteworthy. There was firstly the initiation and expansion of industries in the few urban centres which occurred without disturbing the overwhelming concentration and consistent growth in the metropolitan area of Greater Bangkok. Secondly, there was a vigorous development of irrigation facilities in the most feasible sites which provided an additional 20 000 acres (8000 hectares) of paddy land with an assured supply of water. Finally, there was the rapid expansion in acreage of non-paddy crops, especially of maize, cassava and kenaf whose combined output increased fivefold during the quinquennium[5]. Under the operation of a policy of imposing a heavy premium and levying an export duty on surplus rice, a favourable atmosphere was created for agricultural diversification. With the improvement of the economic infrastructure, an era of evolution from subsistence to commercial farming has begun. Thus, Silcock[6], states: 'One of the most striking changes in the last decade (the 1950s) has been the great increase in the number of farmers who are aware of change and of increased individual income as possibilities. New roads and country buses . . . and the widespread diffusion of battery-operated transistor radios, have all contributed to this change.'

Furthermore, there is nothing in the loosely structured Thai society that opposes the spatial and occupation mobility of the individual.[7] The people do not generally live in extended families nor do they belong to any rigidly defined local organisations. The system of land transfer is flexible and compulsory state education has fostered a strong sense of personal ambition for advancement achieved through individual merit. Internal movements within Thailand are spontaneous, and any inducement to migrate is likely to be indirectly[8].

Considering the combination of these factors, one would no doubt expect a high degree of internal mobility, yet the census data show that less than 4 per cent of the population 5 years of age and over changed their *changwad* of residence between 1955 and 1960. Indeed, not a single *changwad* experienced a population gain or loss through internal interchange by an amount greater than the natural increase over the period (Fig. 5.2). This apparently unresoluble contradiction could be explained by one of two, or a combination of both, sets of reasons. Firstly, the overall and even the physiological density of Thailand is still much lower than in most paddy cultivating countries[9]. It is probable that the farm acreage in most parts of the country can still be increased by clearing new plots in the virgin forests even in the relatively densely settled areas[10]. The crop yield of existing land can be raised through improved farming techniques, better irrigation facilities or a greater use of artificial fertilisers[11]. It is therefore likely that the present population growth has been accommodated locally without generating mass migration from even the hard pressed areas.

On the whole, the level of unit area yield of paddy seems to bear a close relationship to the population density. Despite the universal preference to produce paddy for home consumption and for surplus sales, specialisation in particular cash crops as supplementary sources of income has given rise to marked regional variations in the land-use pattern. Thus, in the hilly north, tobacco growing assumes much importance in the livelihood of the peasants; in the northeast, livestock rearing constitutes an essential part of the farm economy, while coconut and rubber planting is reported on most holdings on the Peninsula[12]. The lack of experience in the planting of certain types of supplementary crops may often be sufficient to dissuade a farmer from taking up rural residence in another part of the country. Furthermore, the average size of the farm holdings shows a considerable variation from one area to another and seems to be significantly correlated inversely to the physiological density. Smith's recent investigations reveal that the smaller the size of the farm, the heavier the investment in terms of unit production[13]. Thus, it may well be that the differences in population pressure have largely been absorbed by the different levels of intensity of land utilisation. In this way the disparity in farm incomes is greatly reduced, thereby dampening the effect of the 'push' factor. Pockets of fast growing population may also be immobilised by non-economic factors. Beneath the thin veneer of a homogeneity of language, ethnic origin, and religion of the Thai race, there are important regional differences in cultural background within the country. Kundstadter[14], observes

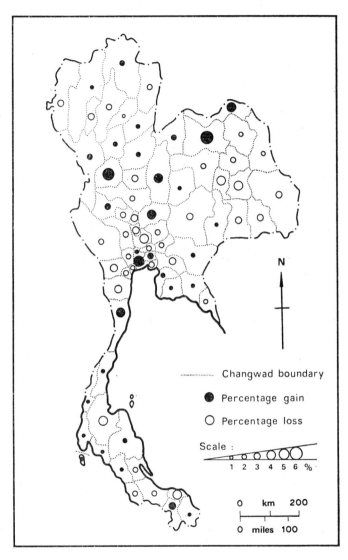

Fig. 5.2   Percentage change by net internal migration, 1955–60.

that 'even within regions that give the outward appearance of uniformity, there may be differences which are important in the minds
of the people involved'. It is conceivable that some economically
attractive areas may prove to be rather unappealing to many in-
tending migrants from other regions, and that the 'pull' factors
operate only at the local level.

Perhaps a more likely explanation for the low degree of internal
mobility in a time of fundamental economic and social change, is
the technical question of definition and classification of the changes
in place of residence. In the 1960 Census 'last place of previous
residence was asked of all persons who had moved to their present
place of usual residence within the 5 years preceding the census
date. The classification of persons who had moved is on the basis
of *last* previous residence'. The term *migrant* has been consistently
applied to 'a person who had changed his *changwad* of residence
within 5 years of the census'. The operative words of 'last *changwad*
of previous residence' introduce discrepancies of two kinds. First,
the *changwads* which range from under 400 square kilometres to
almost 23 000 square kilometres would render the migration data
incomparable. Second, the fact that only one move in the quinquennium was enumerated would have concealed all records of
intermediate moves and return flows over this long period when
rapid changes were occurring in the economy. The census figure of
825 438 instances of inter-*changwad* movement is far removed from
the 5 606 714 migrants quoted by Wichienchareon[15] for the period
of 7 years from 1948 to 1954. The contrast between the 4 per cent
of the 1960 population listed as migrants as against 25 per cent of
the 1956 population is truly startling. However, on closer examination, the two sets of figures do not seem to be entirely incompatible.
In his study of inter-regional migration, Wichienchareon used the
nine-fold administrative regional division of the early 1950s as the
basis of his calculations and discovered that only 8 per cent of the
migrants, or roughly 450 000, moved between the regions. Having
adjusted for the differences in time intervals and the exclusion of the
population under 5 years of age in the 1955–60 figures, the comparable figure for the latter period was found to be even higher than
that for the period 1948–54. Indeed, the fact that recent migration
accounted for almost one-third of those residing in a *changwad*
other than the one in which they were born, indicates that the pace
of internal movement has substantially quickened.

IDENTIFICATION OF MIGRATION REGIONS

As demographic statistics are invariably collected on the basis of administrative units, variations in areal extent, shape of the boundary and internal population distribution may all have considerable effect on the number of migrants entering or leaving the area as well as on the directions of exchange with other units. By grouping together contiguous areal units at the lowest level of data collection many of these irregularities can be eliminated without detracting from the quality of the data. By applying Bogue's[16] concept of change and adaptation involved in the migration process, a meaningful scheme of regionalisation can be devised. Migration regions can be defined as groups of administrative or enumeration units with the maximum internal interaction and a minimum exchange with those in other regions. The underlying principle is that within each migration region, movement from one part to another requires a minimum amount of readjustment in a person's way of life and means of livelihood and hence a greater probability of movement within the migration region should normally be found.

In conventional studies of internal migration, the importance of having to devise a special migration regional scheme prior to the detailed analysis of the trends and the patterns is often overlooked. Some form of existing regional system is usually adopted *in toto*. Intra-regional and inter-regional migrations are therefore generally taken to mean migrations within and between Census Regions which are designed to facilitate enumeration of population *totals* and not devised to throw light on the subject of internal *movements*. In the case of Thailand, because the *changwads* have effectively contained virtually all the local movements within their boundaries, the use of the enormous Census Regions to measure 'inter-regional' migration has grossly underestimated the true magnitude of real inter-regional movements. Although one may agree with Sternstein (see Ref. 1, p. 20) that there appear to have been no mass migrations or seepages of the population to or from any particular region (according to a six-fold system of Settlement Regions), the Census figure of 214 273 inter-regional migrants still seems to be unreasonably low. One of the first principles of regionalisation, as pointed out by Grigg[17], is that the regions should be designed for a specific purpose and they rarely serve two different purposes equally well. There is therefore a need to discover an appropriate scheme of regionalisation for the treatment of intra-regional and inter-regional migrations.

In the present context regionalisation must relate to the exchange of migrants between the basic enumeration units extracted from the census migration tables. In Thailand, it is known that there was a total of 825 438 inter-*changwad* migrants between 1955 and 1960, but the origins and destinations of only 745 717 can be ascertained by cross-tabulation. There is no way of extracting the same information from the 10 per cent residual classified as having arrived 'from other *changwads*' and these are therefore excluded from the analysis. The migrants with known directions of movement were represented in 1093 streams among the 71 *changwads*. The movements were highly reciprocal in nature with a net redistribution equivalent to less than 30 per cent of the gross movement.

To express the inter-relationship between pairs of *changwads* in the light of their mutual interchange of migrants, a common index *W* is accorded to each opposing pair of streams. The *W*-index actually measures the proportional amount of mutual movement between two enumeration units expressed as a percentage of the total migrants having arrived at *and* departed from, the two areas concerned. It ranges from 100 for cases in which all the outflows from a unit are directed to its partner, to 0 where there is no exchange between the specified pair. The value of the *W*-index can be obtained by applying the formula:

$$W_{ij} = \frac{(2m_{ij} + m_{ji})}{\Sigma m_i + \Sigma m_j} \times 100$$

where m_{ij} is the number of emigrants from i to j (or conversely, immigrants from j to i), m_{ji} is the number of emigrants from j to i (that is, the counter-flow) and Σm_i and Σm_j are the total number of migrants of i and j, respectively. As m_{ij} and m_{ji} constitute part of both Σm_i and Σm_j simultaneously, their values need to be adjusted by the constant multiplier 2 in the computation.*

One criticism of this index is that it tends to favour units with larger population totals because of the greater chance of these areas having a more substantial number of migrants than smaller units. However, the index aims at expressing the inter-relatedness in the pattern of movement and not the effect of migration on specific units. Experience shows that there is little discrepancy in using the *W*-index for identification of migration regions compared with other

---

* The calculation of the *W*-index and its subsequent listing have been computerised and a programme developed for the sorting procedure.

methods which depend more directly on the absolute numerical strength of the component streams. Furthermore, the index has proved to be equally convenient in regionalising on the basis of birth place and other similar types of data, and is particularly useful in handling a large number of complicated streams.

The sorting procedure begins with the ranking of pairs of enumerative units in descending order according to their W-value and then a graphic method is employed to reveal the pattern of the linkages. Contiguous pairs with high W-values forming nuclear pairs are first plotted against a vertical scale. Non-contiguous pairs are noted and reserved until the intervening units have emerged in other clusters to which these should then be assigned. Additional members are progressively incorporated until all units have been processed. Before reaching this stage, linkages with fairly high W-values may connect either partner of nuclear pairs with their lower-level associates. These are to be conjoined via a point at the equivalent value on the W-scale. A pattern of linkages soon appears binding together groups of units into well-integrated clusters which indicate the extent of the migrating regions. As the sorting process progresses towards the lower end of the scale, and as the membership of the clusters expands, an increasing amount of 'noise' will begin to creep in, blurring the clear-cut pattern of the clusters. These apparent inconsistencies constituting the 'noise' actually represent migration across the regional boundaries and are therefore inevitable. Discretion must be exercised at this stage to distinguish carefully between 'signal' and 'noise'. Under normal circumstances, these disturbances will only occur at a very low level, say at $W = 8$ as in the present case, and should not be considered serious enough to invalidate the regional scheme. When the sorting process has been completed, that is, when all the areal units have been attributed to their respective clusters, the groups (regions) will remain as distinct entities.

MIGRATION REGIONS OF THAILAND

This graphic analysis on the basis of a mutual exchange index identifies ten migration regions in Thailand (Fig. 5.3). Although the alignment of the regional boundaries does not always coincide with any particular regional system previously devised on the basis of some other parameters, it follows closely the well-recognised lines

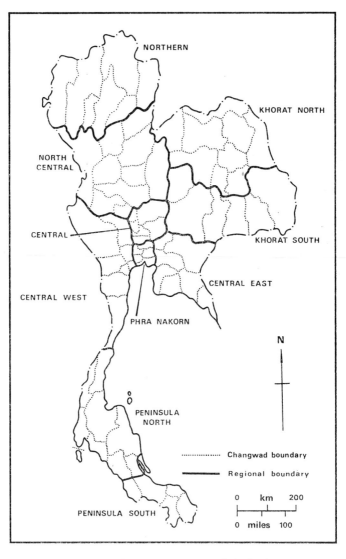

NORTHERN

KHORAT NORTH

NORTH
CENTRAL

CENTRAL

KHORAT SOUTH

CENTRAL EAST

CENTRAL WEST

PHRA NAKORN

N

PENINSULA
NORTH

.... Changwad boundary

──────── Regional boundary

0   km   200

0   miles   100

PENINSULA SOUTH

Fig. 5.3   The migration regions of Thailand.

of regional demarcation in the country. The major physical and cultural divide of the Dong Phrya Yen, separating the Khorat Plateau from the Central Plain has not been violated. The southeastern hills with their distinctive relief and climatic features form a coherent migration region. The seven *changwads* of northern Thailand, with its distinctive local dialect, constitute another separate region, and the administrative boundary between *Changwads* Prachuapkirikhan and Chumphun, commonly considered as the beginning of Peninsular Thailand, also marks the division between two migration regions. In a recent study of the pattern of internal movement in Thailand covering the same period, Chapman and Allen[18] point out that 'the boundary separating the Northern and Central Regions (of the Census) bisects the central plain just below the confluence of the Ping and Nan rivers, while clearly the areas on either side have much closer links with each other than the lower northern *changwats* have with the far North'. They suggest that 'the regional boundary might desirably be shifted north for Census purposes and another region created to extend from the northern boundary of *Changwat* Ayuthia to the northern boundary to *Changwat* Sukhothai'. The result of the present linkage analysis is in complete agreement with Chapman and Allen's observations and has indeed identified their proposed region (the North Central Migration Region extending from *Changwad* Chainat northwards to include *Changwad* Sukhothai, and from *Changwad* Petchbun westwards to *Changwad* Tak).

The levels of inter-*changwad* migration by migration regions differ as widely as the numbers and areal sizes of the *changwads* comprising the regions. About a fifth of the inter-*changwad* migrants were associated with the five small *changwads* of the Phra Nakorn Region, while the two Khorat Regions and the North Central Region accounted for 12 to 16 per cent each and the more remote regions like the Central East, the Northern and the Peninsula South had less than 15 per cent of the migrants between them. However, when expressed in terms of inter-*changwad* migrants inwards and outwards, per thousand residents, the range narrows considerably (Table 5.2). These participation rates are, of course, composite in nature and do not distinguish between the intra-regional and inter-regional components. An attempt is made in the following sections to describe separately the pattern of the migration streams within the regions and between the migration regions. The lack of a comprehensive body of statistical information relating to the various aspects of the local economy that might influence population movements at the *changwad* level makes it difficult, if not hazardous, to explain why each individual stream flowed in the way it did. In this period of rapid economic development in Thailand, major construction projects may by themselves be sufficient to induce substantial transfers of labour from one administrative unit, or even

Table 5.2   Regional Distribution of Inter-Changwad Migrants

Migration Regions	Instances of Inter-Changwad Inward and Outward Movement	Percentage Distribution	Total Inter-Changwad Migrants per 1000 Population
Phra Nakorn	312 210	21·0	11·3
Central	128 578	8·7	8·8
Central East	75 280	5·0	4·8
Central West	127 836	8·6	5·7
North Central	172 688	11·5	5·7
Northern	77 983	5·2	2·6
Khorat North	236 163	15·8	5·2
Khorat South	199 517	13·4	4·5
Peninsula North	99 424	6·7	5·0
Peninsula South	61 755	4·1	4·9

migration region, to another. From the analysis of one single set of migration data, it is virtually impossible to assess what proportion of the changes of residence is indeed permanent in nature, but a cursory inspection of the birth place data seems to confirm that the ten-fold regional scheme derived from the 1955–60 information does reveal the fundamental spatial pattern of internal migration in the country.

INTRA-REGIONAL MIGRATION

Movement among the *changwads* within migration regions is the dominant mode of internal migration in Thailand. The overwhelming majority of the dominant streams from each *changwad* are confined to the limits of the migration regions. Even so, it does not always follow that a net gain or loss by intra-regional migration would be accompanied by a proportionate gain or loss by inter-regional movement. But when the latter is removed from the overall change by inter-*changwad* migration, the simplicity of the pattern of intra-regional balance emerges immediately. Within each migration region, there is at least one of the country's fastest growing *changwads* which is often surrounded by units of the greatest loss. Intra-regional population redistribution is effected by a few significant streams in a rather definite pattern, but geographic contiguity is not usually the decisive factor and the level of reciprocity is often very low.

The mobility rate of the *Phra Nakorn Migration Region* was by far the highest of all regions, but over half of the migrants had merely moved across the Menam Chao Phrya, from one part of the metropolis of Greater Bangkok to another. The residential suburbs in *Changwad* Thonburi gained about 4 per cent of their population by this process. This was probably due to the easier access to the city centre, in *Changwad* Phra Nakorn, by the improved system of public transport. Part of the urban overspill was represented by the gain of *Changwad* Nonthaburi just to the north of the city. The loss of population by *Changwads* Pathumthani and Samut Prakan was the inevitable result of the much wider urbanisation process.

The centre of migration attraction in the *Central Region* was *Changwad* Lopburi. Streams of migrants converged on this *changwad* in numbers roughly proportional to the population totals and densities of their *changwads* of origin. The net outflow of almost two thousand strong from *Changwad* Phranakorn Sri Ayuthia to *Changwad* Saraburi, which did much to compensate for the latter's heavy loss to Lopburi, completes the picture of the major trends of movement in the region.

The *Central East Migration Region* was characterised by the large number of reciprocal streams of small magnitude. Even though the mutual interflow of migrants between the seven *changwads* vis-a-vis their external linkages justifies identifying them as a migration region in their own right, there was a greater amount of interaction among the three paddy cultivating *changwads* on the edge of the Central Plain and among the four rubber and cassava producing *changwads* on the southern coast than between the two groups. However, the industrial and service employment opportunities in the Sri Racha area of *Changwad* Chonburi did much to fuse the two sections into an integral migration unit.

The pattern of internal migration in the *Central West Migration Region* is one of a general shift from the densely populated western edge of the Central Plain towards the less crowded hilly tracts of the west and the south. The major movements were from *Changwad* Suphanburi to *Changwad* Kanchanaburi whose predominant out-flow was towards Ratburi which in turn lost a substantial number of migrants to Prachuapkirikhan. This southernmost *changwad* also drew heavily from non-contiguous *Changwad* Nakorn Pathom. As these *changwads* gained from some neighbouring areas and lost to others at the same time, the net balance of the individual units in the region was but a fraction of the movements involved.

The pattern of internal migration in the *North Central Region* was very similar to that of the Central West Region, but the popu-lation shift was northwards and eastwards. Practically every *chang-wad* was involved in this process at various stages. The six major streams, mostly from one unit into another immediately to the north, accounted for 40 per cent of the 53 273 intra-regional mi-grants. As a result of the shift, the two southern *changwads* of Chainat and Uthaithani lost 5415 and 2327 migrants respectively while the attractive destinations of Kamphangphet and Petchbun gained 10 456 and 4024 migrants from internal sources. The pull of the northern areas was so strong that the intervening *changwads* had all registered heavy losses.

In the *Northern Migration Region*, *Changwad* Chiengrai has both the largest population and the lowest settlement density. Most of the intra-regional migration streams were directed towards this *changwad* which gained 1·4 per cent of its population by net local movement during 1955–60. *Changwad* Chiengmai also experienced a moderate growth by drawing a substantial stream of migrants from nearby *Changwad* Lamphun. The intra-regional mobility is generally very low and no more than 30 000 persons, or just over 1 per cent of the total, were involved in the process of internal movement. The predominantly self-subsistence nature of the economy and the difficulty in inter-valley communication are more likely reasons for the low degree of participation than the larger than average territorial extent of these northern *changwads*.

Although the *Khorat North Region* contains the *changwad* with the largest population gain by intra-regional migration and two of the *changwads* with the most severe loss, the intra-regional migration rate was no higher than the other regions. The pattern of the streams is basically determined by the tremendous outflows from *Changwads* Mahasarakham and Roi-et to *Changwad* Udornthani. *Changwad* Nongkai was the only other *changwad* in the region that attracted a substantial number of migrants. The outflow from *Changwad* Khonkean was the single largest stream in the country after the one from Phra Nakorn to Thonburi, but its effect on the population total was offset by the inflows from Mahasarakham and Roi-et. It seems that in this region, the paddy cultivating *changwads* all lost heavily to those experiencing agricultural commercialisation. As this appears to be the general trend of recent development throughout Thailand, the Khorat North region should be included in future research programmes for detailed study.

Unlike the Khorat North Region where the bulk of the inter-*changwad* migrants were confined within the region, intra-regional, movement in the *Khorat South Migration Region* played only a secondary role in the overall changes in the population totals of the six *changwads* along the Nam Chi valley. As many of the migrants chose not to remain in the region, the internal mobility rate was the lowest of all the regions. Nevertheless, *Changwad* Chaiyaphun with its opportunities in cash crop production and *Changwad* Buriram with its low physiological density in the paddy growing areas, each attracted over 10 000 migrants from neighbouring *changwads*. The internal outflow streams were markedly directional: for example, 58 per cent of the emigrants from *Changwad* Nakornratchsima went to Chaiyaphun and 63 per cent of those from Surin went to Buriram.

The population of the *Peninsula North Migration Region* is heavily concentrated in the two largest *changwads* of Nakorn Sri Thammarat and Surathani, and the majority of the intra-regional migrants were associated with these two administrative units. The outflow stream from the latter to the former was the third largest in the country and accounted for 37 per cent of the intra-regional migrants. The inflows and outflows among the remaining seven *changwads* were not only highly reciprocal but also of such small magnitude that they rarely exceeded 500 migrants in volume. Nevertheless, for these smaller *changwads*, the gain of a thousand or so local migrants makes a significant change in the population total and hence, *Changwads* Trang, Krabi and Ranong all increased their population by over 1 per cent during the quinquennium.

In the *Peninsula South Migration Region*, the pattern of internal movement was basically one of a redistribution in favour of the fast-developing but as yet sparsely populated *Changwads* Yala and Narathiwas. The outflow streams from *Changwad* Patani towards these destinations accounted for 40 per cent of the movements within the region. The two slightly less significant streams were from Patani to *Changwad* Songkla and from Songkla to Yala. The remainder comprised the counterflows of these major currents.

Overall the intra-regional patterns point consistently to a general movement away from the centres of heavy population concentrations, into the more hilly areas formerly unattractive to lowland farmers, but now being developed for upland cash crops. In the more remote regions, the centres of local attraction are often border *changwads*. This apparently centrifugal pattern may be merely coincidental and due more to a process of in filling of sparsely populated areas than to specific political measures.

INTER-REGIONAL MIGRATION

On the basis of the ten migration regions revealed by the linkage analysis, 359 836 inter-*changwad* migrants, or 47 per cent of the 1955–60 total, were involved in the inter-regional movement. Most of these inter-regional migration streams were so small that they were inconsequential in the pattern of population redistribution in the country. In fact, of the 72 identifiable streams, no more than twenty had a magnitude exceeding 5000 migrants, and thirteen of these larger streams were associated with the Phra Nakorn Region in which the metropolis of Greater Bangkok is located, while most of the other more significant streams were either outflows from Khorat South or inflows into North Central. The gain of the Phra Nakorn Region and the loss of the Khorat South Region are both well-known facts, but the important role played by the North Central Region, and to a lesser extent the Central West Region, has hitherto been concealed by the use of the over-extensive Census Regions for analysis of the pattern of inter-regional migration. Although the numerical loss of the Central West Region was not as heavy as that of the Khorat South Region, its *rate* of loss was much higher than the latter. In fact, the rate of emigration experienced by the Khorat South Region was lower than the Central Migration Region (Table 5.3). Perhaps for want of a meaningful regional

Table 5.3   Inter-Regional Migration in Thailand, 1955–60

Region	Net Inter-Regional Migration		Net Migration to Greater Bangkok		Net Migration Elsewhere	
	Actual change	Change per 1000 residents	Actual change	Change per 1000 residents	Actual change	Change per 1000 residents
Phra Nakorn	+66 046	+24·0	—	—	—	—
Central	−14 048	−9·5	−10 935	−7·4	− 3 113	−2·1
Central East	+ 372	+ 0·2	− 7 737	−4·9	+ 8 109	+5·1
Central West	−25 526	−11·4	−17 876	−8·0	− 7 650	−3·4
North Central	+21 328	+ 7·1	− 4 656	−1·5	+25 984	+8·6
Northern	− 891	− 0·3	− 1 688	−0·6	+ 797	+0·3
Khorat North	−12 581	− 2·8	− 6 122	−1·4	− 6 459	−1·4
Khorat South	−38 817	− 8·7	−12 042	−2·7	−26 775	−6·0
Peninsula North	+ 2 108	+ 1·1	− 3 328	−1·7	+ 5 436	+2·7
Peninsula South	+ 2 011	+ 1·6	− 283	−0·2	+ 2 294	+1·8

system, the emigration from the Khorat Plateau has been over-emphasised in previous studies.

The dual trend with a rural-urban metropolitanisation and an inter-rural redistribution component in the pattern of inter-regional migration in Thailand is well recognised. However, there persists a controversy over the issue of whether the shift to the capital should be considered an intra-regional or an inter-regional phenomenon. While Wichienchareon (see Ref. 15, p. 30) asserts that Region 1 (with 11 *changwads*) in the Central Plain, which includes Bangkok, absorbed 38·54 per cent of all the inter-regional migrants, Chapman and Allen (see Ref. 18, p. 7) think that this popular myth of extensive inter-regional transfers to the metropolis should be demolished because the capital, in fact, gained only one-fifth of its net in-migrants from outside the Central Region (with 26 *changwads*). This controversy seems to have arisen not so much from using Census figures for different periods (during which time the trends do not appear to have been fundamentally different), but from the fact that neither commentator has devised a regional system for the specific purpose of analysing the internal migration pattern. Under the present scheme of migration regions as identified by migration linkages, Greater Bangkok is included in a much smaller region, the Phra

Nakorn Migration Region, which has only five *changwads*. For the period between 1955 and 1960, 44 per cent of the inter-regional migrants were attracted to the metropolis and 94 per cent of the gain by Greater Bangkok was derived from *changwads* in other migration regions. Doubtless, the majority of the migrants originated from the three contiguous regions, but the fact that Khorat South contributed 17·3 per cent and Khorat North another 8·7 per cent of the capital's migration gain should not be overlooked.

Participation in the metropolitanisation trend seems to be governed to a large extent by physical distance. The rate of rural–urban migration towards the capital in terms of net loss per thousand residents shows a gradation from under one in the distant Northern and Peninsula South Regions, increasing to over seven in the Central and Central West Regions (Fig. 5.4). The degree of urbanisation in individual *changwads* also appears to have some influence on the rate of flow towards the metropolis. Thus, *changwads* with a comparatively large urban population* like Chiengmai, Nakornratchsima and Lampang had a greater degree of interaction with, and at the same time a heavier loss to, the capital city than their regional norms. Experience of other developing countries indicates that this nascent form of inter-urban migration may gather momentum as other urban centres emerge in the provinces.

With the identification of the North Central Migration Region, a focal point of the inter-rural component in the inter-regional movement is provided. If those inter-regional migrants who did not move to the Phra Nakorn Region are defined as inter-rural regional migrants, then 16·5 per cent of them migrated into the North Central Region. Furthermore, 26 per cent of the region's immigrants originated from the Khorat South, while the other surrounding regions also contributed a substantial share. The pattern of inter-regional migration between the predominantly rural regions is essentially determined by the gain of the North Central and the loss of the Khorat South Regions which underwent changes of similar magnitude (Fig. 5.5). The Central Migration Region, situated between these two areas of intensive migration movement, had both the largest number of immigrants per thousand residents and the highest

* In the Census of 1960, no distinction was made between rural and urban population, but 'municipal' totals are separately listed. 'All municipal areas have some characteristics generally recognised as urban, but some such areas are geographically extensive, with a population more rural than urban.' *Thailand Population Census, 1960, Whole Kingdom*, p. 111.

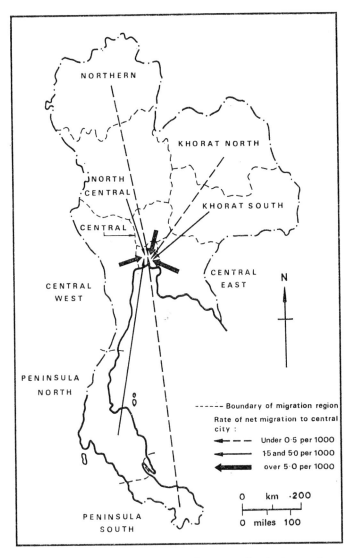

Fig. 5.4 Regional participation in the metropolitanisation trend.

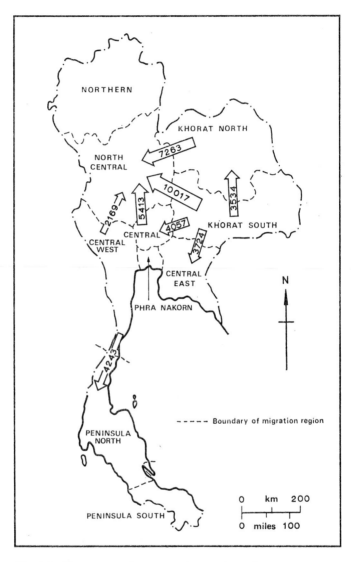

Fig. 5.5 Net migration between predominantly rural migration regions.

emigration rate. The Khorat Region was affected in very much the same way. An interesting direction for future research would be to determine whether these two regions had acted as a clearing house catering for those emigrants of Khorat South moving into the southern and northern parts of the North Central Region respectively.

CONCLUSION

While population pressure is mounting and new opportunities are being created by a rigorous economic development programme, the rate of internal mobility in Thailand in the late 1950s had remained remarkably low. In most *changwads*, changes by net migration between 1955 and 1960 were less than the equivalent of a single year's natural growth. However, the spatial pattern of the numerous migration streams as revealed by the Census migration tables is highly complex and can only be analysed meaningfully on the basis of a system of regions. Migration regions, defined as groups of units with maximum mutual interchange of migrants, provide an adequate and conceptually justifiable basis for a general description of the migration trend in their spatial context.

Beneath the complex of flows and counterflows, there is basically a well-defined pattern in the inter-*changwad* population movement in Thailand, but a full explanatory account of the underlying factors that govern the volume and direction of the migration streams will require a careful examination of a wide range of relevant statistical information or an elaborate scheme of field research.

SOURCE: *Journal of Tropical Geography*, Vol. 31, 1970, pp. 65–78.

REFERENCES

1. L. STERNSTEIN. A critique of Thai population data. *Pacific Viewpoint*, **6** (1965), 15–35.
2. I.L.O. *Report to the Government of Thailand on Internal Migration*. Regular Programme of Technical Assistance, Geneva (1965).
3. GOVERNMENT OF THAILAND (n.d.). *Thailand Official Year Book, 1964*, Bangkok.
4. J. C. CALDWELL. The demographic structure, in SILCOCK, T. H. (ed.), *Thailand: Social and Economic Studies in Development* (1967), p. 41.
5. T. H. SILCOCK. The rice premium and agricultural diversification, in SILCOCK, T. H. (ed.), *Thailand: Social and Economic Studies in Development* (1967).

6. T. H. Silcock (ed.). *Thailand: Social and Economic Studies in Development.* Australian National University Press, Canberra (1967), 2460.

7. J. F. Embree. Thailand—a loosely structured social system. *Am. Anthrop.,* **52** (1950), 181–93.

8. R. Ng. Land settlement projects in Thailand. *Geography,* **53** (1968), 179–82.

9. F. D. Whyte. Monsoon Asia: population and rice, the next 30 years. *Span,* **10** (1967), 138–41.

10. K. Janlekha. *Saraphi: A Survey of Socio-Economic Conditions in a Rural Community in North-East Thailand.* World Land Use Survey Occasional Papers No. 8, Bude (1968).

11. C. A. Fisher. *South-East Asia: A Social, Economic and Political Geography.* Methuen, London (1964), 507–12.

12. Central Statistical Office. *Thailand Population Census, 1960, Whole Kingdom* and *Changwad Series,* Bangkok (1963).
 — (n.d.), *Agricultural Census,* 1963, Bangkok.

13. H. D. Smith. *Agricultural Production and Consumption Patterns Market Potential in Thailand.* Department of Agricultural Economics, University of Maryland (1963).

14. P. Kundstadter (ed.). *Southeast Asian Tribes, Minorities and Nations,* Vol. 1. Princeton University Press, Princeton (1967), 3720.

15. A. Wichienchareon. Movements of population within Thailand. *Journal of Public Administration,* Bangkok (1960), pp. 29–35.

16. D. J. Bogue. Internal migration, in Hauser, P. M. & Duncan, O. D. (eds.). *The Study of Population: An Inventory and Appraisal* (1959), pp. 488–90.

17. D. Grigg. The logic of regional systems. *Ann. Ass. Am. Geogr.,* **55** (1965).

18. E. C. Chapman, and A. C. B. Allen, *Internal Migration in Thailand.* Paper presented to ANZAAS Conference, Hobart (1965).

6 Spatial Patterns of Population in Indian Cities

JOHN E. BRUSH

THE cities of India have entered a period of growth, reflecting the country's general population increase and rising employment in secondary and tertiary economic activities. From 62·4 million in 1951 India's urban population rose to 78·9 million in 1961, an increase of 26·4 per cent. In the 50 years ending in 1961 the increase was more than 200 per cent, or about 53 million. In the same period total population rose from 252 million to 439 million, or about 75 per cent[1]. Today India probably ranks fifth among the nations of the world in number of urban inhabitants, exceeded only by the United States, the Soviet Union, the People's Republic of China, and possibly Japan. Although the proportion of India's people living in cities and towns remains 18 per cent of the total, and although there is evidence of a deceleration in the rate of urban increase during the census decade 1951–1961 as compared with the preceding two decades, the number of city and town dwellers increased at a rate that exceeded the general population growth rate of 21·6 per cent[2]. It is probable that an ever-increasing share of India's expected population growth in the next several decades will be absorbed in its urban places.

In the process of growth the urban centres of India are undergoing transition from their old morphological and functional patterns, derived in part from pre-modern South Asian traditions and in part from British colonial rule, to patterns commensurate with the goals and capabilities of national independence. The new shape of urban India may be seen in such planned industrial towns as Jamshedpur, Durgapur, Rourkela, and Bhilai, or in the administrative showplace of Chandigarh. However, most Indian cities present a mixed pattern of development in which growth has occurred with little control and no systematic planning[3]. Change is slow, and expansion lags[4].

Indian and foreign scholars have described and analysed the

For References to this chapter, see page 131.

geography of India's urban areas and the socio-economic characteristics of its urban population. The state of knowledge as of 1960 is
summarised in a useful volume of papers prepared by twenty-three
academic specialists and government officers for an international
conference held in that year at Berkeley, California[5]. Reference
should also be made to the growing body of studies of particular
urban centres carried out by geographers, sociologists, and economists in the last few years[6]. J. F. Bulsara has collated and summarised the findings from nine of the socio-economic surveys sponsored
in the late 1950s by the Planning Commission of the Central Government of India[7]. Official recognition of the problems of housing congestion, poverty and the deficiency of basic urban amenities has
resulted in the publication of census monographs on Madras[8] and
Kanpur[9]. Master plans for development have been completed in
Ahmedabad, Asansol, Bangalore, Bombay, Calcutta, Delhi, Durgapur, Gaya, Hubli, Patna and Siliguri[10].

OBJECTIVES

The purpose of the present inquiry is to analyse the spatial patterns
of Indian intra-urban population distribution and its change as
exemplified by selected cities (Table 6.1)[11]. I had the opportunity in
1966 to travel widely in India in order to gather statistical data and
to gain knowledge of urban conditions. The urban centres for which
it was possible to obtain maps and areal statistics for municipal
wards or other census divisions are either in the four northern states
of West Bengal, Bihar, Uttar Pradesh and the former Punjab, or
in the four peninsular states of Gujarat, Maharashtra, Mysore, and
Madras. They range in size from metropolises with more than a
million inhabitants, such as Bombay, Calcutta, and Madras, to small
municipalities with fewer than 100 000, such as Chandigarh, Dhanbad, and Dharwar. Although the 22 centres constitute less than 1 per
cent of the 2700 urban settlements recognised in the 1961 census, the
19 Class I cities (population exceeding 100 000) analysed here represent about one in six of 107 cities of this size class in the whole of
India. Differences among the cities under study in origin, growth
history, and economy make it possible to draw some instructive
comparisons. Changes through time can be observed from data
available for ten of these urban areas.

I am concerned with two aspects of population variation in Indian

Table 6.1 Population of Selected Urban Areas in India

City, State	Population 1961	Area (*Acres*)	Administrative Status*
Ahmedabad, Gujarat	1 155 344	22 986	MC
Allahabad, Uttar Pradesh	411 966	15 415	MC
Bangalore, Mysore	864 203	17 575	MC
Bombay, Maharashtra	4 152 056	108 160	MC
Bombay Island	2 771 933	16 751	—
Calcutta, West Bengal	2 927 289	24 493	MC
Calcutta Metropolitan District	5 967 000	166 610	PA
Chandigarh, Administered by Central Government	89 321	6 581	M
Coimbatore, Madras	286 305	5 671	M
Dhanbad, Bihar	57 352	6 684	M
Dharwar, Mysore	77 163	4 160	M
Gaya, Bihar	151 105	7 283	M
Howrah, West Bengal	512 598	7 392	MC
Hubli, Mysore	170 109	6 016	M
Hyderabad–Secunderabad, Andhra Pradesh	1 129 345	40 437	MC
Jamshedpur, Bihar	303 516	19 200	TA
Kanpur, Uttar Pradesh[a]	807 356	18 932	MC
Lucknow, Uttar Pradesh	595 440	19 882	MC
Madras, Madras	1 729 141	31 814	MC
Patna, Bihar (1951)	297 436	11 227	MC
Poona, Maharashtra[b]	597 419	27 190	MC
Sholapur, Maharashtra	337 583	6 139	M
Tiruchirapalli, Madras	249 862	5 747	M
Varanasi, Uttar Pradesh	471 258	18 259	MC

Source: Census of India 1961, except for Patna, for which source is Census of India 1951.

* MC: Municipal Corporation; M: Municipality; TA: Town Area; PA: Planning Area.

[a] Kanpur city only. Total area of Kanpur Municipal Corporation according to the 1961 census is 72 960 acres, with a population of 971 062.

[b] Greater Poona.

cities: first, the density gradients from the highest levels in or near the centre of the city; second, intra-urban density changes that accompany growth of area and increase of population in the city as a whole.

Interpretation of the patterns of population distribution and change in the cities of India must take account of existing models of urban structure. Usually a downward gradient is to be expected from the greatest concentrations per unit area in or near the centre out towards the periphery, in conformance with the negative exponential rule* first proposed by Bleicher[12]. Later Clark,[13] and later still Berry, Simmons, and Tennant[14], found the rule to be a satisfactory description of the density gradients observed in some hundred cities in various parts of the world, including India.

The second aspect of urban population variation in India is differential change in intra-urban distribution through time. Newling[15] has offered evidence of an inverse relationship between population density and growth rates. Both in Pittsburgh, Pennsylvania, and in Kingston, Jamaica, he observed that population density tended to decrease in the central units where it exceeded fifty persons per acre, and to increase in the outer units where it fell below this level, which he has called the 'critical density'. In other words, general population growth in an urban area is accompanied by decrease at the centre and diminution of the density gradient. However, Berry and his colleagues observed continuous increase of density in the central wards of Calcutta from 1881 to 1951, in contrast with Western cities; for example Chicago, where Winsborough[16] found that the central density increased from 1860 to 1910 and thereafter decreased as metropolitan sprawl advanced. Clark also presented evidence of deconcentration of urban population in Western cities, which he interpreted as the result of economic factors, especially transportation improvement. In a later study Clark[17] discussed the worldwide phenomenon of outward movement of population from cities to suburbs and presented evidence that the density gradient in Poona declined between 1881 and 1953 (?), which he interpreted to mean that dispersion had occurred. However, faced with contrary evidence in Asian cities, Berry has theorised that non-Western, and particularly Indian, cities have a pattern of growth characterised by rising residential concentration in the city centre concurrently with outward expansion and peripheral population increase.

Analysis of new data from India will enable confirmation or refutation of these observations and clarify the trends of intra-urban population growth that obtain under a wide variety of circumstances.

* Population density is a negative exponential function of distance from the city centre in the equation $D^d = D_0 e^{-bd}$, where D^d is the population density at distance d, D_0 is the population density at the centre of the city, e is the base of natural logarithms, and b, the density gradient, is an exponent expressing the rate of change of density with increasing distance from the centre of the city.

PROCEDURE

The first step in population-density analysis of a city, beyond obtaining the areal and population statistics for municipal wards or other census divisions, is finding the location of the nodal point to which the spatial structure of economic activity and population can be related. Presumably there is one point, usually in a commercial area with a major street intersection or public square, in the vicinity of which communication and interchange are at maximum concentration and land values are highest. However, the geographical pattern of most Indian cities is not simple because of the dualism introduced by British administration side by side with indigenous economic factors. There is not often a clear-cut nodal point in the central business district, a high-value location of the kind identifiable in most American cities. So far as possible, I have accepted as the nodal point in each city under examination that so identified by the authors of planning studies or monographs on that city, or I have relied on the advice of well-informed local officials and resident scholars, supplemented by field reconnaissance. In some cities more than one nodal point must be recognised because of the pronounced dualism of the geographical pattern.

Having found the nodal point(s) of a city, compass arcs of one-tenth of a mile were described to determine, to the nearest twentieth of a mile, the median distance from the city centre for each statistical unit. Air-line distances were taken as the basis for calculations without adjustment for ground distances except where water barriers restricted accessibility between the centre and certain other parts of the city. Thus the statistical units of each city could be arranged in order of distance from the centre, and the data on population densities be analysed.

Results are presented from analysis of the 1961 census data for gross population density in twenty-one urban areas (Table 6.2) and for residential population density in two of these areas, Greater Poona and Hubli, and in Tiruchirapalli, for which the residential density data are available (Table 6.3). These data were treated in terms of the linear regression $Y = a+bX$; where Y is the population density, expressed as a logarithm of the number of persons per acre, a is a constant and b a variable, both expressed as logarithms and derived from the density data, and X is the distance, expressed in miles.

Table 6.2 Regressions of Gross Population Density in Selected Urban Areas

City or urban area	Number of Statistical units	Estimating equation			Persons per acre Miles from centre						Coefficient of Correlation	Coefficient of Determination	Significance of F Ratio
		log a	log b	log Sxy	0	1	2	3	4	5			
Ahmedabad	45	2·6407	−0·5038	0·3780	437·2	136·7	43·0	13·5	4·2	—	0·82	0·67	**
Allahabad	27	2·1267	−0·2768	0·3798	130·8	70·8	37·4	19·8	10·5	5·5	0·68	0·46	**
Bangalore	50	2·3520	−0·2738	0·3455	224·9	119·7	63·7	33·9	18·1	—	0·62	0·39	**
Greater Bombay	88	2·6751	−0·0988	0·4447	473·3	377·0	300·2	239·1	190·5	151·7	0·83	0·69	**
Bombay Island[a]	38	2·5921	−0·0713	0·4074	390·9	331·7	281·7	238·9	202·7	172·0	0·32	0·10	*
Calcutta Metropolitan District[b]	143	2·2436	−0·0596	0·4361	175·2	152·8	133·2	116·1	101·2	88·2	0·67	0·45	**
Calcutta City	80	2·6154	−0·1596	0·2922	412·4	285·6	197·8	137·0	94·9	65·6	0·57	0·33	**
Chandigarh	28	1·4366	−0·4549	0·5124	27·3	9·6	3·4	—	—	—	0·39	0·15	*
Coimbatore	30	2·2160	−0·2989	0·2818	164·0	82·6	41·5	20·9	—	—	0·63	0·39	**
Dhanbad	27	1·8780	−0·9122	0·3703	75·5	9·2	—	—	—	—	0·70	0·48	**
Dharwar	10	2·2689	−1·0267	0·1855	185·7	17·5	1·6	—	—	—	0·92	0·85	**
Gaya	10	2·2640	−0·6015	0·2718	183·6	46·0	11·2	—	—	—	0·78	0·62	**
Howrah	10	2·3764	−0·3444	0·2875	237·9	107·6	48·7	22·0	10·0	—	0·65	0·43	*
Hubli	9	2·5212	−0·9656	0·1465	33 ·1	35·9	3·9	—	—	—	0·96	0·92	**

Hyderabad–Secunderabad	35	2·1086	−0·2430	0·3805	131·4	73·4	41·9	24·0	13·7	7·6	0·63	0·40	**
Jamshedpur	39	1·6911	−0·1619	0·4179	49·1	33·7	23·3	16·5	11·8	7·6	0·38	0·15	*
Kanpur[c]	116	2·6330	−0·4294	0·4199	429·5	159·9	59·5	22·6	8·4	3·1	0·57	0·33	**
Lucknow	32	2·3608	−0·3810	0·3531	229·5	97·7	40·6	16·9	7·0	—	0·70	0·49	**
Madras	100	2·4318	−0·1643	0·2722	270·3	185·1	126·8	86·9	59·5	40·8	0·69	0·47	**
Patna (1951)	37	1·7392	−0·0571	0·3810	54·9	48·1	42·2	37·0	32·4	28·4	0·28	0·07	+
Greater Poona[d]	38	2·4796	−0·5047	0·5490	301·7	94·4	29·5	9·2	3·0	—	0·81	0·65	**
Sholapur	16	2·6453	−0·7960	0·2201	441·9	70·6	11·3	—	—	—	0·90	0·81	**
Varanasi[e]	30	2·4233	−0·4644	0·3016	265·0	91·0	31·2	10·7	3·7	1·3	0·87	0·76	**

Source: Computations by the author, based on reports from municipal or town-planning offices, based on Census of India 1961, except for Patna, for which source is Census of India 1951.

** F ratio exceeds 1 per cent level; * exceeds 5 per cent level; + exceeds 10 per cent level.

[a] Includes only 38 census sections, comprising Bombay Island.

[b] Includes 80 municipal wards of Calcutta City, 10 wards of Howrah, and 53 other municipal and nonmunicipal urban areas in Calcutta Metropolitan District.

[c] Includes only 116 of 136 census blocks in Kanpur city area.

[d] Includes 36 municipal wards, Poona Cantonment and Kirkee Cantonment.

[e] Includes 27 wards in Varanasi municipal area, also cantonment, railway colony and Banaras Hindu University areas.

Table 6.3 Group 1 Cities: Regressions of Residential Population Density

City or urban area	Number of Statistical Units	Estimating equation			Persons per acre Miles from centre						Coefficient of Correlation	Coefficient of Determination	Significance of F Ratio
		log a	log b	log Sxy	0	1	2	3	4	5			
Greater Poona[a]	34	2·7224	−0·1368	0·4222	527·7	386·0	281·8	205·7	150·1	109·6	0·45	0·21	**
Tiruchirapalli[b]	8	2·5576	−0·3646	0·1399	361·0	155·9	67·4	—	—	—	0·81	0·65	*
Hubli[c]	41	2·3661	−0·5203	0·2529	232·0	70·1	21·1	—	—	—	0·69	0·48	**

Source: Reports from municipal or town-planning offices, based on Census of India 1961. Residential density is computed for area occupied by dwellings and associated structures exclusive of streets, public parks, agricultural land, and other open space.

** F ratio exceeds 1 per cent level; * exceeds 5 per cent level.
[a] Includes only the 34 municipal wards for which data are available.
[b] Gross population density data are not available for wards of Tiruchirapalli.
[c] Residential population density data are given for census 'circles', units that are smaller than wards.

Calculations were done at Rutgers University on the IBM 7040 computer, using a stepwise regression programme in Fortran known as BMDO2R of the University of California Health Sciences Computing Facility, version of 17 December 1965, as modified at Rutgers[18]. This programme not only provided the desired correlation coefficients and certain measures of significance of the results but was also convenient for treatment of the successive time series data where available. The relationships of population density to distance proved to be statistically significant at the 5 per cent level of probability, except for Patna, where the significance exceeded 10 per cent probability. In addition, I have calculated two- or three-part regressions for selected cities in an attempt to secure a better fit. I obtained the logarithmic means of density by distance increments in all the urban areas in order to compare distinctive features of particular cities with the generalised gradients as determined by simple regression.

RESULTS

Although the results show that the density-distance relationships have statistical significance and generally conform to the Bleicher-Clark model based on negative exponential decline of density with increase of distance from the city centre, four patterns of deviation from the model are found. The first, and most common, configuration occurs in cities where the highest density of population is found in a compact central area, situated in or adjacent to an indigenous bazaar. Within one or two miles from the centre the gradient slopes sharply downward to the periphery (Fig. 6.1, Group 1). This pattern, well exemplified by Ahmedabad and Poona, is representative of the majority of Indian cities. A different pattern, resembling that of Western cities, is found in the British-built port cities of Bombay, Calcutta, and Madras, where the central business district is occupied in part by banks and office buildings and the population density is relatively low (Fig. 6.1, Group 2). Within the first mile or mile and a half (2 or 3 kilometres) density may reach an extremely high level (the maximum occurs in Bombay, 1520 persons per acre [3750 persons per hectare]), but beyond that it declines gradually over a distance of 8 kilometres or more. The third configuration is found in cities with two distinct nodes of population concentration, one around a bazaar of traditional type, the indigenous city, and the other around a former British centre that may be two miles distant or more (Fig. 6.1, Group 3). Hyderabad–Secunderabad and Bangalore are examples of such dualism, in which two distinct density gradients can be recognised. The fourth pattern, which exists in the modern planned cities of Jamshedpur

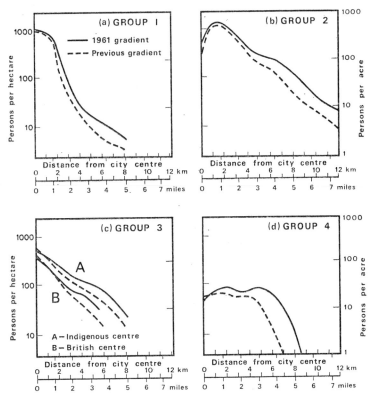

Fig. 6.1　Patterns of change in population density gradients of Indian cities.

and Chandigarh, is distinguished by low population density throughout the urban area, with little or no concentration in the central business district or in the industrial and administrative areas (Fig. 6.1, Group 4).

Examination of the data for changes of population density with time tends to support Berry's observation that progressive intra-urban concentration in India is concurrent with growth of the total number of inhabitants of municipal areas for cities of the first group. But the tendency is less marked or is absent in the other groups. In Bombay and Madras, though concentration is increasing in the central wards, expansion is accelerating on the periphery; in metropolitan Calcutta growth seems to be more concentrated. In the binuclear cities of the third group deconcentration has been occurring. In the cities of the fourth group low population density is maintained through control of land use and housing, and growth is largely confined to the periphery.

Thus the pattern of population growth in Indian cities is too complex and varied to conform to a single model. Discussion of further details of the spatial and temporal patterns will clarify this conclusion.

GROUP 1 CITIES

The spatial pattern most frequently observed in Indian cities, both large and small, is that of a single densely populated core area and a sharp gradient down to the thinly settled margin. This occurs typically in cities of pre-British origin, such as Ahmedabad, Poona, Varanasi, Sholapur, Tiruchirapalli and Coimbatore. It may also occur in settlements of recent origin, such as Kanpur, Howrah and Dhanbad, all of which grew during the nineteenth and twentieth centuries, or in cities where the centre of growth has shifted away from a pre-British settlement, as, for example, in Hubli, Gaya and Dharwar. Mean density in the central wards within the first quarter or half mile of the nodal point may be as high as 400–500 persons per acre (1000–1250 persons per hectare); in the peripheral wards only one or two miles ($1\frac{1}{2}$ to 3 kilometres) distant it may be less than 10 per acre (24 per hectare). Thus the ratio between gross density in the centre and that on the periphery can be more than 50:1, and it is usually more than 15:1 or 10:1.

It is noteworthy also that the general density gradient, when treated in terms of the regression analysis, usually shows higher correlations and higher levels of statistical significance in Group 1 cities than in other cities (Table 6.2). Except in Kanpur, Howrah, and Coimbatore, the coefficient of correlation in Group 1 cities is at least 0·7, whereas in the other groups a correlation as high as 0·7 is rare. In all Class 1 cities except Howrah the F ratio obtained from analysis of variance is in excess of the 1 per cent level of chance occurrence. Thus not only are Class 1 cities characterised by a steep density gradient, but the ward variations conform closely to the negative exponential rule (Figs. 6.2 and 6.4).

However, the configuration of specific cities shows important departures from the rule. Maximum density does not necessarily exist in the central bazaar (for example, in Kanpur, Varanasi, Coimbatore and Dharwar) but is found in wards between a quarter

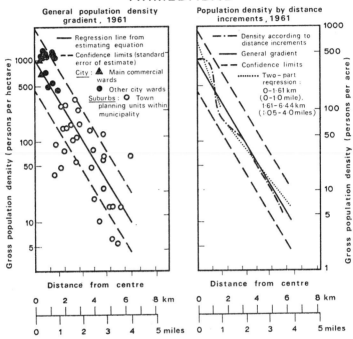

AHMEDABAD

Figs. 6.2 and 6.3   Population density: Ahmedabad

of a mile and half a mile (0·4 and 0·8 kilometre) from the centre. In other cities the density gradient flattens noticeably (for example, in Ahmedabad, Poona, Sholapur and Gaya) to produce a population plateau within the first half mile or three-quarters of a mile (0·8 to 1·2 kilometre) from the centre. The only clearly concave gradient is that of Dhanbad, a sprawling small city which has a compact nucleus in the central bazaar. The typical density gradient of Class 1 cities is convex.

A closer look at Ahmedabad and Poona reveals certain additional variations in population distribution (Figs. 6.3 and 6.5). In each of these cities the main commercial ward(s) shows a distinctly lower population density than the surrounding wards of the pre-modern city. However, all the wards in the old city within a mile (1·5 kilometre) radius of the centre are more densely populated than the suburban areas. In Greater Poona the discontinuity between old

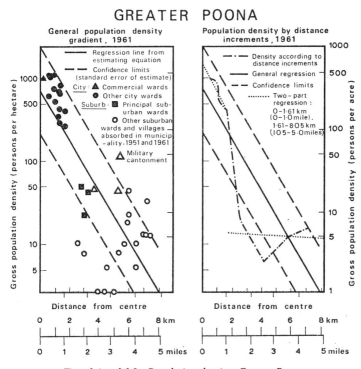

Figs. 6.4 and 6.5   Population density: Greater Poona

city and suburban or cantonment areas is so abrupt that the density gradient is strongly distorted and the regression lines computed for the two parts of the urban area fall far from one another (Fig. 6.5). In Ahmedabad the discontinuity between city and suburbs can be recognised, but it is much less pronounced, and the regression lines do not differ markedly (Fig. 6.3). This feature of spatial structure of population in Ahmedabad can be explained by the early establishment of cotton textile mills outside the city walls and the consequent spread of housing for the mill workers. The relatively late start of industrial development and suburban sprawl in Poona has yet to bring about as much change in the basic difference of population distance in the city and in its semi-rural environs.

Analysis of the observed patterns of net residential density in Poona, Hubli and Tiruchirapalli further elucidates our understanding of the spatial structure of urban population in India. In Poona and Hubli, where comparisons are possible between net and gross density, it is noteworthy that the gradient of net density based on regression is less steep, and the relationship of density to distance from the city centre is less significant, than the gradient of gross density. (Compare coefficients of correlation and determination for Poona and Hubli, Tables 6.2 and 6.3.) In Tiruchirapalli, where only residential density information is available, the significance of the F ratio falls between the 1 per cent and 5 per cent levels. This means that distance from the central bazaar area is a less effective explanation for net population concentration observed within built-up residential areas than for gross population concentration. In other words, the people living in the peripheral wards three to five miles from the centre of Greater Poona are living in fairly compact clusters with 100 to 200 persons per acre (250 to 500 persons per hectare) (Tables 6.3 and 6.4). Yet at one to two miles (1·5 to 3 kilometres) from the centre residential density is markedly lower. The ward data of mean density by distance increments for all three cities show that maximum residential density occurs in the central bazaar area.

These geographical relationships may be interpreted in the following way. In the heart of a traditional Indian city, with typically mixed commercial and residential land use, as exemplified by Poona, residential land use is partly displaced by commerce and other activities, which are sufficiently concentrated to reduce the gross density of population. Somewhat removed from the nodal point of banking and trade in the ring of maximum gross density, residential density goes up to 800 persons per acre (2000 persons per hectare), though the most extreme residential congestion may exist (1150 persons per acre [2850 persons per hectare] in Poona) in the central commercial area. Immediately outside the old city in the area of recent urban growth residential density falls below 100 persons per acre (250 persons per hectare), but beyond this urban-rural transition belt the residential density again rises to as much as 200 per acre (500 per hectare). The inversion of the profile of density by

Table 6.4   Group 1 Cities: Variation in Residential Population Density by Distance Increments

| | | | | | | Persons per acre Miles from city centre | | | | |
City	0·00–0·25	0·30–0·50	0·55–0·75	0·80–1·00	1·05–1·50	1·55–2·00	2·05–3·00	3·05–4·00	4·05–5·00
Greater Poona	1150·0	781·0	452·5	564·0	46·1		140·6	207·0	167·2
Tiruchirapalli	246·2		193·8		158·6		63·1	—	—
Hubli	206·7	150·8	100·1	73·7	28·6	48·0	—	—	—

Source: Computations by the author, based on Census of India 1961.

distance increments in suburban Poona is due to the fact that the
inner suburbs have not yet received much spillover from the crowded
central city and remain occupied largely by relatively affluent and
spacious upper-class housing tracts, while the residents of the outermost suburbs are either agricultural villagers living in compact
villages or low-paid industrial workers living in close and unplanned settlement clusters on the margin of the developed urban
area. Most of this outermost area around Poona remains in
cultivated fields or open wasteland, which explains the low level of
gross density.

It is not possible to present here a full account of the growth of
the five cities of Group 1 for which data on density changes are at
hand (Table 6.5). Let it suffice to point out a few facts. In 1881
Poona's population was recorded as 99 421; 50 years later it had
increased to 213 680, with little change of area. By 1961 the old
city had been enlarged more than ten times, from 2390 acres to
27 190 acres, and the population had grown to 597 419, but without
any large shift of people into areas incorporated into Greater Poona.
In the three decades 1931–1961 Howrah more than doubled its
population, from 224 873 to 512 598, with an expansion of area
from 6400 acres to 7392 acres (2589 to 2991 hectares). In the same
three decades Gaya grew from 88 005 to 151 105, without any
change in municipal area. In the decade 1951–1961 Hubli increased
from 129 609 to 170 109 and Dharwar from 66 571 to 77 163, with
little change in area.

Analysis of the temporal changes of population density in these
five cities reveals a pattern of concurrent growth in the central and
peripheral areas, with one minor exception, central Howrah 1941–
1951. The general gradients have tended to move upward in parallel
fashion from census to census. The correlations and statistical
significance of the relationship of density to distance are normally
high, except in Howrah. Change in the statistical base of computations for Poona detracts from complete reliability of comparison
of results for the several census dates. But the length of the record
for Poona and the clearly defined upward shift of the density profiles
for Poona City from 1881 to 1961 confirm the conclusion drawn
from shorter-term evidence in the other four cities. It is clear that a
large share of population growth in Indian cities has been absorbed
into existing urban areas, resulting in progressive congestion in the
previously occupied tracts.

Table 6.5 Group 1 Cities: Temporal Changes in Gross Population Density by Distance Increments

City	Census date	Persons per acre *Miles from city centre*						
		0·00–0·25	0·30–0·50	0·55–0·75	0·80–1·00	1·05–1·50	1·55–2·00	2·05–2·50
Poona City	1961	409·0	395·2	224·3	180·8	—	— —	—
	1951	352·0	322·7	187·8	118·6	—	— —	—
	1941	233·0	204·5	136·2	74·2	—	— —	—
	1931	185·0	157·7	87·9	53·8	—	— —	—
	1881	159·0	109·1	44·0	39·2	—	— —	—
Howrah	1961	208·3		94·2		90·1	46·1	
	1951	176·4		83·9		88·6	39·9	
	1941	182·4		78·8		73·1	26·8	
	1931	110·4		47·4		44·2	15·3	
Hubli	1961	163·3		55·8	72·9	11·3	11·8	—
	1951	124·5		42·6	55·7	8·5	9·0	—
Gaya	1961	92·2		78·5		39·6	9·3	—
	1951	90·3		74·1		34·4	7·4	—
	1931	57·5		44·4		22·9	5·3	—
Dharwar	1961	74·5	81·1	39·5	21·6	10·1	4·7	—
	1951	64·2	69·9	34·1	18·7	8·7	4·0	—

Source: Computations by the author.

GROUP 2 CITIES

Three of India's four largest cities make up Group 2. The Greater Bombay Corporation ranks first in population and area among the municipal units in this category (Table 6.1), but it would be second if the Calcutta Metropolitan District were to be consolidated into one giant administrative unit of nearly six million persons. The third-largest metropolitan city by any reckoning is Delhi, together with New Delhi and Delhi Cantonment, containing in all 2 359 408 inhabitants in 1961 and occupying some 80 690 acres (32 650 hectares). Unfortunately, Greater Delhi cannot be analysed here because of the current unavailability of statistical base maps. Undoubtedly it would belong with Group 2 cities because of the high concentration of population in the pre-British city of Delhi. Madras, which ranks fourth, resembles Bombay and Calcutta in having had a long and close association with British rule in the subcontinent. It is therefore understandable that the spatial structure of the three Group 2 cities should be similar to the Western pattern.

Closer examination of the density profiles in the three cities according to distance increments reveals the basic features: a mean low of 71 to 193 persons per acre (175 to 477 persons per hectare) in the central business district within half a mile (0·8 kilometre) of the centre; a mean maximum of 369 (912 hectares) for Calcutta and 248 (613 hectares) for Madras in the second half mile (0·8 kilometre) and 615 (1520 hectares) in the third half mile (0·8 kilometre) for Bombay; and beyond these peaks there is a somewhat irregular decline of density. Although the correlations for Greater Bombay, the Calcutta Metropolitan District and Madras (Table 6.2) are shown to be significant, it is evident that the profiles of density by distance increments in Bombay and Madras are much more in conformity with the general gradients as determined by regression. The pattern of density in Calcutta and the contiguous urban belts of the Hooghly riverain shows a distinct concentration within the first 7 or 8 miles (11 or 13 kilometres), beyond which the profile flattens out (Fig. 6.6). The contrast between the general gradients and the mean densities according to distance increments indicates that the spatial structure of Greater Bombay (Fig. 6.7) is much more unified than that of Metropolitan Calcutta. Both urban areas are centred at waterfronts, and both have developed on confined natural sites. The original growth of Bombay on an insular site and the subsequent expansion to Salsette Island along two rail lines bear some similarity to Calcutta's situation between the river and the salt marshes and the restrictions to expansion along the parallel banks of the Hooghly, especially in Howrah and the adjacent suburbs north and south.

However, the flatness of the density profile in much of Metropolitan Calcutta reflects the low concentration in the Hooghly river towns, which have grown up as industrial satellites rather than as

Table 6.6 Temporal Changes in Gross Density of Population by Distance Increments
Bombay Island and Madras

Urban area	Census date	Persons per acre Miles from city centre												
		0·00–0·50	0·55–1·00	1·05–1·50	1·55–2·00	2·05–2·50	2·55–3·00	3·05–3·50	3·55–4·00	4·05–4·50	4·55–5·00	5·05–6·00	6·05–7·00	7·05–8·00
Bombay Island	1961	123·8	204·1	614·6	494·3	245·1	189·6	84·1		169·0		215·6	136·1	110·0
	1951	98·9	174·4	588·8	467·7	192·1	134·8	49·6		151·7		165·2	87·2	97·0
	1941	65·2	131·2	401·5	350·4	126·8	105·1	27·5		76·3		97·1	47·8	35·0
	1931	42·4	90·0	360·1	266·4	115·2	71·3		74·9				31·5	
	1921	51·0	160·3	359·2	284·0	164·4	68·2		76·0				30·0	
	1911	44·2	164·8	320·7	252·2	112·7	69·2		56·9				20·2	
	1901	40·9	120·4	272·6	206·0	124·8	52·2		36·6				14·7	
	1891	48·1	144·4	369·7	264·5	132·8	52·2		25·2				11·9	
	1881	52·4	147·4	393·7	271·7	115·6	29·5		18·8				9·1	
Madras	1961	70·9	248·0	128·2	158·7	133·5	99·8	58·8	79·7	63·5	28·6	52·8	21·8	12·1
	1951	124·6	170·2	225·8	121·6	116·6	52·8	42·2	92·4	23·8		18·2	11·2	

Source: Computations by the author.

suburbs of the metropolis. These differences are clarified by fitting three-part regressions to each of the two density profiles (Figs. 6.6 and 6.7).

Temporal changes in density of Bombay Island and Madras City (Table 6.6) indicate that concentrations have been rising recently in or near the central area of each city, while growth has occurred in

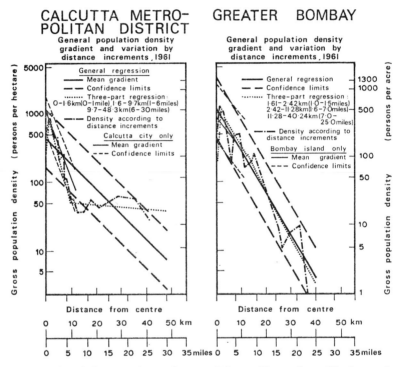

Figs. 6.6 and 6.7 *Population density: Calcutta Metropolitan District; and Greater Bombay.*

the outer areas. The unusually long and continuous record for Bombay Island (Figs. 6.8 and 6.9) shows that from 1881 to 1961 there was a persistent contrast of densities in the central business district—that is, 'The Fort'—and in the adjacent 'City' between 1 and 2 miles (1½ and 3 kilometres) distant, and a progressive rise in density in the remaining area. During the 40 years from 1881 to 1921 the increase of population, from 773 196 to 1 175 851, was largely absorbed by expansion in the central and northern parts of the city. Between 1921 and 1961 the population of the Island grew to 2 771 933, bringing about the extreme concentrations recorded in the most recent census. The spillover of Greater Bombay to the vast new areas of Salsette Island, which began before 1951 and accelerated in the following census decade, has been insufficient to relieve the pressure on Bombay Island. Unquestionably Bombay

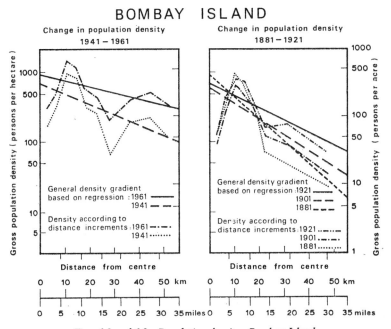

Figs. 6.8 and 6.9   Population density: Bombay Island.

Island contains the apex of India's population concentration. The maxima in several census divisions range from 750 persons per acre (1850 persons per hectare) up to 1520 (3760 per hectare) in one division, Bhuleshwar, which comprises 43·22 acres (17 hectares) with 65 681 inhabitants (1961). The maximum density in the most congested ward of Calcutta in 1961 was about 750 persons per acre (1850 persons per hectare); in Madras the maximum in any ward was below 500 (1200 per hectare). In Madras, although the total population grew from 1 416 056 in 1951 to 1 729 141 in 1961, the density change was proportionately greater in the area beyond 3·5 miles (5·5 kilometres) from the city centre than in the inner area. A drop of density is observed in the vicinity of Parry's Corner in the central business district, but the most congested areas show increases during the decade.

GROUP 3 CITIES

The spatial patterns of the dual-centred cities differ from those in the preceding groups, first, in their generally low density levels, and second, in a tendency towards dispersion rather than concentration of population. The central densities computed by regression analysis show consistently lower levels of aggregate population than those for comparable cities of Group 1. Compare, for example, Bangalore with Kanpur, Lucknow with Poona, Allahabad with Varanasi, Patna with Sholapur (Table 6.2). In each of the above four Group 3 cities the regression analysis is based on distance measurements from the one dominant centre of population concentration. Another noticeable feature is the usually lower correlation coefficients of Group 3 cities and the less significant statistical relationships between density and distance. Patna stands out as the lowest among all cities for which results of regression are presented (Table 6.2). In the case of Hyderabad–Secunderabad the results given are based on merging of measurements of distances taken from either of the two centres of the urban area, whichever proved to be closer to each statistical unit. The results of computation based on measurements from one centre only (Mahatma Ghandi Road) in Hyderabad–Secunderabad are not recorded here because they proved to be without statistical significance, serving to demonstrate the high degree of population decentralisation in the twin-city area. Thus the regression obtained for Hyderabad–Secunderabad is a merging of the two gradients, treated as if there were one centre.

Examination of the density of population by distance increments in Group 3 cities reveals binodal profiles. In Hyderabad the main centre of population density is the walled city, containing the former Nizam's palace, and Secunderabad, in the former British civil cantonment, is secondary. In Bangalore the old centre of the city (Chickpet), with a density exceeding 750 persons per hectare, is clearly dominant over the former British civil and military station, some 2 miles distant. In Lucknow the British-based centre of population and commercial activity has displaced the old chowk, or market, less than 3 km away, where trade flourished in the heyday of the

Table 6.7　Temporal Changes in Regressions of Gross Population Density, Hyderabad–Secunderabad and Bangalore

City centre	Census Date	Number of Statistical Units (N)	Estimating equation			Persons per acre Miles from centre					Coefficient of Correlation	Coefficient of Determination	Significance of F Ratio
			log a	log b	log Sxy	0	1	2	3	4			
Hyderabad (Old City)	1961	19	2·1423	−0·2257	0·3518	138·8	82·5	49·1	29·2	17·4	0·65	0·42	**
	1951	19	2·3048	−0·0626	0·3430	201·7	92·4	42·3	19·4	8·9	0·80	0·63	**
Secunderabad	1961	16	2·1367	−0·3244	0·4087	137·0	64·9	30·8	14·6	7·1	0·67	0·45	**
	1951	16	2·1371	−0·3696	0·4366	137·1	58·6	25·0	10·7	4·6	0·70	0·48	**
Bangalore (Old City)	1961	28	2·4290	−0·3682	0·2539	268·6	115·0	49·3	21·1	9·0	0·70	0·49	**
	1951	28	2·4588	−0·4261	0·2867	287·6	107·8	40·4	15·2	5·7	0·71	0·50	**
Bangalore Civil and Military Station	1961	22	2·2144	−0·4552	0·3493	163·9	58·8	20·6	7·2	—	0·69	0·47	**
	1951	22	2·2405	−0·5332	0·3805	174·0	51·0	14·9	4·4	—	0·71	0·51	**

Source: Computations by the author.
** F ratio exceeds 1 per cent level.

Nawabs, before British rule, and where a secondary concentration of population persists. Similar displacement of a pre-British centre has occurred in modern Allahabad, which has almost completely superseded the old city, more than 2 miles distant. In Patna the British administrative centre, on the Ganges River more than 4

Table 6.8   Temporal Changes in Gross Density of Population by Distance Increments, Hyderabad–Secunderabad and Bangalore

City centre	Census date	Persons per acre *Miles from city centre*						
		0·00–0·50	0·55–1·00	1·05–1·50	1·55–2·00	2·05–3·00	3·05–4·00	4·05–6·00
Hyderabad (Old City)	1961	147·8	118·1	29·9		48·1	35·5	10·1
	1951	150·7	117·2	27·8		44·6	28·2	3·2
Secunderabad	1961	119·5	68·4	33·8		32·5	13·0	—
	1951	122·6	67·0	24·0		24·3	10·2	—
Bangalore (Old City)	1961	305·9	89·3	67·1	61·8	69·1	—	—
	1951	322·8	89·9	59·0	44·6	63·3	—	—
Bangalore Civil and Military Station	1961	213·5	55·0	22·9	32·7	20·5	—	—
	1951	253·6	45·1	18·8	22·1	16·2	—	—

Source: Computations by the author.

miles upstream from the old city, combined with the attraction of the riverbank site produced an attenuated pattern of development.

The two largest cities of Group 3 thus have been analysed in terms of the two existing density gradients (Tables 6.7 and 6.8). In each city it is the indigenous centre that is dominant. The results show somewhat higher correlation coefficients, and thus higher levels of statistical significance.

Temporal changes (1951–1961) in density according to distance increments show in both Hyderabad–Secunderabad and Bangalore a trend towards decline of the centres of population and increase in the interstitial and peripheral areas of lower density (Fig. 6.10 and Table 6.8). Such a pattern of population redistribution is unlike

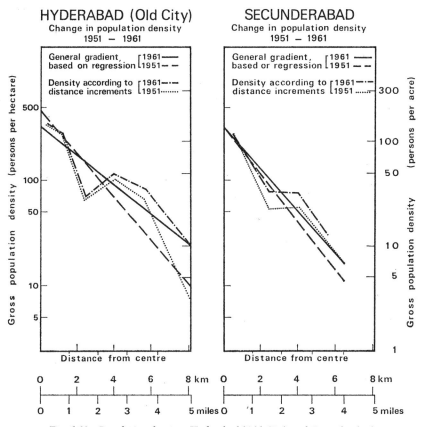

Fig. 6.10 Population density: Hyderabad (Old City) and Secunderabad.

the patterns observed in Group 1 and Group 2 cities. It appears that the comparatively sprawling polynuclear development, reported by various scholars in describing these two urban areas, is associated with diminishing density gradients and little or no change in municipal area, though total population was growing. In the decade 1951–1961 the area of the Hyderabad–Secunderabad Municipal Corporation remained 40 437 acres (16 364 hectares), but the population grew from 1 008 640 to 1 129 345. In the same decade the Bangalore Municipal Corporation was changed from 17 450 acres (7062 hectares) to 17 575 acres (7112 hectares), and the population rose from 778 072 to 864 203.

GROUP 4 CITIES

If we turn now to the last group of cities, it is possible to appreciate their atypical qualities. In neither Jamshedpur nor Chandigarh does the correlation of distance and density (Table 6.2) show highly significant statistical relationships. In both cities the coefficient of determination is 0·15, which means that only 15 per cent of the variance of population density is explained by distance from the city centre. Although the 1961 density gradient indicates a generally low level in Jamshedpur, declining from about 49 persons per acre (121 persons per hectare) to 8 (19 per hectare) at the margin, a more accurate profile of density according to distance increments rises from a central density of 27 (67 per hectare) to a maximum of 35 (86 per hectare) within the first mile (1·5 kilometre) and drops to 4 (1 per hectare) at the margin. Chandigarh shows a still lower gradient and a similarly convex profile of density by distance increments. Owing to changes in 1961 of the statistical units on which the computations for 1941 and 1951 are based, the earlier density profiles for Jamshedpur are not strictly comparable. However, the general gradients determined by regression show little change in the central densities, while the recorded changes in density according to distance increments show more abrupt increases on the periphery of Jamshedpur.

The pattern of population distribution in Jamshedpur relates to stages of planned growth around the main industrial plant and administrative offices of the Tata Iron and Steel Company. Sixty-five years ago the 19 200-acre (7770 hectares) tract on which stands today a 'company town' of more than 300 000 inhabitants was an agricultural area with a few thousand villagers. Once the location of the iron and steel works had been fixed, the company offices, retail business centres, and residential tracts were developed in successive stages. By 1941 the population of the area under company control had grown to some 160 000, and by 1961 it exceeded 300 000. Subsidiary and allied manufacturing industries have been located 3 km or more from the iron and steel works. The expansion of the residential areas and retail centres has been kept widely dispersed and not allowed to concentrate in or near the initial areas of development. Thus the urban–industrial complex has remained a 'garden city', largely free of the congestion that so commonly characterises Indian cities.

It is too early to judge the results of governmental planning and control in the model city of Chandigarh, built since independence to serve initially as the administrative capital for the Punjab and now temporarily for the two states of the Punjab and Haryana. The plan of Chandigarh restricts residential use of land in the central commercial area and in the main administrative area. Some private construction is permitted, but land-use zoning and building regulation prevent densities from rising above 30 persons per acre (70 persons per hectare). In the public housing tracts for families of low income, densities are well below 50 persons per acre (120 persons per hectare). Additions are planned in peripheral areas to permit the orderly growth of Chandigarh.

SOURCE: *Geographical Review*, Vol. 58, 1968, pp. 362–91.

REFERENCES

1. Census of India 1961, Vol. 1, India, Part II-A (i), General Population Tables, Delhi 1964. All data are applicable to the present area of India.
2. JOHN E. BRUSH. Some Dimensions of Urban Population Pressure in India. Paper presented at the symposium of the International Geographical Union's Commission on Cartography and Geography of World Population held at The Pennsylvania State University, September 17–23, 1957.
3. GERALD BREESE (1963). Urban Development Problems in India. *Ann. Assoc. Am. Geogr.*, **53**, pp. 253–65.
4. NIRMAL KUMAR BOSE (1965). Calcutta: A Premature Metropolis. *Scient. Am.*, **213**, No. 3, pp. 91–102.
5. ROY TURNER (ed.) (1962). *India's Urban Future*. Berkeley and Los Angeles.
6. S. MANZOOR ALAM (1965). *Hyderabad-Secunderabad (Twin Cities): A Study in Urban Geography*, Bombay; A. BOPEGAMAGE, Delhi: A Study in Urban Sociology. *Univ. of Bombay Publs., Social Ser.* No. 7, Bombay 1957; B. R. DHEKNEY, *Hubli City: A Study in Urban Economic Life*, Dharwar 1959; D. R. GADGIL, *Poona: A Socio-Economic Survey, Part I*, Gokhale Inst. of Politics and Economics Publ. No. 12, Poona 1945; idem: *Poona: A Socio-Economic Survey, Part II*, ibid. No. 25, 1952; idem: *Sholapur City: Socio-Economic Studies*, Poona 1965; S. KESAVA IYENGAR, *A Socio-Economic Survey of Hyderabad-Secunderabad City Area*, Hyderabad 1957; V. A. JANAKI and Z. A. SAYED, *The Geography of Padra Town*, Baroda 1962; D. T. LAKDAWALA, J. C. SANDESARA, V. N. KOTHARI, and P. A. NAIR, *Work, Wages and Well-Being in an Indian Metropolis: Economic Survey of Bombay City*, Univ. of Bombay, Ser. in Economics No. 11, Bombay 1963; D. N. MAJUMDAR, *Social Contours of an Industrial City: Social Survey of Kanpur*, Bombay 1960; P. C. MALHOTRA, *Socio-Economic Survey of Bhopal City and Bairagarh*, New York 1964; H. C. MALKANI, *A Socio-Economic Survey of Baroda City*, Baroda 1957; B. R. MISRA, *Report on Socio-Economic Survey of Jamshedpur City*, Patna 1959; MOHAMMAD MOHSIN, *Chittaranjan: A Study in Urban Sociology*, Bombay 1964; RADHAKAMAL MUKERJEE and BALJIT SINGH, *Social Profiles of a Metropolis: Social and Economic Structure of Lucknow, Capital of Uttar Pradesh*, New York 1961; C. RAJAGOPALAN, *The Greater Bombay: A Study in Suburban Ecology*, Bombay 1962; V. K.

R. V. Rao and P. B. Desai; Greater Delhi: A Study in Urbanisation 1940–57, New York 1965; S. N. Sen, *The City of Calcutta: A Socio-Economic Survey 1954–55 to 1957–58*, Calcutta 1961; N. V. Sovani, D. P. Apte, and G. R. Pendse, *Poona: A Re-Survey: The Changing Pattern of Employment and Earnings*, Gokhale Inst. of Politics and Economics Publ. No. 34, Poona 1956; R. L. Singh, *Banaras: A Study in Urban Geography*, Banaras 1955; idem: *Bangalore: An Urban Survey*, Varanasi 1964; Ujagir Singh, *Allahabad: A Study in Urban Geography*, Varanasi 1961.

7. Jal F. Bulsara, *Problems of Rapid Urbanisation in India*, Bombay 1964.
8. 'Slums of Madras City', Census of India 1961, Vol. 9, Madras, Part XI-C (Delhi, 1965).
9. 'Special Report on Kanpur City', Census of India 1961, Vol. 15, Uttar Pradesh, Part X (Delhi, 1965).
10. Development Plan. Ahmedabad Municipal Corporation, Ahmedabad *c.* 1962; Interim Development Plan, Asansol-Durgapur. Asansol Planning Organisation, Government of West Bengal, Development and Planning Department, Asansol 1966; The Outline Development Plan for the Bangalore Metropolitan Region. Bangalore Town Planning Office, Government of Mysore, Bangalore 1963; Report on the Development Plan for Greater Bombay. Bombay Municipal Corporation 1964; Memorandum on Development Plan, Calcutta Metropolitan District, 1966–1971. Calcutta Development and Planning (Town and Country Planning) Department, Government of West Bengal, Calcutta 1965; Basic Development Plan for the Calcutta Metropolitan District 1966–1986. Calcutta Metropolitan Planning Organisation, Government of West Bengal, Calcutta 1966; Master Plan for Delhi. Delhi Development Authority, Town Planning Organisation, Delhi 1962; Work Studies Relating to the Master Plan for Delhi. 3 vols., *ibid.* 1964; Draft Master Plan. Gaya Improvement Trust, prepared under direction of J. C. P. Sinha, Government of Bihar, Patna *c.* 1965; Master Plan for Hubli-Dharwar, 1965. Government of Mysore, Town Planning Department, Hubli 1965, mimeographed; Master Plan Patna. 2 vols., Patna Improvement Trust, Patna *c.* 1962; Interim Development Plan for Siliguri. Siliguri Planning Organisation, Town and Country Planning, Government of West Bengal, Siliguri 1965.
11. It has not been possible to include here all the tabular material compiled for this study. Readers who are interested may obtain copies of eight supplementary tables from the author.
12. Heinrich Bleicher, *Statische Beschreibung der Stadt Frankfurt am Main und ihrer Bevölkerung*, Frankfurt am Main 1892.
13. Colin Clark, Urban population densities, *J. R. Statist. Soc.*, Ser. A, **114** (1951), 490–6. See also his Urban population densities, *Bull. Inst. Int. Statist.* **36** (1958), Part 4, 60–8.
14. Brian J. L. Berry, James W. Simmons, and Robert J. Tennant, Urban population densities: structure and change, *Geogr. Rev.*, **53** (1963), 389–405.
15. Bruce E. Newlings, Urban growth and spatial structure: mathematical models and empirical evidence, *Geogr. Rev.*, **56** (1966), 213–25.
16. Halliman H. Winsborough, 'A Comparative Study of Urban Population Densities' (unpublished Ph.D. dissertation, Department of Sociology, University of Chicago 1961).
17. Colin Clark, The location of industries and population. *Tn Plann. Rev.*, **35** (1964–65), 195–218; reference to Poona on p. 214.
18. Map analysis and computations were supported by a grant from the Rutgers Research Council during 1967–68.

7 The Economic Expansion of Jinja, Uganda

B. S. HOYLE

THE municipality of Jinja, second town of Uganda, with an estimated population of 50 000, stands at an altitude of 3750 feet on the east shore of the Victoria Nile at the point where the river formerly issued from Lake Victoria in the Ripon Falls. (*Jinja* is the Luganda word for 'stone'. This is taken to refer either to the rocks of the Ripon and Owen Falls or, more probably, to a sacrificial stone on a hilltop overlooking the town.) Over a century ago John Hanning Speke, discoverer of the source of the Nile, recorded that these falls constituted

> by far the most interesting sight I had seen in Africa . . . that attracted one to it for hours—the roar of the waters, the thousands of passenger-fish, leaping at the falls with all their might, the Wasoga and Waganda fishermen coming out in boats and taking post on all the rocks with rod and hook, hippopotami and crocodiles lying sleepily on the water, the ferry at work above the falls, and cattle driven down to drink at the margin of the lake—made . . . as interesting a picture as one could wish to see.
>
> The expedition had now performed its functions. I saw that old father Nile without any doubt rises in the Victoria N'yanza. . .[1]

Thus 'the subject of so much speculation, and the object of so many explorers'[2] was revealed to the outside world.

The thick riverain forests have now been cleared, and the fauna dispersed. The ferry to which Speke made reference—an ancient and essential link between the rival states on the two shores, used at times by the Kabaka Mutesa's armies when raiding Busoga from the west[3]—has been replaced by a railway bridge and by a road that traverses the crest of the Owen Falls Dam. The Ripon Falls are submerged under the higher Nile waters behind the dam.

For References to this chapter, see page 140. The author has revised the text of his original article for this volume, and the References have been reorganised.

HISTORICAL BACKGROUND

In the earliest years of the present century the economic significance of Jinja was slight. A British post had been established in 1893 at Chief Luba's fort nearby (later rebuilt as Fort Thruston), but Iganga, a little way to the northeast, became the first headquarters of the then Central Province of Uganda in 1900. The establishment of a lake steamer service between Jinja and Port Florence (Kisumu), the port that in 1901 became the terminus of the railway from the coast, focused attention on the significance of Jinja's location with respect to transportation, and the administrative headquarters were accordingly opened at Jinja in that year. Two years later the newly formed Uganda Company introduced cotton into Uganda as a cash crop (first into Buganda, and subsequently into the Eastern Province), and in 1904 the first export of cotton was recorded; previous trade to the coast had been largely in ivory. Even at this early date the geographical potentialities of Jinja were apparent. In 1908 Winston Churchill wrote, with considerable perspicacity: 'Jinja is destined to become a very important place in the future economy of Central Africa. . . . In years to come the shores of this splendid bay may be crowned with long rows of comfortable tropical villas and imposing offices, and the gorge of the Nile crowded with factories and warehouses'[4].

The opening in 1912 of the 61 mile (98 kilometres) long Busoga Railway represented an important step forward, which helped to consolidate Busoga as a cotton growing and ginning area; this railway connected Jinja with the Lake Kyoga steamer services at Namasagali and thus provided a link in the chain of north–south communications with the Sudan. The significance of Jinja as a transport focus was further emphasised by the completion in 1928 of a direct railway connection with Kenya and the coast. In 1931 this line was continued westward to Kampala and northward from Tororo to Soroti, and became a basic factor in the subsequent economic expansion of the country as a whole. The lake steamer services were, of course, adversely affected by these developments, but whereas in 1925 goods traffic of the port of Jinja amounted to only 15 000 tons, the total tonnage of goods handled at the Jinja railway station in 1961 reached 69 000.

RECENT DEVELOPMENTS

The economic growth of Jinja, previously unspectacular and due almost entirely to the expansion of commercial activities, has been considerably accelerated since the mid-1950s. The town has become a focus of modern manufacturing industry and the seat of some of Uganda's larger industrial concerns. The basis for these developments was the decision taken in 1947 to proceed with the construction of a dam and hydroelectric power station at the point where the Nile leaves Lake Victoria. With reference to this site, Churchill had commented earlier that 'there is power enough to gin all the cotton and saw all the wood in Uganda, and it is here that one of the principal emporia of tropical produce will certainly be created. . . . It would be perfectly easy to harness the whole river and let the Nile begin its long and beneficient journey to the sea by leaping through a turbine. It is possible that nowhere else in the world could so enormous a mass of water be held up by so little masonry'[5].

By providing large quantities of industrial power at economic rates the completion of the Owen Falls Dam at Jinja in 1954 marked a major turning point in the economic development of the town and of the country[6]. The dam has not raised the level of Lake Victoria, though it has caused the submergence of the Ripon Falls and the Owen Falls. The generating station has an installed capacity of 150 000 kilowats (in ten sets of 15 000 kilowatts each). The scheme led to an unprecedented boom in building and commerce in Jinja and had many complex social repercussions. The provision of a basic power grid in southern Uganda opened up wide possibilities of industrial production. Considerable expansion has taken place, notably in Kampala, Jinja, and Tororo. On the basis of United Kingdom and World Bank loans totalling £5·5 million, power lines were extended, and by the end of 1963 electricity supplies from Owen Falls were available in Fort Portal in the west, in Gulu in the north, beyond Masaka in the south, and beyond Mbale in the east. Valuable income is also derived from the export of bulk supplies of power to western Kenya and Nairobi.* However, the present

---

* The rate at which this export takes place is highly favourable to Kenya. In 1962, 42 per cent of the output of Owen Falls went to Kenya, but the revenue derived from this sale accounted for only 13·4 per cent of the Uganda Electricity Board's total income for that year. Nevertheless, the Kenya bulk supply is an

potential output of the station no longer greatly exceeds demands, and proposals to develop further hydroelectric power stations along the Victoria Nile have been investigated.

Most of the industrial establishments that have grown up in Jinja and elsewhere in Uganda as a result of the stimulus provided by electricity supplies have been promoted and largely financed by the Uganda government through the Uganda Development Corporation. The largest single consumer of electricity is the smelter that treats copper concentrates from Kilembe, in the foothills of the Ruwenzori massif. An ore concentrator is situated at Kilembe and a roasting plant 8 miles (13 kilometres) away at Kasese. The development of the industry was made possible by the 208 mile (334 kilometre) westward extension of the railway from Kampala to Kasese in 1956. The copper smelter at Jinja came into operation in the same year, and in 1962 production reached 15 231 tons (15 475 tonnes) of blister copper, which added almost £4 million to the country's export earnings. Unfortunately, the prospects for further expansion appear at present to be slight in spite of recent new ore discoveries; at the current rate of working, ore reserves will become exhausted in the mid-1970s. Moreover, there seems to be no likelihood whatsoever that any other mineral will assume a major position in the economy of Uganda. In assessing the prospects of the copper industry, the members of the International Bank's economic mission to Uganda commented in 1961 that 'the failure of Kilembe would make it even more difficult to attract overseas capital to other mineral developments'[7], in addition to intensifying labour problems and resulting in a serious loss of national income.

A second major enterprise, which came into production at Jinja in 1956, is a long-projected cotton-textile factory which uses entirely local raw material. Initially it proved difficult to sell cloth produced at Jinja, since Africans preferred to buy cheaper Indian cloth and Asian traders were reluctant to handle locally produced material; production costs were high at first as a result of the small output and the relatively high level of industrial wages. These difficulties have been largely overcome, and demand has increased to such an

economic proposition; without it, tariffs in Uganda would be much higher. Kenya is responsible for transmission costs from the Uganda–Kenya border. The agreement between Uganda and Kenya under which this sale takes place is under review.

extent in recent years that the size of the original plant has been doubled, and a second major textile mill has been built.

Other large industrial developments at Jinja are brewing (of beer), grain conditioning and oil milling, sugar refining, and tea and coffee processing. Tobacco curing and cigarette manufacture represent an important undertaking, and there are several light-engineering concerns. A plywood factory and a steel rolling mill were opened in the 1960s—both the first of their kind in East Africa. Additional expansion has involved a total investment of more than £5 million, and recent developments have included a flour mill, a tool factory and papermaking and matchmaking factories.

These various developments have been accommodated in two distinct industrial zones: one on the west bank of the Nile, within Buganda, and the other on the east side of the river beyond the central commercial and residential zones (Fig. 7.1). The cultivation of cash crops such as cotton, coffee, sugar and tea is a prominent feature of the agricultural landscape in the Jinja area; the primary processing of these products has given rise to a group of major undertakings. It is interesting to note that cash-crop production and processing remain concentrated in the areas served by the first railway link with the coast—a legacy from the earliest days of Uganda's economic development. Sugar, first planted near Jinja in 1921, has been highly successful; 40 years later the extensive Lugazi and Kakira estates together produced a record crop of 95 000 tons. The Muljibhai Madhvani group of companies, founded on sugar cultivation, employed more than 11 000 people in the 1960s; its subsidiary developments included a farm boarding school, a commercial college, grain mills, soap and glass factories, and the steel rolling mill mentioned earlier. The Madhvani organisation was the basis of much of the planned development of Jinja.

LOCATIONAL FACTORS

The Luganda phrase *Kiyira bive bugagga*, inscribed on the coat of arms of the municipality of Jinja, signifies that 'the Nile is wealth', and it is true that Speke's 'magnificent stream', harnessed to produce electricity and channelled into industry, is a prime factor in the recent economic growth of the town. However, the precise extent to which the availability of virtually unlimited supplies of electricity has acted as an industrial locational factor for Jinja itself is open to debate. The Uganda Electricity Board offers a special uniform tariff, irrespective of distance from Owen Falls, to relatively small-scale

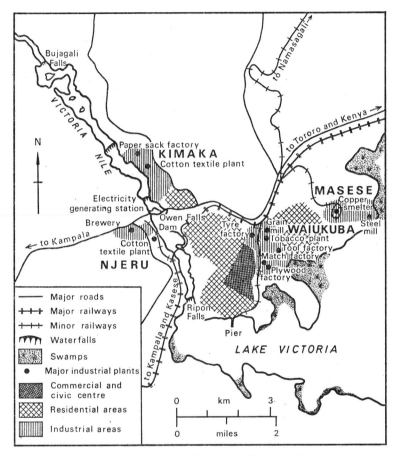

Fig. 7.1   Urban regions and principle industrial establishment of Jinja. Two distinct industrial areas have developed, one on each side of the central commercial and residential core.

industrial consumers: the cost of power does not normally exceed about 8 per cent of the total annual expenses of a small concern. But although the availability of a good supply of electricity is clearly a prime consideration for these industries, its cost is not a vital factor. For large-scale industries, to whose manufacturing techniques electricity provides a major contribution, power costs form a much higher proportion of total expenses. There are distinct savings in locating such consumers near Owen Falls; short, inexpensive private power lines can be easily laid and are less susceptible to interruption than long-distance lines. The policy of the Uganda Electricity Board is therefore to consider special tariff arrangements, by private agreement, for any potential large-scale consumer of electricity in the Jinja area; similar agreements may be concluded with consumers farther afield—for example, at Tororo—but obviously in these cases the transmission costs, and therefore the tariff charges, are higher. It would appear that a definite financial incentive exists to attract the larger industrial establishments to Jinja —the copper smelter, the textile factories and the steel rolling mill are cases in point—but that this incentive does not extend to smaller industrial concerns.

Apart from electricity, the geographical basis for Jinja's 'miniature economic revolution', which has 'telescoped into the space of a few years processes which elsewhere have occurred only in decades'[8], is to be found in the simultaneous occurrence in the area of a number of additional factors; these include the general situation of the town in a highly productive agricultural area forming part of the economically focal lake zone of Uganda[9], the ready availability of a plentiful supply of water and of land for industrial use, the presence of a large and hardworking labour force, and the site of the town at a transport node where internal Busoga and Buganda routeways converge and where the principal railway and road routes from Uganda to Kenya and the coast cross the Nile route to the Sudan, a location that facilitates both the collection of raw materials and the distribution of finished products. There is some evidence, however, to show that in certain cases, notably that of the steel rolling mill, the decisive locational factors are much more a matter of financial circumstance, government policy and administrative convenience than of geography.

PRESENT AND FUTURE PROSPECTS

The considerable industrial potential of Jinja has now been partly demonstrated, but industrialisation is still very much in its initial stages. Although Churchill's prophecies have been translated into reality, and although government encouragement has been both positive and continuous, the optimism engendered in 1954 by the provision of electricity has not been entirely justified by subsequent events, and the confidently expected industrial revolution has not taken place on the scale envisaged. The Owen Falls scheme has not yet become truly profitable, since the expected level of sales to large industrial consumers has not been attained; this is partly because a projected steel mill at Tororo was never built, and also because a railway, and not a power line, was built to the western region. Had these two early projects come to fruition, it is possible that the full capacity of Owen Falls would have been absorbed at an earlier date. In contrast with the late 1940s and early 1950s, the 1960s have been marked by relative economic stagnation in Uganda, shown particularly by a lack of confidence in the country on the part of overseas investors and, within Uganda, by a slight decline in per capita income. In common with most other African towns, Jinja has encountered social problems, rarely foreseen and always difficult of solution, as a result of the rapid intermixture of traditional African societies and the new urban culture, and in association with the essentially migratory character of industrial labour. Nevertheless, Jinja represents in some senses an epitome of the tremendous economic and social advances that have taken place in Uganda during the remarkable hundred years since Speke was at Mutesa's court and at the Ripon Falls.

SOURCE: *Geographical Review*, Vol. 53, 1963, pp. 377–88; revised for this volume, summer 1973.

REFERENCES

1. JOHN HANNING SPEKE (1863). *Journal of the Discovery of the Source of the Nile.* Edinburgh and London, pp. 466–7.
2. Ibid. (1864). *What Led to the Discovery of the Source of the Nile.* Edinburgh and London, p. 307. For a useful summary of earlier ideas and contributions towards the solution of the Nile mystery, see B. W. LANGLANDS (1962). Concepts of the Nile, *Uganda Journ.*, Vol. 26, pp. 1–22.
3. Speke approached the Nile through Buganda from the Kabaka's court at Mengo (Kampala) and did not cross to the east, or Busoga, shore of the river. The first white man to visit the site of the present town of Jinja was Henry M. Stanley in 1875.
4. WINSTON SPENCER CHURCHILL. *My African Journey.* London (1908), p. 119. A new edition of this fascinating book was published in 1962 by the Holland

Press (Neville Spearman Ltd.), London. The passages quoted occur on pages 80–1 of this new edition.

5. *Ibid.*, 119–20.

6. DAVID N. MCMASTER (1955). Some Effects of the Owen Falls Scheme, Uganda. *Geography*, **40** (1955), pp. 123–6.

7. *The Economic Development of Uganda: Report of a Mission Organised by the International Bank for Reconstruction and Development at the Request of the Government of Uganda.* Baltimore 1962, p. 269; Entebbe, Uganda 1961, p. 212.

8. CYRIL and RHONA SOFER. Jinja Transformed: A Social Survey of a Multi-Racial Township, *East African Studies No. 4*, East African Institute of Social Research, Kampala (1955), p. 113.

9. An interesting examination of the comparative economic progress of Buganda and the other three regions of Uganda is provided by A. M. O'CONNOR (1963). Regional inequalities in economic development in Uganda. *East African Geogr. Rev.*, No. 1, pp. 33–44; also 'Recent railway construction in tropical Africa' in *Transport and Development* (ed. B. S. Hoyle) Macmillan, London (1973).

8 The Craft Structure of a Traditional Yoruba Town

JENNIFER M. BRAY

UNTIL the present century, craft industries in Yorubaland were carried out only in towns, as in mediaeval Europe, and this greater complexity of economic activity has been used as a criterion for the definition of a Yoruba urban centre[1]. The aim of this article is to analyse the craft structure of a traditional Yoruba town, taking as an example men's weaving in Iseyin. It is based on a questionnaire survey of a random sample of ninety weaving compounds as listed in the 1966 tax returns.

In the discussion of a craft, as of a factory industry, the elements of industrial structure fall basically into three groups: the unit of production; supply factors and the organisation of production; and demand factors and the organisation of marketing. The spatial implications of industrial structure are reflected in the morphology of a town, that is, in its internal landscape, and in the dispersion or concentration of the units of production and industrial workers. In a pre-industrial town, the location of craft establishments may be determined only in part by economic factors, and will mainly reflect social structure and organisation, together with the town's technological base, particularly the media of communication[2]. One site frequently serves several purposes and the location of craft production units may be closely related to that of public buildings and services such as markets, places of worship and centres of administration. The social and economic organisation of a society is a function of its culture and of the stage of economic development. In the pre-industrial cities of Europe, craft production took place within a rigid and inflexible system of apprentices, journeymen and master craftsmen[3] and membership of a particular family grouping, rather than economic advantage, was often the most stringent condition of entry into an industry. In Africa today it is possible that the varying levels of education of different generations may be playing a part in breaking down the rigid social stratification and

For References to this chapter, see page 158.

class consciousness which prevent the diffusion of technology and the horizontal mobility of occupation.

Some investigations have been made into the economic structure and morphology of pre-industrial cities in Europe and China[4], and also into the social organisation of the Yoruba peoples[5]. This paper, however, provides a detailed case study of one craft industry, to show how far social and economic factors have together influenced the location and functioning of the weaving industry, both at the various stages of production and in the organisation of production and marketing.

THE TOWN OF ISEYIN

Iseyin, situated 89 km (56 miles) north-west of the city of Ibadan, is a traditional Yoruba settlement with a low level of economic specialisation and little division of labour other than according to sex. There are no factories, little service employment and few amenities such as electricity and a private piped-water supply; only two tarred roads serve the town and elsewhere a maze of laterite paths links the compounds and quarters. One of the most distinctive features is the number of its inhabitants who are engaged in farming. In 1966, 88 per cent of the male taxpayers recorded farming as their primary occupation, although in some cases they may help only with planting and the harvest.

Iseyin had a considerable impetus to growth during the Ilorin raids on Oyo country in the 1830s and again during the 1850s, when Egba country was invaded by raiders from southern Dahomey. The town was under the protection of the Alafin of Oyo and refugees fled to its easily defended site. These decades coincided with the spread of Islam into Yorubaland and the refugees included *malams* from Oyo and Ogbomosho, many of whom were also weavers: they taught Arabic and passed on their traditional weaving techniques to the local people.

As the settlement expanded, the compound became the visible expression of the lineage of the founder member. Quarters consisted of groups of compounds and each usually had its own chief. The names of neighbouring villages which were absorbed into the growing township have been retained in the present quarters, for example, Sagbo and Malete. New quarters were added as the population increased and sixteen are now normally recognised, although traditional delimitation of these quarters does not always coincide with divisions imposed by recent features such as tarred roads.

Iseyin is now a town under the influence of modern media of communication—by road, radio and the postal services—with the large cities of Ibadan and Lagos. European contact is reflected in the numerous small trading stores, the inevitable bars and petrol filling stations. The status of the town is further raised by the importance of its daily night market[6] and it is considered by the Yorubas themselves to be an *ilu*, a town, rather than an *aba* or *abule*, a hamlet or village[7].

The total population of Iseyin is probably approaching 60 000, including some 28 000 taxpayers. According to the 1966 tax returns, the town has 1540 full-time weavers, drawn from 188 of the 670 compounds. It is probable, however, that at least 6000 more people can weave and do so intermittently: these include boys who are too young to feature in the tax records and men who weave as a subsidiary occupation to farming or trading. An estimated figure of 27 per cent of the total male population should therefore include both full-time and part-time weavers in Iseyin.

THE LOCALISATION OF PRODUCTION UNITS

The economic organisation of the Yoruba peoples is based on the core of their social structure, the lineage or *idile*, which comprises all those who can trace their descent from a common male ancestor[8]. Since the lineage may now have several hundred members, it is often not coincident with the residential extended family compound or *agbo ile*, which forms the organisational framework for the weaving industry. As a result of overcrowding in the original compound, sons have moved away to build new houses for themselves and their children. These may either cluster around the old compound and so form a lineage agglomeration of buildings, or be located in a separate quarter of the town.

The extended family compound is the unit of production for weaving itself and for the intermediate processes of spinning and dyeing. The place of residence is also the workplace, whether there is a row of fixed looms in the central open space of a compound or a single portable loom alongside the house. Some weavers, however, have a subsidiary occupation such as tailoring or trading for which a shop is rented from the local council or a private owner. These shops are situated near the market place and along the two tarred roads through Iseyin: the loom is set up outside the shop and the weaver works there during the day.

There is considerable variation in the morphology of the weaving compounds (Fig. 8.1). Only in the farming quarters of Iseyin does the outer wall surrounding the large square compound still remain. Elsewhere, this has been destroyed owing to population pressure on building land, revealing a complex pattern of individual houses.

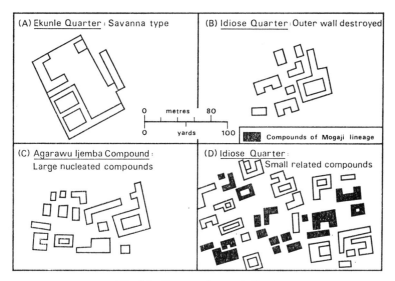

Fig. 8.1   Compound types in Iseyin.

Where weaving is an old-established craft in a lineage and the original house was built on a site with adequate room for later expansion, the production unit is one large nucleated compound such as Agarawu-Ijemba. Where there was limited space for the erection of new looms on the original site, there is now one large unit and several smaller but related compounds in a near-by quarter of the town. If weaving has been introduced within the last 60 years, particularly into an area of high building density, there is commonly a group of small related compounds which are dispersed over one or more quarters of Iseyin, for example, those of Mogaji lineage. These location patterns have considerable economic significance.

There is a marked concentration of weaving compounds in certain wards and quarters of Iseyin (Fig. 8.2). In Adabo, 91 of the 138 compounds (66 per cent) include weavers and 73 have at least four craftsmen, the minimum number for which a row of fixed looms is normally erected. In Koso-Ijemba, 76 of the 188 compounds (38 per cent) have weavers but only 45 compounds have more than four craftsmen. The other two wards show a very low concentration. In Isalu, only 18 of the 167 compounds (11 per cent) have weavers and

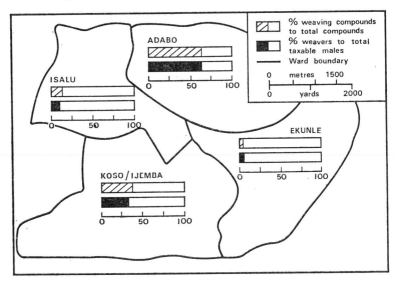

Fig. 8.2   Concentration of weavers and weaving compounds in Iseyin, by wards.

half of these have less than four craftsmen. In Ekunle, only 3 out of 177 compounds record any weavers and none has more than four.

These figures correspond quite closely to those for the proportion of weavers to total occupied males, as recorded in the 1966 tax returns (Fig. 8.2). Of the male workers in Adabo, 64·5 per cent were returned as weavers. The proportions in the other wards were: Koso-Ijemba, 34·6 per cent; Isalu, 8·3 per cent; Ekunle, 3·3 per cent.

There is, too, some localisation of production units within the wards (Fig. 8.3). In Adabo, there are few weavers in Dunmola quarter and in Adabo itself. The latter includes a large part of the market place, while Dunmola families on the eastern periphery of the town are predominantly farmers and the craftsmen in this quarter are blacksmiths. In Koso-Ijemba, most weavers are found in the two quarters of the same name. The people of the former villages of Sagbo, Malete and Ilado have remained farmers and even in Koso most of the weaving families still own farmland. In Isalu, the majority of the eighteen weaving compounds are located in Oke Eyin, adjacent to the high concentration in Oke Oja quarter of Adabo ward. It is in the quarters without a conspicuous concentration of craftsmen that most of the part-time weaving takes place.

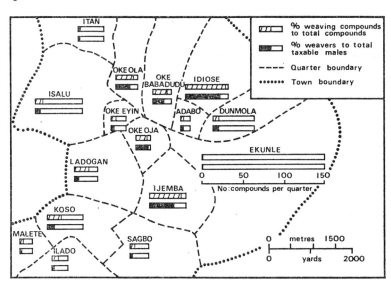

Fig. 8.3 Concentration of weavers and weaving compounds in Iseyin, by quarters.

There is very little mobility between compounds. If men leave their father's house because of overcrowding or a family dispute, they normally move to their mother's compound and never to their wives' families. Alternatively, they may build a new house away from the original compound. All married women live in their husband's house.

There are numerous 'stranger' settlers in the weaving compounds in Iseyin, many of whom have had previous trading contacts with the town and may still act as middlemen for their new compound. Some were also weavers, particularly migrants from the towns of Ijebu-Ode, Ibadan, Oyo, Ilorin and Shaki. Those who were farmers and hunters, or who followed other crafts such as that of blacksmith, originated from smaller villages near Iseyin such as Ipapo, Okeho and Ago-Are. 'Stranger' settlers have often married into the compound and their sons have become weavers. If a family or a group of brothers migrated to Iseyin, the move was usually made at a time when a new compound was being founded and the size of the initial population was more flexible; only single men have settled in established compounds with little room for newcomers.

A Yoruba woman is expected to follow her own profession and women's work is an indispensable part of preliminary weaving processes: they alone may roll and spin raw cotton and use the locally prepared blue and brown dyes. Almost all the weavers in Iseyin are Moslems and each man is allowed to take up to four wives. Included in the sample were forty-seven traders, thirty-nine spinners and fourteen dyers: only five women recorded other work, namely, four meat sellers and one clerk. These figures are misleading, however, as although few women both spin and dye, trading in food or petty goods may be associated with either occupation, particularly in the wet season when the demand for thread by weavers is low. There are no restrictions on the family from which a man may take a wife, but there is a high degree of selection from other weaving compounds. Women from these families can usually spin or dye and are able to assist their future husbands.

Almost half of the weaving families also own farmland. These families include a proportion of farmers ranging from 10 to 90 per cent of their total male population. Only 20 per cent of the farms are in the outer farming zone, *oko egan*, more than 8 km (5 miles) from the town[9]: the remainder lie within this radius, in the *oko etile* zone. There is a significant concentration of those compounds which do own farmland. In Koso quarter, in particular, and also in Adabo and Idiose, the majority of weaving compounds have farms attached. In Ijemba, Oke Oja and Oke Ola, on the other hand, such compounds are in the minority. With one exception, the land of all the compounds in Koso is located to the south-west of Iseyin, near the former village of Koso itself. About 40 per cent of the farms of Idiose quarter are also located in this district because at the time of the founding of the weaving compounds, in the early decades of the nineteenth century, there was more uncleared land than Koso farmers themselves could cultivate and they gave land to Idiose families. On all farms, food crops are the most important, but from only fifteen is there a surplus for sale. No cotton is grown on weavers' farms and only eleven have an income from the sale of cash crops such as cocoa, cassia and palm oil.

THE STAGES OF PRODUCTION

The production processes comprise spinning, dyeing and weaving, together with ancillary services such as tailoring. It is in the preliminary weaving processes and supplementary services that the greatest degree of areal specialisation is shown.

Spinning

The harvesting of locally grown *Ishan* cotton takes place from late November until February. Although no craftsmen use this cotton exclusively, 79 per cent of the weavers use it in a mixture with imported thread. The price of a packet of local cotton is only 60p., compared with £1.05 for imported thread: the former, however, has many knots and breaks easily since it is spun by hand and not by machine.

All spinning is women's work and often those who are no longer capable of heavy work in the compound are employed in this way. Of the ninety sample compounds, fifty-eight have spinners who work on an individual basis and of the thirty-two families with no spinners, thirteen use only imported thread and nineteen also weave with local cotton. Fifteen buy spun thread from the nearest compound as and when they need it; the other four all buy from Aiyegoro in Oke Ola, the family which also dyes for them (Fig. 8.4).

There is little specialisation among spinning compounds since Iseyin cotton is used only sporadically by the weavers. This is reflected in the fact that thirty-two of the fifty-eight spinners, particularly the younger women, are part-time traders. There is also a degree of seasonality in the women's work since the main cotton harvest is in the dry season, which coincides with the period of the weavers' maximum potential output.

Factory-spun cotton is now used by all weavers. This was formerly imported from India but Nigeria is now spinning its own white, red and black cotton at the mills in Apapa and Kaduna. Twenty-seven per cent of the weavers buy this cotton in Ibadan or Lagos at one of the expatriate trading stores, such as the United Africa Company or G. B. Ollivant. A further 41 per cent buy regularly at the periodic markets in these two cities. There are also three shops in Iseyin which retail thread only and a store run by members of the Oreofero co-operative society; all these shops are located on the tarred roads through Iseyin. Cotton is also sold, in smaller quantities and with

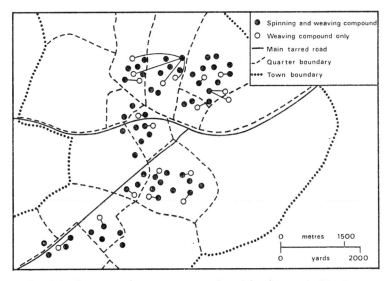

Fig. 8.4 Spinning and weaving compounds and families supplied by them.

irregular supply, at numerous general trading stores. There are certain large compounds which buy white cotton in bales of 100 packets in Ibadan and Lagos and sell a variable surplus to other weavers. Fifteen compounds are acknowledged as thread suppliers in this way and are dispersed over all the weaving quarters.

Dyeing

All-white cloth is not a feature of Iseyin weaving and the local dye made from brown tree bark is the most common base colour in traditional patterns. Less than 5 per cent of the weavers prefer to buy imported brown yarn.

Half the sample compounds have dyers who can prepare the vats, but since 95 per cent of the weavers use brown cotton, there is some specialisation at this stage of production. All vats are prepared to order and the same price is charged by all dyers. There are no economies of scale which are passed on to the weavers, as the cost function does not decrease with the number of vats in operation and there is therefore little competition between compounds.

Seven large dyeing compounds, each able to supply up to fifty weavers, featured in the sample (Fig. 8.5) and include Aiyegoro and Ileyinka, both of whom supply fifteen weavers within the compound and also serve men from Koso quarter to the south-west and non-related families in adjacent quarters. The small compounds with dyers in Koso can supply only their own craftsmen or near-by related

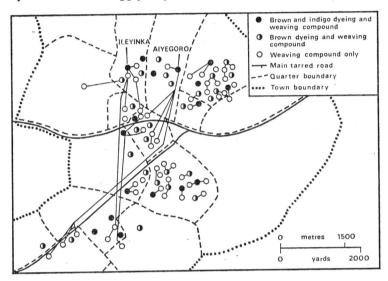

Fig. 8.5   Brown dyeing and weaving compounds and families supplied by them.

compounds where the women are spinners or traders. Since a high proportion of the compounds in Ijemba quarter have their own dyers or can obtain thread from neighbouring families, the two largest compounds, Agarawu and Mogaji, primarily serve part-time weavers from Ekunle. The three large compounds in Oke Ola and Idiose serve Isalu, Oke Eyin and Dunmola farmers/weavers. Frequently there is also specialisation within a group of dispersed but related lineage branches: one family spins and a second dyes for all the other compounds.

The use of blue-black indigo dye is less widespread. Both because they prefer the colour and also because they have no dyers in their compound, 25 per cent of the weavers use only imported black thread. A further 20 per cent buy imported thread but then dip it into a local vat for a few hours to produce a deeper shade. Only 55 per cent of the weavers use the local dye exclusively.

Compounds with women who can prepare the indigo vats are also less widespread. Only one-third have their own dyers and three-quarters of these women are also traders, since the total demand for thread is insufficient to keep them fully occupied. Two-thirds of the compounds with indigo vats coincide with those where brown vats

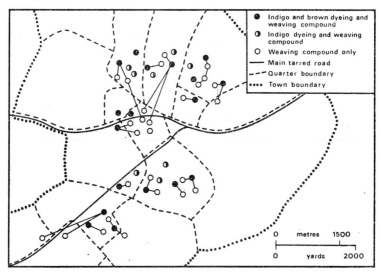

Fig. 8.6   Indigo dyeing and weaving compounds and families supplied by them.

are also in production, including the seven largest, and only one-third therefore specialises in indigo. Localisation of production occurs primarily among groups of near-by or related compounds (Fig. 8.6). Both Aiyegoro and Ileyinka supply fewer compounds and all are in adjacent quarters; in Koso, the three compounds with their own vats meet all the requirements of that quarter. Dyers of Ijemba and Oke Ola still supply part-time weavers of Ekunle and Isalu respectively.

A comparison of the patterns of compounds where indigo dyeing and brown dyeing take place therefore indicates that fewer production units of the former serve a more localised area among the full-time weavers. To meet the higher and steady demand for brown cotton, large weaving and dyeing families supply smaller units in an area that extends beyond the boundary of the quarter and is often independent of the location of related lineage branches.

The use of imported dye is one of the few occupations which is shared between men and women and the colours are used for the central stripes of traditional patterns. Yarn is required only in small quantities and is dyed in a shallow calabash. Only 18 per cent of the compounds, however, regularly use imported dyes and all of them also prepare either brown or indigo vats. Two-thirds of the families buy tins of dye when required for a special order and do not stock permanent supplies. The others take white thread to a trader or weavers in their own quarter, who keep small supplies of dye primarily for their own use.

Ancillary Services

When a length of weaving has been completed, it is cut into strips of between 1 and 1·8 m in length: these strips are 10 cm wide and fourteen of them are joined together to make one wrapper, *iro*. Only five of the ninety sample weavers sell their cloth in bundles of strips or as an uncut length and only six still sew the strips together by hand: the remainder market their cloth as sewn wrappers. These wrappers are then made into garments.

In 1966, a total of eighty-four men in Iseyin recorded tailoring as their primary occupation: thirty-eight live in Adabo ward, twenty-eight in Koso-Ijemba, nineteen in Isalu and two in Ekunle. The concentration of tailors in the groups of weaving quarters is highly significant. Nineteen of the sample weavers are part-time tailors and there are also several seamstresses in the town. The tailors supply the weavers in addition to meeting the clothing requirements of the town's population.

Of the nineteen sample weavers who are also tailors, fifteen work in their own compound, while the other four rent shops; three of these are located on the main road to Shaki and the fourth on the Eruwa road. The men who work in the compounds do little sewing other than joining strips of woven cloth, but those who rent shops also engage in general tailoring, including work with imported material. This difference is a function of accessibility by road and the advantages of a central site in the town.

Almost half the sample weaving compounds include a tailor within their branch of the lineage. Of these thirty-nine men, thirty-two work in one of the family houses and seven rent shops near the

market place. In the compounds without tailors, three-quarters of
the weavers take cloth to one of the central shops and the remainder
use tailors from near-by compounds, whether or not they are relatives. As far as possible, however, the sewing of strips is carried out
within the weaving compounds themselves.

The embroidery of *agbada*, a man's outer garment, is restricted to
certain families and is a full-time occupation; two compounds,
Alufa in Idiose and Oloro in Ijemba, both have more than nine
craftsmen. The location of this trade is determined solely by the
location of family land.

There are also related trades. Carpenters and carvers both supply
looms and tools such as shuttles, bobbins and reels, and also carry
out loom repairs. Three carpenters have workshops on the main
Oyo–Shaki road and make chairs and tables in addition to looms;
the remainder of these craftsmen are dispersed among all quarters
of the town since the majority of their customers are non-weavers.
A few items such as warping pegs and *eya*, which is used to produce
a pattern of holes in a cloth, are required from blacksmiths or goldsmiths. Only one weaving family includes blacksmiths in the same
compound and these are 'stranger' settlers. There are three groups
of smiths in Iseyin, a total of some fifty men; two groups work in
Dumola quarter on the Oyo road and the third in Ijemba, near the
boundary with Ekunle farming quarter. The goldsmiths usually
work as individuals and are found in Koso, Ladogan and Oke Ola
quarters.

THE ORGANISATION OF PRODUCTION AND MARKETING

Entrepreneurs

The system of entrepreneurs is a response to the shortage of capital
in circulation and to the need for cotton thread among boys who
have recently completed their training. There is no class of professional moneylenders in Iseyin; the accumulation of savings is
thus an internal family concern and borrowing takes place among
relatives. Entrepreneurs buy cotton thread and sell finished cloth
for young weavers and take a small commission on each transaction.
These men continue to work as one of a row of weavers in their own
compound but have no supervisory role over either standards of
weaving or patterns woven.

Fifty-six of the ninety weavers are entrepreneurs who are found in every weaving quarter of Iseyin (Fig. 8.7). This proportion is slightly misleading, however, as no young children were included in the sample. The system itself operates partly within the compound unit of production: 76 per cent of the entrepreneurs supply cotton only to members of their own family, each to an average of five people, and in some instances these included an adult craftsman. The head man of a compound may be either the sole or the most

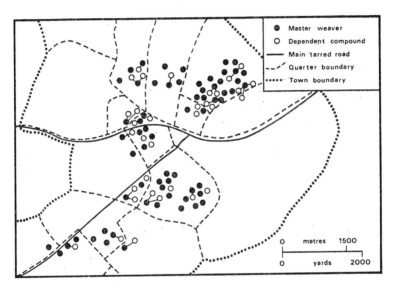

Fig. 8.7   Master weavers and weaving compounds supplied by them.

important entrepreneur, thus adding a managerial function to his social position; the remaining entrepreneurs also serve weavers from other compounds, who in all cases are from the same quarter and over two-thirds of them are related.

The location of entrepreneurs corresponds closely to that of the large weaving compounds in Iseyin, that is, those with more than ten craftsmen. In these families, the total turnover of cotton and cloth is high and there are opportunities for more than one entrepreneur. The larger compounds also have more children in training and an enterprising weaver can supervise young men other than his own sons.

Co-operative Societies

Weavers' co-operative societies are a relatively new feature in the organisation of traditional cloth production in Iseyin. There are now four societies in the town, all registered since 1963. Membership is not compulsory but shows clear areal concentration within quarters. Oreofero, for example, draws weavers from fifteen compounds in Oke Oja quarter, located on both sides of the main road to Shaki: Emilere is based in Ijemba quarter while Otitoloju draws its members from Oke Babadudu and Oke Ola: the majority of Ifelodun weavers live in Adabo and Idiose quarters. Since there is no co-operative which caters for weavers from Koso ward, men from this area also belong to Ifelodun, but membership of each society is otherwise centred on groups of related lineage branches.

The societies make loans to their members for advance payment for cotton thread purchase and usually also act as buying and selling organisations with their own traders. Oreofero has a shop on the main Shaki road which sells cotton at one price to members and at a higher price to non-members. Close co-operation between weavers has thus given rise to a centralised function on a site that is sufficiently attractive to draw additional non-member customers.

Trading Associations

Traditional cloth is sold through both private and public sale. The former includes direct orders for religious festivals and family ceremonies. Of the full-time weavers, 62 per cent sell cloth publicly in the Iseyin night market. Wrappers are also sent to the periodic markets in Ibadan and Lagos: the Lagos market takes place every 32 days and *Oje* market in Ibadan every 16 days.

All trade to Ibadan and Lagos is in the hands of two societies, *Egbe Ibadan* and *Egbe Eko*. Only their members may sell cloth in the markets and the same weaver cannot belong to both groups. In December 1966, they had 311 and 335 members respectively, that is, just over 40 per cent of all full-time weavers in Iseyin. Over half the traders in both associations live in Idiose, Oke Babadudu and Oke Ola quarters and less than 4 per cent are from the farming quarters of the town. There is no areal differentiation of membership between the societies. Part-time weavers produce so little cloth in comparison with full-time craftsmen that they give their wrappers to traders in neighbouring compounds and do not themselves travel to the markets.

Only 8 per cent of the weaving compounds have traders in both associations; 52 per cent have members of *Egbe Ibadan*, but only two compounds, both in Koso quarter, have members of *Egbe Eko* only. One-third of the compounds are without traders, yet 93 per cent of these families sell cloth in Ibadan and 35 per cent sell in Lagos; such families send their wrappers through neighbouring families whether or not they are related.

CONCLUSIONS

The most striking feature of the industrial structure of Iseyin is the concentration into distinct areas of workers in a craft industry that employs up to 27 per cent of the town's male population, for six quarters contain over 85 per cent of the full-time weavers. The unit of production is the residential compound or patrilineal group cooperative and, since there is no spatial variation in land values within the town and hence no point of least cost production, location is determined by the location of family land. In certain ancillary services such as tailoring, there may be advantages of a central site if these services are also required by non-weavers.

There are varying degrees of specialisation and of interdependence between production units. Few weaving compounds have neither spinners nor dyers and there is an even dispersion of those families with which all three processes are associated. In other families, there is specialisation in either spinning or dyeing within the quarter or within a group of related lineage branches. The location of spinning and dyeing units and of the families supplied by them depends upon the degree of social cohesion within the lineage, or between compounds in any one quarter, rather than on economic controls. Where there is interdependence between quarters, this is usually owing to the scale of production and to the advantages of size and compactness of a compound.

The traditional organisation of production and marketing also reflects the functioning of the industry on the basis of the residential compound. There is, however, increasing opportunity for entrepreneurial initiative whereby weavers may extend their patronage to neighbouring or non-related families. Yet no organisation that embraces more than a single compound involves any move in the unit of production itself.

It might be expected that employment in craft weaving would

show a decline since the introduction of free primary education and the opportunities for some school leavers in the large cities in new trades such as tailoring and secretarial work, many of which have their own apprenticeship system[10]. Only eight new looms were erected in Iseyin in 1966, with no addition to the number of units in production. However, there are approximately 800 weavers' sons in training, all under the age of 15 years, and of those of primary school age, 85 per cent are at school. Unless they are to join the pool of unemployed school leavers in Lagos and Ibadan or new employment is created in Iseyin, it seems likely that a high proportion of these boys will continue to work at the family looms in Iseyin and that there will be little change in the organisation and functioning of this industry.

SOURCE: *Transactions of the Institute of British Geographers*, **46**, 1969, pp. 179–93.

REFERENCES

1. A. L. MABOGUNJE. *Yoruba towns*. Ibadan (1962), p. 3.
2. G. SJOBERG. *The pre-industrial city*. Glencoe (1960), p. 323.
3. H. PIRENNE. *Economic and social history of mediaeval Europe* (1936), p. 189.
4. J. S. BURGESS. *The guilds of Peking*. New York (1928).
5. P. C. LLOYD. Craft organization in Yoruba towns. *Africa* 23 (1953), 30–44.
6. B. W. HODDER. This distribution of markets in Yorubaland, *Scott. geogr. Mag*. 81 (1965), 48–59.
7. G. J. A. OJO. *Yoruba Culture* (1966), p. 127.
8. P. C. LLOYD. The Yoruba lineage. *Africa* 25 (1955), 235–51.
9. S. GODDARD. Town-farm relationships in Yorubaland: a case study from Oyo. *Africa* 25 (1965), 29–37.
10. A. CALLAWAY. From traditional crafts to modern industries. *Odu* 2 (1965), 28–57.

9 Unemployment in Less Developed Countries: A Case Study of a Poor District of Tehran

WILLIAM H. BARTSCH

UNEMPLOYMENT is today considered perhaps the most serious of the problems afflicting less developed countries and one that is believed to be steadily worsening as the gap between the rapidly rising numbers pressing for work and new employment opportunities being created widens[1]. Yet surveys conducted in recent years in these countries do not indicate levels of unemployment much higher than found in many developed countries today or any perceptible trend towards significant increases[2]. Even in the urban areas, where such unemployment is regarded to be most serious, very high rates are not reported[3].

How does one explain this discrepancy between what is generally believed and what surveys in these countries indicate? It is submitted here that the problem lies primarily in the type of methodology used to measure unemployment in less developed nations. Simply stated, it is the writer's (and others') view that the definitions and concepts of unemployment formulated in developed countries are poor techniques for determining the true degree of worklessness in less developed countries where quite different socio-economic conditions prevail[4].

CONVENTIONAL DEFINITIONS OF UNEMPLOYMENT

Definitions of unemployment generally require that to be recorded as unemployed, a respondent must also be taking active measures to find employment during a specific reference period, usually the week preceding the enumerator's call. Yet those familiar with the socio-economic realities of less developed countries know that considerable numbers of persons seeking work may not take active

For References to this chapter, see page 166; the references in the original article have been reorganised.

steps to find employment because they believe that no work opportunities in their region exist or because they do not know where to apply for work, given the imperfect state of knowledge in the labour markets of such countries. Furthermore, with no specific information on job openings in their locality during the reference period of the survey, other unemployed persons who are usually actively seeking work may have not been so during this period and thus would not have been recorded as unemployed by the survey either. (In developed countries, the unemployed are generally continuously in search of work, given the more perfect state of knowledge of job opportunities and the requirement of unemployed insurance schemes that they should actively seek work each week if they are to receive financial benefits.)

Developed countries' concepts of unemployment also assume that job-seekers unable to find work may remain in a state of unemployment, since in such countries provision of unemployment insurance benefits meets the living needs of such persons during periods of worklessness. However, in less developed countries no such benefits are paid to the unemployed, and the very low income level of the great majority of families makes recourse to unemployment—except for short periods—virtually impossible for those unable to find a job or discharged from their previous employment. Except in the case of immigrants to urban areas—most of whom have the option of returning to their village pursuits if unable to find work—low-income job-seekers must create work for themselves in any activity that will provide a bare subsistence income[5]. Indeed, an individual worker will even be willing to work for *less* than subsistence earnings if he is a member of a family in which more than one person is employed and all incomes are pooled, since he will be able to live on an inadequate income under such conditions, given the economies of scale in family living expenditures and assuming that total family income is adequate to meet total minimum expenditure requirements. Similarly, single women living together, sharing expenses and pooling incomes, can survive on individual earnings that would otherwise fall short of their needs.

No differentiation is made in recording wage employment in developed countries as between 'stable', or 'continuing', wage employment and 'irregular' wage employment, in view of relative unimportance of the latter in such countries. However, in developing countries a considerable part of total wage employment is on a day-to-day (such as is typical in construction work and agriculture) or short-term basis.* While some in irregular wage employment prefer such an arrangement, most can be assumed to desire continuous wage employment and thus experience frequent periods of unemployment over the year.

TESTING AN IMPROVED METHODOLOGY

While carrying out research on the employment situation in Iran during 1966–7, the writer had the opportunity to test a revised definition of unemployment and some new criteria he believed would draw out various aspects of the worklessness situation in a poor district of Tehran. This district, Ku-ye 9 Aban, is a model community established by the Iranian Government to house the slum dwellers of Tehran city. At a cost of 415 million rials ($5·5 million), 3450 low-cost 3-room housing units and associated social infrastructure were built during 1965–6 by the Government and by early 1967 inhabitants of all the shanty town areas of Tehran were transferred to the community and their slum quarters demolished. Each former slum family was able to purchase its new house through instalment payments of 500 rials ($6·67) a month over 15 years. The liberal financial arrangements were designed to ease the hardship for a community whose income situation was so adverse[6].

In August 1967 the writer arranged for the conducting of a 10 per cent sample survey of the households of Ku-ye 9 Aban, whose population at that time was estimated at 21 000. The survey was carried out by a person who was known to, and enjoyed the confidence of, the inhabitants of the community. (In Iran, distrust of surveys and the motives of those conducting them results frequently in incorrect answering and consequent reduced validity of the surveys.) Questions were kept simple and few in number. Included were those to gauge the worklessness situation: (1) 'Are you unemployed and seeking work?' (with no requirement to be actively seeking work), (2) 'Did you only take up self-employment following failure to gain wage employment?' (asked of the self-employed),

---

* In Iran, many workshops and smaller factories discharge new employees after only a few months so as to avoid having to pay social insurance charges required by law for permanent wage employees. This practice is probably typical of other less developed countries with similar legal requirements for payment of social insurance.

and (3) 'Are you employed on a continuous or irregular basis?' (asked of the wage-employed).

RESULTS OF THE SURVEY

As might be expected in the case of former slum-dwellers, almost all of the adults sampled were of rural origin. Of the heads of the households, 85·3 per cent had been born in a village and 83·5 per cent of their mates were also rural-born. On the average there were 6·4 persons to each household, as compared to an average 4·8 for Tehran city and 5·0 for Tehran's District 7 (which includes Ku-ye 9 Aban) in November 1966, according to the census of that date[7]. The age structure was also considerably more youthful than for Tehran or District 7, with 43·7 per cent of the population under 10 years of age, as compared to 29·0 and 35·8 per cent for Tehran and District 7, respectively.

Labour force participation rates, that is the ratio of economically active persons (employed plus unemployed) to population, were considerably higher for Ku-ye 9 Aban's population aged 10 years and over than was the case for Tehran and District 7 according to the November 1966 census. In the case of males, 79·5 per cent were economically active, as compared to 69·6 and 75·1 per cent for Tehran and District 7, respectively. The difference for women was spectacular: 51·0 per cent of Ku-ye 9 Aban's females aged 10 and over were recorded as active, as against only 8·9 per cent for Tehran and 3·3 per cent for District 7 in 1966. The very high rate of labour force participation for Ku-ye 9 Aban's women is due largely to the heavy incidence of unemployment among them reported by the survey (see below), which counted workless persons as unemployed whether they were actively or inactively seeking work. But it is also attributable to the very high rate of employment—the ratio of employed persons to population aged 10 years and older—of such women: 24·9 per cent. Such high rates of labour force participation on the part of males and, in particular, females are not surprising, given Ku-ye 9 Aban's poverty situation: the urgent need for income dictates that a much higher share of dependants of working age (wives, children) seek employment than is the case for relatively better-off Iranian families[8].

With no condition stipulating active search for work, rates of unemployment in Ku-ye 9 Aban as indicated by the survey were much greater than those of the 1966 census for Tehran and District 7, in which it was stipulated that respondents should have been actively seeking work during the preceding week to be recorded as unemployed.* For males, 14·3 per cent of the economically active aged 10 and over were reported as unemployed, as compared to 5·4 per cent for District 7 and 4·8 per cent for Tehran city. A phenomenal 51·2 per cent of Ku-ye 9 Aban's economically active women were reported as unemployed, as opposed to only 5·0 per cent for those of District 7 and 4·1 per cent for Tehran city. Most of these unemployed women were housewives who were not actively seeking work, but who wanted employment to supplement the meagre earnings (if any) of the head of household. In the event of finding work, they had arrangements to leave their children with a neighbour during working hours.

The incidence of self-employment was also considerably higher in Ku-ye 9 Aban than in Tehran city or District 7. Of employed males, 26·7 per cent were self-employed, as against 20·1 per cent for Tehran and 20·9 per cent for District 7. In the case of working females, 17·2 per cent were self-employed, as compared to 6·2 per cent for Tehran and 14·2 per cent for District 7. That such high levels of self-employment in Ku-ye 9 Aban derive from the inability to gain wage employment is clear from the results of the survey: 80·6 per cent of the male, and 77·3 per cent of the female, self-employed reported that they had only taken up self-employment after failing to gain preferred wage employment. The pressure of poverty combined with freedom of entry into self-employment and low capital requirements[9] account for the high incidence of such 'forced', or 'involuntary', self-employment, which may be looked upon as a form of 'disguised' unemployment ('disguised' in the sense that, if they could have received unemployment benefits, they would have been able to remain unemployed and wait for a wage employment offer).

Most of Ku-ye 9 Aban's wage employed were only in irregular employment, subject to loss of livelihood when the work assignment was completed or short-term contract expired. In the case of males,

---

* In making these comparisons, the writer does not wish to imply that the rates of employment of Tehran and District 7 would necessarily have been as high as those for Ku-ye 9 Aban if census definitions had been as unrestrictive as in his survey; indeed, they probably would not have been, given the acute employment/poverty situation in the community.

45·2 per cent were reported in such 'intermittent' wage employment[10], while for females the incidence was 72·0 per cent. (It would appear that the large numbers of domestic servants in the female workforce were reported as in irregular wage employment, because they were subject to discharge at any time by their employers.) Thus over the course of a year, a large part of the wage employed must have experienced periods of worklessness for varying periods of time.

Table 9.1 below summarises the incidence of various forms of unemployment in Ku-ye 9 Aban, as discussed above. It can be seen that over 70 per cent of the community's economically active population 10 years of age and over was either in open or 'disguised' unemployment or was intermittently (un)employed.

Table 9.1   Components of Worklessness of Labour Force by Sex

Ku-ye 9 Aban August 1967 Survey
(In per cent of labour force)

Category of worklessness	Males	Females	Both sexes
Unemployed	14·3	51·2	28·6
Self-employed Rejects of Wage Employment	19·1	6·8	14·3
Irregularly Wage Employed	28·0	28·8	28·3
Total	61·3	86·8	71·2

CONCLUSION

By including more searching questions than used at present in labour force inquiries, as well as by relaxing the current definition of unemployment used, it has been possible to assess more realistically the worklessness situation of an urban area of a less developed country. While the application of this revised methodology to the extreme case of a poverty-stricken community has dramatised the extent of the worklessness, applying this revised methodology to any urban community of a less developed country would certainly result in findings of much higher rates of worklessness than can be gained by continuing to adhere to concepts and definitions of unemployment really only suitable in the developed countries.

The writer's attempt to probe more deeply and realistically into the worklessness situation in a less developed country should be regarded only as a rudimentary first step in improving methods of assessing worklessness in such countries, however. Use of definitions as developed here should be refined and tested for suitability by statisticians before being used in large-scale surveys of the labour force. For instance, the definition of 'intermittently unemployed' should specify that the wage-employed person in question in fact *wanted* continuous wage employment. (Some, in fact, prefer irregular employment.) Furthermore, the definition must spell out more clearly who are to be regarded as the intermittently (un)employed. The contractual arrangement between the worker and his employer would appear to be the best basis for formulating such a definition[11].

Other modifications in surveys would be useful in characterising unemployment more clearly and meaningfully. For example, labour force surveys might inquire as to the minimum wage acceptable to the unemployed (and the involuntarily self-employed), i.e. the wage at which they would be willing to accept wage employment, and for what type of wage employment they are available at this wage, since these restrictions will affect the formulation of effective remedial policies. Furthermore, in order to give a time dimension to the situation of worklessness, surveys should indicate for how long such persons have been unemployed, involuntarily self-employed, and intermittently (un)employed. The question on this aspect would relate only to the point in time of the survey, of course; if it were desired to view the situation over the period of a year, stock-and-flow surveys should be introduced that could identify not only the *numbers* completely idle in forced self-employment and intermittently idle at different times of the year, but also the *man-day distribution of the labour time* offered by the labour force as between employment and unemployment at these times and for the year as a whole. This would provide data on the extent of 'visible underemployment' among the workforce over the year. Such data are particularly valuable in assessing the manpower situation in the rural areas where such visible underemployment is most widespread[12].

Even should these additions to, and modifications of, questions in labour force surveys be introduced in an effort to improve the methodology of assessing worklessness in less developed countries, it should be recognised that the results will not be entirely satisfactory for their rural areas because of the socio-economic conditions there that make it difficult to distinguish between employment and unemployment or even to know what constitutes participation in the labour force. Where the rural population is mainly self-employed or in unpaid family activities, there is a fine line of distinction between being in or out of the labour force, or being employed or unemployed, made even more difficult to determine as the result of the constant shifting of the rural population over the year between different statuses. The ILO is currently engaged in a research project to re-examine and assess these basic concepts in terms of their applicability to the less developed countries. Similarly, the OECD Development Centre is carrying out a project, the objective of which is to determine the most useful and relevant means of assessing employment and unemployment in such countries.

These considerations notwithstanding, it seems clear that the improved techniques suggested here, using modified definitions and including new concepts, can go a long way in bringing more clearly to light the nature and dimensions of the worklessness problem in less developed countries, particularly in their urban areas. The governments of these countries should consider reappraising the relevance of their current surveys of the labour force and unemployment[13] in the light of the suggestions made here, with a view to formulating effective and appropriate policies to overcome the rising tide of worklessness in their labour forces.

SOURCE: *International Development Review*, **13**, No. 1, 1971, pp. 19–22.

REFERENCES

1. Growing concern for the employment situation in less developed countries has characterised recent policy statements by the United Nations and its specialised agencies, including the FAO, the World Bank, and the ILO. In response to what it regards as a growing threat, the ILO in 1969 launched its World Employment Programme aimed at accelerating the rate of employment-creation, and within this context in 1970 carried out the first of a number of planned country missions (to Colombia) for developing comprehensive strategies to overcome the employment problem in less developed countries. A similar concern with the unemployment problem was expressed by the Pearson Commission in its report, *Partners in Development*, which termed the problem 'urgent'. Both the World Bank and the OECD Development Centre are devoting considerable research effort during the Second Development Decade to analysis of unemployment in LDCs, reflecting the rising concern with the problem.

2. For instance, unemployment (excluding the seasonally unemployed) as a percentage of the economically-active population in Iran in November 1966 was only 3·7 per cent, according to the census of that date, as compared with 2·6 per cent in the census of November 1956. Annual surveys of unemployment in the United Arab Republic, Korea, Philippines, and Taiwan during the 1960s show rates varying from 1·5 to 8·4 per cent only, with no trend towards increase. See DAVID TURNHAM. 'The Employment Problem in Less Developed Countries: A Review of Evidence', Unpublished-Roneo OECD Development Centre, Paris, June 1970, p. 56.

3. Iranian urban unemployment as reported by censuses increased only slightly between 1956 and 1966, or from 4·5 per cent to 4·9 per cent. Rates for the urban areas of Chile in 1968, Panama in 1963–4, Venezuela in 1969, Ceylon in 1968, India in 1961–2, Malaya in 1965, and Philippines in 1965, were 6, 10·4, 7·9, 15·0, 3·2, 9·8, and 11·6 per cent, respectively. See TURNHAM. *Op. cit.*, pp. 58–60.

4. In his recent study of conditions in southeast Asia, *Asian Drama*, London 1968, GUNNAR MYRDAL is also highly critical of the use of Western definitions and concepts of unemployment in less developed countries. See pp. 1020, 1024–5. Similarly, the OECD regards the concept of unemployment used in industrial countries as 'inappropriate' for most LDCs. See OECD. *Development Assistance: 1970 Review*, Paris December 1970, p. 117.

5. A situation noted, among others, by MYRDAL. *Op. cit.*, pp. 1020 and 1120; JAN L. SADIE. 'Labor Supply and Employment in Less Developed Countries,' *The Annals of the American Academy of Political and Social Science*, January 1967, pp. 127–8; and INTERNATIONAL LABOUR OFFICE. *Employment and Economic Growth*, Geneva 1964, p. 124.

6. Of 944 employed men in two of the slum communities subsequently razed (Behjatabad and Salsabil), 84·5 per cent were reported by surveys of the Ministry of Development and Housing in 1965 as earning 100 rials ($1·33) or less a day when minimum needs for food alone in that year for a family of four in Tehran were estimated at 137 rials ($1·83) by a Ministry of Labour investigation. The supplementary earnings of the considerable number of wives and children in the two communities who were also working (396 persons) may be assumed to have brought family incomes up to a subsistence level.

7. All figures for Tehran City and its District 7 quoted in this article derive from data in Plan Organisation, Iranian Statistical Centre, *National Census of Population and Housing*, November 1966, Volume 10, Tehran Shahrestan, Tehran, August 1967.

8. The writer is currently engaged in a study of the relationship between head of household income and labour force participation rates in less developed countries, using data for the urban areas of Iran. In Ku-ye 9 Aban, the 1967 survey also showed that 4·6 per cent of boys under the age of 10 were economically active, a real poverty indicator.

9. For instance, the Ku-ye 9 Aban day maid employed by the writer's Iranian parents-in-law asked them to lend her 1000 rials ($13·33) so that her unemployed husband could buy a stock of watermelons and start a street sales business.

10. About half of the wage employed males in the two slum districts surveyed in 1965 (see Note 6) were construction workers, typically subject to day-to-day employment and discharge on completion of the work assignment.

11. See, for instance, the views of the ILO on this subject in UNITED NATIONS. *Handbook of Household Surveys*, Studies in Methods, Series F, No. 10,

New York 1964, p. 83. Useful guidelines in determining whether a respondent should be classified unemployed or not are also included in this *Handbook*, p. 77.

12. For an example of how such data might be shown in tabular form, see WILLIAM H. BARTSCH and LOTHAR E. RICHTER. 'An Outline of Rural Manpower Assessment and Planning in Developing Countries,' *International Labour Review*, **103**, No. 1, January 1971, Table 1, p. 74.

13. Indeed, the Indian Government has already initiated action along these lines, setting up recently a Committee of Experts on Unemployment Estimates, reporting to its Planning Commission, charged with making recommendations for improving the methodology currently in use for surveying unemployment.

10 The Role of Urbanisation in Economic Development: Some International Comparisons

BERT F. HOSELITZ

1

RAPID urban growth is a relatively new phenomenon in India. Up to the end of the First World War some urban growth took place, but neither the proportion of the total population in urban places nor the rate of increase of the urban population itself was startling. With the decade 1921 to 1931, urbanisation became a noticeable phenomenon in India, and the rate of urban growth has accelerated with each decade since then. Moreover, the cities and larger towns (that is, urban places with more than 20 000 inhabitants) have grown more rapidly than those with only quasi-urban features. These trends of urban growth in India during the last few decades are presented in Table 10.1.

Two facts, above all, should be noted: (1) The percentage variation of the total population living in urban places has been increasing each decade since 1901, and (2) the rate of increase during the five decades 1901 to 1951 in towns with 20 000 or more inhabitants has been almost twice as fast as the rate of growth of all urban places together (that is, 112 per cent as against 59 per cent). These data apparently understate the rate of urban growth somewhat, since the Indian census, on which these data are based, does not list population of metropolitan areas, but only of towns and town groups, and we may assume that data for metropolitan areas would show a more rapid rate of growth, especially of the larger cities and towns.

A datum which is often selected from these figures is the fact that in 1901 (or 1891) the proportion of the urban population of India was around 10 per cent, and that this proportion was roughly similar to the share of the urban population in the United States in 1840. But, whereas in the five decades between 1840 and 1890 the share

For References to this chapter, see page 190.

Table 10.1   Urban Growth in India since 1881

Year	British India			India (boundaries of 1948)	
	Percentage of urban population	Per cent variation per decade		Percentage of urban population in towns 20 000+	Percentage variation per decade in towns 20 000+
	(1)	(2)	(3)	(4)	(5)
1881	9·3				
1891	9·4				
1901	10·0	10·91		5·61	
1911	9·4	10·57	−3·12	5·48	−2·32
1921	10·2	11·38	7·66	6·08	10·95
1931	11·1	12·13	6·59	6·97	14·64
1941	12·8	13·91	14·67	8·88	27·40
1951		17·34	24·66	11·89	33·90
1901–51			58·94		111·94

Sources: Column 1, KINGSLEY DAVIS (1951). *The Population of India and Pakistan*, Princeton, p. 127; columns 2–5, ASHISH BOSE (1959). The Process of Urbanisation in India, doctoral dissertation, University of Delhi, p. 167.

of the urban population in the United States rose from 10·8 per cent to 35·1 per cent, in India it rose only from 10·9 per cent in 1901 to 17·3 per cent in 1951. Hence the rate of urbanisation in India was much slower than in the United States, though the parallel is somewhat vitiated by the fact that in India the rate of urbanisation accelerated from 1901 onwards, whereas in the United States from 1840 to 1890 it tended to slow down gradually[1].

The purpose of these comparisons is either to determine the comparative speed of urban growth in India, as against the United States, or to extrapolate from American past experience the future trends of Indian urban growth. But there are a number of reasons why comparisons between the United States and India have serious shortcomings. Culturally the United States and India are very different, and it would be difficult to select two countries more different in social structure. The growth of the United States falls entirely in the period of modern capitalism; there are no survivals in American culture of previous feudal or tribal systems of social organisation; moreover, though an overwhelming proportion of the American population did live in rural areas in the eighteenth and early nineteenth centuries, rural America was at that time culturally an outlying province of Britain and Europe. Even in the early stages of American history, the urban centres played an overwhelming role culturally, and, as Lampard has pointed out, from the very early times the United States had an essentially urban civilisation[2]. Finally, and most importantly, the growth of American society in the nineteenth century took place through the settlement of new land. Urban growth was not merely a process of already existing urban centres growing larger; new cities were founded, and this was possible and necessary because of the spatial expansion of the population over previously uninhabited country. The experience of urban growth in countries like the United States, Canada, or Australia is relevant if comparisons are made with Siberia or Brazil, or perhaps even the western portions of China, but not if our concern is with India, a country which in its main outlines has maintained a fairly stable settlement pattern for hundreds and even thousands of years. Moreover, unlike American society, which fundamentally is a modern society, Indian society has roots which go back deep into its past. Though Harappa and Mohenjo Daro are irrevocably gone, we should not forget that Banaras was a principal urban centre in the time of the Buddha; that Patna, a state capital in modern India, is located on the site of Pataliputra, the capital of the Magadha empire; and that Delhi, the national capital of India, was once Indraprastha, one of the legendary capitals of the Mahabharata.

Comparisons between India and the United States, whether they deal with historical or contemporary trends, must, therefore, be highly imperfect, because of the profound differences in culture and traditions of the two societies. Similar though somewhat less profound differences exist if India is contrasted with Europe. Europe had a feudal social structure not so long ago, and its society was organised along tribal lines at a time when India had seen the rise and fall of empires which embraced a large portion of the subcontinent. Moreover, in many European countries we will encounter manifold traditions which date back to a time in which most of the population lived in more or less self-contained village communities and in which the few scattered urban centres, rather than specialising in the production of finished goods and exchange with the countryside, performed mainly administrative functions for sur-rounding territories. As we shall see later, a wide distance separates the European and the Indian city culturally and administratively. But, in terms of social structure and even in terms of demographic developments, the countries of Europe in the nineteenth century are less distant from twentieth-century India, and hence patterns of urbanisation in nineteenth-century Europe are more appropriate as a yardstick of developments in modern India than corresponding data from the United States.

In Tables 10.2 and 10.3 are presented some data on the rate of urban growth in various countries during the nineteenth and twentieth centuries. In Table 10.2 urban places with more than

Table 10.2   Population in Cities with over 20 000 Inhabitants in Selected Countries (in per cent of total population)

Country	c. 1800	c. 1850	c. 1890	c. 1920	c. 1950
England and Wales	16·9	34·9	53·7		
Scotland	13·9	27·7	42·4		
Ireland	5·9	8·7	15·3		
France	6·8	10·7	21·1		
Belgium	8·7	16·6	26·0		
Netherlands	24·5	21·6	29·4		
Germany	4·6	13·0	21·9		
Prussia	6·0	7·8	23·0		
Bavaria	3·7	6·1	15·8		
Switzerland	1·5	5·4	13·2		
Sweden	3·0	3·4	10·8		
Denmark	10·9	9·6	20·2		
Norway	0·0	4·2	13·8		
Scandinavia	4·1	4·9	13·8		
Spain	9·8	9·6	18·0		
Portugal	10·4	10·6	8·0		
Iberian peninsula	9·9	9·8	15·5		
Austria	4·4	4·2	12·0		
Hungary	2·3	4·6	10·6		
Austro-Hungarian Empire	3·5	4·4	11·5		
Russia	2·4	3·6	7·2		
United States	3·8	9·8	23·8		
India			4·8	6·1	11·9

Sources: For countries other than India, ADNA F. WEBER. *The Growth of Cities in the Nineteenth Century*, New York (1899), *passim*; for India, BOSE. *Op. cit.*, p. 170.

Table 10.3   Increase of Population in Cities with more than 100 000 Inhabitants (selected countries, selected periods)

Country	Factor by which population multiplied in cities of 100 000 in 1925			Factor by which city population is multiplied in period cited	
	c. 1815 (*1*)	*c. 1870* (*2*)	*c. 1925* (*3*)	*Period* (*4*)	*Multiplicand* (*5*)
England and Wales	1·0	5·4	12·5	1800–50	5·3
Scotland	1·0	3·7	6·7		
Ireland	1·0	1·8	3·0		
France	1·0	2·3	4·2	1850–90	2·8
Belgium	1·0	2·9	7·4	1850–90	2·3
Netherlands	1·0	1·7	4·8	1850–90	3·4
Germany					
(frontiers of 1914)	1·0	3·0	11·8	1850–90	6·0
Prussia				1850–90	8·6
Bavaria				1850–90	4·5
Switzerland	1·0	3·3	10·6		
Scandinavia	1·0	2·3	8·4		
Austria					
(frontiers of 1914)	1·0	2·7	8·1	1850–90	3·4
Hungary					
(frontiers of 1914)	1·0	1·6	4·3	1850–90	3·2
Russia				1850–90	3·2
Poland	1·0	2·7	14·1		
United States				1850–90	7·0
		1901	1951		
British India				1890–1955	6·1
India		1·0	2·84	1901–51	4·9

Sources: Columns 1–3 (for all countries except India), HELMUT HAUFE. *Die Bevölkerung Europas*, Berlin (1936), pp. 225–6; columns 4–5 (for all countries except India), WEBER. *Op. cit., passim*; columns 1–5 (for India), *Census of India, 1951*, I, Part II-A, and International Urban Research. *The World's Metropolitan Areas*, University of California Press, Berkeley and Los Angeles (1959), pp. 47–9, 52.

20 000 inhabitants are considered, since smaller towns frequently do not exhibit genuine urban characteristics in terms of social structure or even economic specialisation. Though in many countries the census authorities have designated much smaller central places as 'urban', it was decided to confine our comparisons to places with 20 000 inhabitants or more, in order to avoid differences arising from different definitions of 'urban' and 'rural', and in order to enhance the probability that only places with genuine urban features would be included.

Table 10.2 shows that the share of population in these effectively urban places increased in India during the sixty-year period 1891 to 1951 from 4·8 per cent to 11·9 per cent, or in round figures from almost 5 per cent to almost 12 per cent. In most European countries the rate of growth was somewhat faster. If we omit from consideration those countries which already had more than 10 per cent of their population in urban places of more than 20 000 inhabitants at the beginning of the nineteenth century, we find that in Germany the rate of population increase in these effectively urban centres during the last fifty years from 1800 to 1850 was faster than in India, and that in Austria–Hungary the rate of population growth was about the same as in India, but took only forty years, from 1850 to 1890. Proportions of the effective urban population similar to those in India in 1890 were found in Scandinavia in 1850, and in Switzerland in 1850. In both regions the rate of urban growth was faster than in India during the last sixty years, since in Scandinavia the effectively urbanised share of the population grew to 13·8 per cent in forty years, and in Switzerland to 13·2 per cent in the same forty years. On the other hand, the rate of urban growth in Russia was approximately equal to that of India.

Considering the entire experience of European urban growth durng the nineteenth century we may conclude, however, that with the exception of a few cases (e.g., Britain, Germany, Belgium and the Netherlands, and, to a lesser extent, France) India's rate of effective urbanisation during the last fifty to sixty years follows, on the whole, the same pattern as that established in Europe during the period of incipient industrialisation in each country. Thus, although India's urban population in the first half of this century grew at a somewhat slower rate than the urban population of Europe during most of the nineteenth century, the rate of urbanisation in India is not abnormally slow, and is commensurate in general magnitude with European growth rates. Moreover, the speed of urban growth in India (as can be seen from column 5 of Table 10.1) has increased considerably in successive decades, and this pattern again repeats the experience of most European countries. Hence from the purely demographic standpoint India's progress of effective urbanisation shows approximately the same characteristics as the corresponding trends in the various European countries.

In Table 10.3 are presented some data on urbanisation in still larger urban centres, i.e., in places with populations of more than 100 000 inhabitants, which in conformance with Indian practice we will designate as 'cities'. Table 10.3 is composed of two parts; the first three columns show the rate of multiplication of population which at the end point was residing in cities of more than 100 000 inhabitants, and the last two columns show the multiplication of population resident in urban centres with more than 100 000 population at the starting and the final points of the period indicated. In other words, in the first three columns are described the growth rates of cities which ended up with populations of more than 100 000, though at earlier dates some might not have contained 100 000 inhabitants. In the last column we take the population resident at the beginning of the period in all places with more than 100 000 inhabitants and compare it with the population resident at the end of the period in all places having more than 100 000 inhabitants. (The beginning and end dates of the period are given in column 4.) On the whole, the two parts of Table 10.3 show a fairly high concordance; the periods selected for the last two columns of Table 10.3 are those which showed in each country the fastest rate of city growth as compared with other periods.

Table 10.3, like Table 10.2, shows that the demographic trend in India's large cities in the last half-century resembles rather closely that of the large cities in European countries. In the first fifty years of this century the population living in Indian cities which now have more than one lakh population almost tripled. This record compares roughly with that of Belgium, Austria and Germany in the first half of the nineteenth century, and exceeds the rate of growth of population of large cities in Hungary, Ireland and Scandinavia in the same period.

Similarly, the rate of growth of the city population in India during the twentieth century does not fall behind comparable growth rates in European countries during the period of their most rapid urbanisation. From the sociological standpoint this section of Table 10.3 is more significant than the first three columns. It shows by what factor the population resident in large cities was multiplied over a period of forty to fifty years. In other words, it shows that in the first fifty years of this century the population of India in cities of one lakh or more population increased almost fivefold, and that in the sixty-five years from 1890 to 1955 this population in the territory of the former British India increased more than sixfold. Not many European countries show such high rates of growth, though in the United States the population in cities of more than 100 000 inhabitants increased sevenfold in the forty years from 1850 to 1890 and in Prussia the rate of increase in the same period was even more than eight-and-a-half-fold.

These rates of growth are of great significance. Students of urbanisation are agreed that, to the extent to which the process of modernisation is mediated through urban centres, the larger cities play a more crucial role, and that, in general, the larger a city, the more important is its general mediating function in the process of social change and acculturation. To some extent, therefore, the rapidity with which a country modernises, or at least with which psychological attitudes favourable to modernisation are created, is dependent upon the growth of its cities and especially the large cities. And here the performance of India in the most recent past does not seem to lag behind analogous periods in many European countries; if we add to this, moreover, that urbanisation has been increasingly rapid in the last two or three decades (a fact which emerges from Table 10.1) and may be expected to continue at even higher speed than in the recent past, the gradual development of a large urban sector in Indian society will constitute one of the important 'environmental' preconditions for rapid modernisation.

2

We may conclude that on the strictly demographic level the over-all trends of Indian urbanisation in the first half of the twentiety century show substantial similarities with analogous periods in the urbanisation process in Europe. We now shall turn to the consideration of whether the social and economic conditions of the process of urbanisation also show analogies, and what similarities and differences in the two processes may appear.

An important difference between European countries in earlier phases of economic development and India at the present is revealed by Table 10.4. There the approximate distribution of the labour force in eight European countries is presented at a time when the proportion of their population in urban centres with more than

Table 10.4   Distribution of Labour Force and Share of Urbanisation (selected countries)

Country	Year	Percentage of working force			Per cent of population in towns with over 20 000 inhabitants
		Agri- culture	*Manu- facturing*	*Services*	
Austria	1890	43	30	27	12·0
Ireland	1851	47	34	19	8·7
France	1856	53	29	19	c. 10·7
Norway	1890	55	22	23	13·8
Sweden	1890	62	22	16	10·8
Switzerland	1888	33	45	22	13·2
Portugal	1890	65	19	16	8·0
Hungary	1900	59	17	24	c. 10·6
Average (unweighted)		52·1	27·3	20·6	11·0
India	1951	70·6	10·7	18·7	11·9

Source: Columns 1–3, SIMON KUZNETS. Quantitative Aspects of the Economic Growth of Nations, 2: Industrial Distribution of National Product and Labor Force. *Economic Development and Cultural Change*, 5, No. 4 (July, 1957), Supplement, pp. 77, 82–90; column 4, Table 10.2 of this paper.

20 000 inhabitants was roughly the same as that of India in 1951. Some of these countries were substantially industrialised, but other countries were chiefly producers and exporters of primary products, as shown in Table 10.4.

What is important to note is that at a time when the degree of urbanisation was roughly the same in these countries as in India now, the share of the labour force in manufacturing was substantially larger than in India in 1951 and the share of the labour force in agriculture was substantially smaller. In more explicit terms, whereas at a roughly equivalent degree of urbanisation in the European countries only a little more than half of the population derived its livelihood from agriculture, more than two thirds of the population derived their livelihood from agriculture in India in 1951; and whereas more than a quarter of the European population derived its livelihood from manufacturing, only a tenth of India's population depended upon manufacturing for its livelihood.

It is, of course, true that precise comparisons of this kind are imperfect, that the classification of the labour force is somewhat arbitrary, and that the differences may be somewhat smaller than shown in the table. But the difference in the relative weight of industry and agriculture is so striking between late-nineteenth-century Europe and mid-twentieth-century India that even the correction of inaccuracies in classification would not lead to a very substantial change in the picture.

Given the degree of urbanisation, the countries of Europe were more industrialised than India is now. The lag in industrial development, as compared with late-nineteenth-century Europe, is not only exhibited by the lesser degree of industrialisation in India's countryside, but also in her cities. A rough composition of the urban occupational structure can be gained from the distribution of livelihood classes among which the urban population is distributed. The Indian census presents eight livelihood classes, the first four of which are designated as 'agricultural classes' and include farmers, tenants, agricultural labourers and landowners. The fifth class is composed of persons depending upon manufacturing, the sixth on commerce, the seventh on transport and the eighth on miscellaneous services. Only 40 per cent of India's total population in livelihood class 5 resides in cities, and the corresponding figures for livelihood classes 6, 7, and 8 are 60·2 per cent, 66·3 per cent and 50·2 per cent, respectively. In other words, the majority of persons depending upon manufacturing live in rural areas, as do one half of those depending upon services, two fifths of those depending upon commerce and one third of those depending upon transport.

If we look at these data from a different standpoint, that is, from that of the occupational composition of the urban population, we find that 25 per cent of this population depends upon manufacturing, 20 per cent upon commerce, 6 per cent upon transport, 35 per cent upon miscellaneous services and the remaining 14 per cent upon agriculture and landownership. To be sure, the proportion of population dependent upon manufacturing increases as the size of the city increases, but even in cities of the largest size (i.e., cities with more than 100 000 inhabitants) only 29 per cent of the population derives its livelihood from manufacturing, and the proportion of this class declines to 24·9 per cent in towns with population of 50 000 to 100 000 inhabitants and to 22·9 per cent in towns with 20 000 to 50 000 inhabitants. Similar decreases of a few percentage points with declining city size can be noted in other typically urban occupational groups, that is, transport, commerce and other services. In towns with populations below 10 000 inhabitants less than one fifth of the population depends upon manufacturing for a livelihood and more than one third on various forms of agricultural occupations[3].

In contrast to this, the proportion of persons deriving their livelihood from manufacturing and mining in Germany in 1882 showed the following numerical characteristics: in cities of more than 100 000 inhabitants 47·3 per cent derived its livelihood from what the Indian census would call class 5 livelihood (manufacturing and mining), in towns between 20 000 and 100 000 inhabitants this proportion was 52·8 per cent, and in towns between 5000 and 20 000 inhabitants it was 53·6 per cent. In other words, roughly half the urban populations (rather than a quarter as in India) depended upon manufacturing and mining[4].

In brief, one of the characteristics of India's economy, as compared with that of late-nineteenth-century Europe is its lower level of industrialisation, not only in the rural areas, but also in the cities. This means that urban growth has proceeded with a smaller relative accumulation of industrial capital in urban centres, and this in turn has the consequence that relatively fewer employment opportunities in manufacturing and related occupations become available in urban areas for immigrants to the cities. To this should be added that the external aspects of manufacturing in India and in late-nineteenth-century Europe are also different. We have no comprehensive data on the distribution of persons occupied in manufacturing in India as between plants of different size. But it is well known that a large portion of the Indian labour force in manufacturing is employed in the so-called 'unorganised' sector, that is, in small cottage or handicraft-type shops, employing usually few, if any, employees who are not members of the owner's family. Though this is true of almost all enterprises located in rural areas and small towns, it is also true of a large proportion of enterprises engaged in manufacturing in cities and large towns. Important reasons for the preponderance of so many small-scale enterprises are the very inefficient capital market, the absence or malfunctioning of effective institutions for combining many small capitals into one of larger size, and the overall low level of saving in the community. These factors tend, moreover, to inhibit the development of many external economies in urban areas which are generally acknowledged to have been important factors in the economic development of Western countries. Moreover, the small size of many industrial firms also prevents the exploitation of internal economies, that is, economies of scale of production. Thus, the comparatively low level of urban industrialisation, combined with the preponderance of many small enterprises in industry, places impediments in the path of economic development in India which were either absent or much less significant in comparable periods in the Western more highly developed countries.

The scarcity of capital and the small size of many industrial enterprises is the result of yet another difference between India and the countries of Europe during their early phase of industrialisation. Both in nineteenth-century Europe and in present-day India a sizable portion of the urban population is composed of migrants. We have noted earlier the very rapid rates of growth of large towns and cities, and it is quite clear that a multiplication of the urban population by several times in a few decades can take place only because constant sizeable migration to the cities occurs. In Europe, capital formation in urban areas occurred with sufficient rapidity so that the new arrivals sooner or later could find employment in industry or associated occupations. To be sure, there were often violent fluctuations in industrial employment due to the business cycle, and, quite apart from this, there was never a smooth correlation between additions to the urban labour force and additions to the urban capital stock providing employment for the newcomers. This means that during the nineteenth century, when European cities grew so rapidly, there were sometimes prolonged periods of excess labour supply in urban areas; but in the long run the period of European industrialisation and urbanisation must be regarded as one characterised by a shortage of labour—especially if it is compared with present-day India. In other words, in spite of temporary hardships and misery which new arrivals to the urban labour force may have encountered in nineteenth-century Europe, in the long run profitable employment opportunities opened up for them.

This, in turn, had the result of creating an open and well-functioning labour market in European cities, and also made possible a substantial degree of upward social mobility through economic achievements. In present-day India these conditions are absent in most cities, or at best present only to a very limited degree in a few. The simultaneous presence of small, cottage-type enterprises and large factories producing similar or identical commodities, but with a much lower net productivity of labour in the former, leads to great variations in earnings between the large, modern plants and the small, more primitive ones. This disrupts the labour market, and strong tendencies favouring the development of noncompeting groups make themselves felt. This development, in turn, impedes social mobility and at the same time tends to contribute to misallocation of resources and, often, to prolonged unemployment. A fractionalised, internally disrupted labour market exists in many Indian cities not only for unskilled or semiskilled labour, but even for more highly skilled (especially white-collar) occupations; and a portion (though by no means all) of the so-called 'educated unemployment' of Indian cities is attributable to the imperfections in the mechanism of allocating human resources.

Compared with European cities during a corresponding period of economic development, the cities of India, therefore, show the following economic features: urban industry is less developed and is characterised by a larger number of small-scale and cottage-type enterprises; the urban labour force, therefore, is made up of a smaller portion of industrial workers and a larger portion of persons in miscellaneous, usually menial, unskilled services; the urban labour market is fractionalised and composed of mutually noncompeting groups, thus impeding optimum allocation of resources and preventing upward social mobility and relief in the amount of unemployment. All these features make economic development more difficult in India today than was the case in Europe in the nineteenth century. They also are a cause for the lower level of earnings and productivity in Indian urban occupations.

Why, in view of these relative disadvantages, do urban centres, and especially the larger urban centres, grow at approximately the same pace as did the cities of Europe in the nineteenth century?

Though part of the growth is due to the natural increase of population, we have seen that sizeable migration to the cities does take place. Moreover, the bulk of cityward migrants are young males in the early ages of their active working life[5]. There is considerable discussion of whether 'push' factors or 'pull' factors prevail in inducing persons to move to the cities of India, and this discussion is somewhat repetitive of arguments raised in Europe in the nineteenth century. I believe that in both cases the proponents of the preponderance of push factors are more accurate, but the actual conditions and development in rural areas, which tended to push the population out, are different.

The main reason for Indians leaving the villages is the high population density in agricultural regions and the smallness of the amount of land available to cultivators—in brief, the sheer excess of human resources on the land. In Europe there also developed an imbalance between human and nonhuman resources in agriculture, not because of excessive agricultural population density, but because of the rationalisation of agriculture and the creation of larger-sized farms. By the end of the third quarter of the nineteenth century, 74 per cent of all farmland in England and Wales was in farms of 100 acres and more. At around 1890, 44·9 per cent of all agricultural land of France was in farms of that size, and in eastern Germany between 55 and 60 per cent of all agricultural land was in farms of more than 100 hectares (about 250 acres)[6]. In other words, in Europe large-scale agriculture was on the rise. The small- and middle-sized grain farmers became increasingly squeezed and turned to the production of specialised crops (wine, vegetables or fruits) or high-grade foods (meat, dairy products, eggs). This had the result of improving greatly the efficiency of agriculture, and, though the total income of small farmers and agricultural labourers did not catch up with that of urban workers and employees, the rural population did, on the whole, participate in the rising living standards resulting from economic growth. The rationalisation of agriculture also caused them to participate in technical progress and the associated rise in the productivity of labour. Thus, the agricultural sector participated fully in the fruits of the industrial revolution, although in many parts of Europe there appeared various lags and leakages in relative farm incomes. Protection was resorted to in order to overcome, at least partially, these frictions. The important point, however, is that not only was more capital applied to agriculture as economic growth progressed, but education spread to the countryside rapidly, communications were swiftly improved, the rural population became increasingly familiar with machines and their operation, and the cultural gap which divided city and country became narrowed.

In India the pressures which are operative on the cityward migrants are of a very different kind from those predominant in nineteenth-century Europe. Here it is not the modernisation of agriculture which leads to a geographical and functional redistribution of the labour force of the country, but the sheer pressure of population—the low (and declining) man-land ratio[7]. Some idea of the contrasting pressure of human resources on land, as between European countries in the nineteenth century and present-day Indi- is presented in a paper which appeared elsewhere and which showa that the countries of northern and western Europe had available roughly from 3 to 5 times as much cultivable land per farm houses hold in the mid-nineteenth century as is available today for each Indian farm household[8]. This means not only that the short-run effects of population growth exerted less pressure on existing agricultural resources in Europe than in India, but also that it was easier to produce and mobilise a food surplus on European farms which could be made available for the urban population. This, in turn, meant that the entire outlook of the European farmer, from the outset of rapid industrialisation, could be more directly oriented towards marketing all or part of his crop, rather than producing primarily for his subsistence. Here, again, the most important aspect is not the purely economic one, but the sociocultural one. The greater degree of commercialisation of agriculture produced attitudes among the farm population which made them more responsive to fluctuations in relative prices and more receptive to innovations in techniques of agricultural production. Hence European agriculture showed a much greater degree of flexibility in its resource-allocation patterns, and could therefore take part more effectively in the all-pervasive process of economic growth than can Indian agriculture, which today is so largely oriented towards subsistence production.

These conditions determine differences in the reasons for rural-urban migration in Europe and India, as well as differences in the quality of migrants. Though some European writers in the nineteenth century made much of the sociocultural rural-urban differences which were presumed to prevail then, these were different from those prevailing in India today, since in overall attitudes and values the newcomers to European cities and towns were little different from those of the urban population. In India, on the other hand, the cultural impact exerted by the city on the countryside is small, and the attitudes of a large part of Indian urbanites towards educational standards, innovation, capital formation and entrepreneurship are little different from those of the rural population. In brief, in Europe urban cultural values tended to overwhelm and gradually eliminate those of the countryside. In India we find a small, highly urban sector with very new and modern values, and close beside it a mass of urbanites whose distance from rural culture and social structure is almost nil. It is often said that India lives in her villages. This is true not only of her rural population, but also of a large sector of her urban people.

3

These observations bring us to the third aspect of the role of the cities, their cultural and social impact. It has been shown in the preceding sections of this paper that, although the demographic patterns of urban growth in twentieth-century India and in nineteenth-century Europe were rather similar, the underlying economic conditions accompanying this process of urbanisation differed considerably. Social and cultural conditions are associated more closely with economic than with demographic changes, and for this reason it would not be surprising to find that differences between European and Indian urbanisation in the sociocultural sphere also are greater than in the demographic field. One of the factors which contributes to this difference is that many of the largest and most important cities of India were foreign creations, imposed upon Indian society from the outside, rather than natural growths within the native social structure. This is not to say that Bombay, Madras and Calcutta—and other large cities of India—are not thoroughly Indian today. But the outlook of the urban elite in these and other large centres differs from that of the rural elite and the elite in small towns. And in a country like India, where educated persons are still in a minority, the attitudes and opinions of the elite play a very important role in setting the general cultural framework for a society. The urban elite in the large centres is westernised, has a

European or at least European-style education, often uses English as a language of communication, and is far removed in attitudes and style of life from the peasants and the mass of poorer urban workers. The elite in the rural areas and in smaller towns is less removed from the common people, it speaks one of the vernacular languages, and in its religious practices, its social views, and even its ordinary daily behaviour patterns is closer to the masses. To be sure, there are differences in wealth and power between the elite and the common people even in the countryside or the small towns, but the cultural and behavioural gap is narrower and in many instances completely absent. This means that the distance between the dominant ideology in Indian cities and the Indian countryside is great, and that the overcoming of this gap for the newly arrived migrants is difficult, often requiring more than a generation to be accomplished.

This has the consequence that the urban population in India is made up of several layers of differentially 'urbanised' persons. In particular, there exist within the confines of large cities considerable sectors of persons who culturally—that is, in attitudes, values and behaviour—are villagers. Some of them have come recently from a village, others may have resided in a city for some time, and still others may have been born there. Since these persons have still a village outlook, they often have not severed their ties with the village. Many of them return more or less regularly to their villages. Even though they were born in the city, some keep alive their interest in property in the village their parents came from and maintain close ties with the extended family, parts of which continue to live in the ancestral home. These groups also have not overcome the general economic outlook of villagers. They are employed as unskilled workers, and they form usually the most poorly paid sector of the population. They have unsteady and irregular employment, a large proportion of them is illiterate, and, in spite of the impact of the demonstration effect upon them, they have patterns of consumption which are little removed from those of villagers.

In Indian cities there are several intermediate groups between these completely village-like 'urbanites' and the sophisticated, westernised members of the metropolitan elites who resemble in many aspects persons in similar social positions in the great cities of the West. These intermediate groups tend to narrow the gap somewhat between the extremes. Moreover, there existed a cultural gap even in the cities of nineteenth-century Europe. But it was never so wide and so persistent as in India.

Next in importance to the wide gap between urban elite and rural culture in India is the great variety of particularistic groups. Indian society is notably dissected into groups whose behaviour patterns, customs, occupations and even food practices vary. Some of the lines separating these groups are the result of linguistic and tribal differences, but within the linguistic or tribal grouping there are sharp differences of caste, or jati. It is irrelevant for our purposes how this variety of small caste groups, each with its own rules and norms, has originated; that is, whether it is the result of fission and segmentation of earlier larger groups or, as Iravati Karve argues, is the result of a process of constant addition and agglomeration of new groups. It is equally irrelevant whether this great variety of small subgroups is the result of some religious or ritual theory or is the outcome of the political heterogeneity and absence of effective political control over large areas in India's history. It is a fact that caste is important in many parts of India, especially in the rural parts; that caste is hierarchically organised; that it tends to establish barriers to free movement and free interaction; and that—in spite of official condemnation of 'communalism'—caste still manifests its strength in many fields of social action.

In urban centres, largely through the impact of Western values, but partly also under the influence of economic necessity, the divisive features of caste have become greatly mitigated in many public contacts, but have been largely maintained in private, more intimate relations. Persons of different castes will work together and visit the cinema or theatre together, but they will not (or only rarely and in unusual circumstances) visit each other's homes, intermarry or form close friendships. The migrants who come to the city, and who usually leave behind a strongly caste-ridden society, come into a situation in which their caste relations are ambiguous. They soon learn, however, that in private relationships the ordinary divisions set up by caste are, on the whole, valid also in the city. In more concrete terms, neighbours, friends among whom one may visit, and persons from whom one can receive aid or counsel in adversity or difficulty are normally only persons belonging to the same caste or, at most, a related caste. Hence arrangements for living are made in which the rural settlement patterns are, in part, transferred to the city. In Europe, in contrast, caste never existed. Discrimination in the choice of living space took place there also, but a person could and did move out of certain neighbourhoods if and when his economic and social position permitted. Though there is a tendency for this to happen also in India, it is usually possible only for persons in the highest social positions or with relatively great wealth, and many Indian cities, especially many of the smaller cities and medium-sized towns, are spatially comparable to agglomerations of larger and smaller villages rather than to organically interrelated population centres.

There is yet a third socio-cultural difference between Europe and India, relating primarily to the cultural tradition of towns and cities. In Europe, at least in western and central Europe, towns very early became independent political bodies. In territories where the central power was weak, for example, Italy and Germany, the degree of political autonomy of urban centres was high, but it was also in evidence in the more highly centralised monarchies of England and France. The city-state is a European invention, and the city-state was never formally stronger than in mediaeval Europe. Moreover, the mediaeval city-state, unlike the ancient city-state, did not arise out of a combination of tribes, but through contract. One of the points forcefully stressed by Max Weber, in describing the uniqueness of the European mediaeval city, is the fact that its origin is an usurpation of rights by burghers who formed a sworn fraternity, thus exempting themselves from the effective overlordship of some territorial ruler. To be sure, city charters often appeared as grants of a lord, who in this way saved face, but, as Weber points out, the effective instrument in the formation of the Occidental city was the *conjuratio*, the sworn contract by the citizens for purposes of joint protection and defence, even—in extreme cases—against the lord[9]. This resulted in the establishment of an independent government of the urban community which could own property and tax the citizens. It meant that some representative body of the citizens was charged with taking measures for the common defence, that this body could impose laws and ordinances, that it provided for special economic privileges of the citizens, and that it was responsible for the construction of walls and moats and streets and squares—in brief, for public works for and on behalf of the citizens.

Thus, in Europe, urban institutions developed which made for the unified rational administration of the city; city governments developed which had as their function the regulation of relations among citizens and between citizens and strangers; and authorities were constituted which were responsible for the provision of structures and other public works in the common interest of all citizens. Though this cannot be called planning in the modern sense, it was the forerunner of modern city planning. One needs only to look at maps showing the successive extensions of city walls in mediaeval cities to see that these new walls were planned with the ecological pattern of the entire city in mind; that not only the economic and civic-political needs of the community, but also its recreational and aesthetic needs, were considered[10].

India never had a tradition of urban self-government of this kind. The Indian cities always were appendages to a court or other administrative centre, to a temple or other place of worship or pilgrimage, or to a colony of merchants. To be sure, many of the functions which were performed by European cities were also performed by Indian cities. Just as the preindustrial cities of Europe, so the cities of India had principally governmental or religious, educational or cultural functions, but at the same time were economic centres, that is, nuclei of trade. Especially the cities newly founded by Europeans were markets, and the victory of the British over the Dutch and French in Bengal ultimately decided the rise of Calcutta. But, although Indian cities functionally performed a role similar to that of the preindustrial cities of Europe, they never had the political and administrative autonomy of European cities, never developed governments of their own, and never created institutions representing exclusively the civic interests of their inhabitants. Even where we have instances of city planning in India—as, for example, in Jaipur or Lucknow—the plan embraces not the city as a whole, but merely a small area around the court or a central area in which the royal palace and the main cult buildings had their site. Ecological planning of the city as a whole is a concept which first was introduced into India with the foundation of New Delhi in 1911.

Let me summarise. When we turn to the socio-political sphere and contrast the process of urbanisation in India with that of nineteenth-century Europe, again we find several crucial differences. First, the cultural gap between the dominant city elite and the rural masses is even greater in India than was the case in Europe in its early stages of industrialisation. This makes the adjustment problems for cityward migrants in India more difficult, but it also produces in the urban population an intermediate sector of very imperfectly committed urbanites. Secondly, Indian society is much more broken up into mutually exclusive groups than was European society. Class barriers in nineteenth-century Europe were high and often difficult to surmount, but caste barriers are even more nearly impervious. Though in certain urban roles caste tends to lose its vigour, it maintains itself in others and hence continues to play a divisive role, fractionalising the urban population—especially in housing and community-living aspects[11]. Thirdly, India has no tradition of urban autonomy and urban independence in administration. Such concepts as zoning or the provision of parks, open spaces, and other public amenities for community use have been absent from Indian thinking and are only now being introduced. Urban finances have, in the past, been deplorable, and urban tax receipts continue to be insufficient even for the installation and maintenance of vital services. Major public works in urban areas, to the extent to which they were undertaken at all, were the result of action not by the citizens or their representatives, but by some ruler or other powerful person who had his residence in a city or town. Indian cities, even in the very recent past, thus have not grown in any orderly fashion, but—like Indian society as depicted by Iravati Karve—by addition and agglomeration.

The result is that Indian cities—even some of the largest ones—show sizeable quarters which have preserved their rural character and in which life is carried on under general conditions only little different from those of the village. This in turn is reflected in the style of life and attitudes of that part of the urban population which has not broken its ties with village life and is only partially and incompletely 'urbanised'. Hence the cultural impact of the 'city' in the modernisation process in India is exerted upon a population which is culturally and psychologically farther removed from accepting change than was the European population in the nineteenth century and hence under much less favourable environmental conditions than was the case in Europe. Moreover, whereas the cultural elements produced in the European city were elaborations of already indigenous culture complexes, in India many of the new cultural elements come from a foreign culture. These cultural impediments are added to other obstacles in the path to rapid economic growth in India . . .

SOURCE: Roy Turner (ed.), *India's Urban Future*, University of California Press, Berkeley and Los Angeles, 1962, pp. 157–76.

REFERENCES

1. See ASHISH BOSE. The Process of Urbanisation in India, doctoral dissertation, University of Delhi (1959), pp. 168–9. A similar comparison between Indian and United States urban growth, although not with the period 1840–90, but an earlier period (1790–1850), is made by KINGSLEY DAVIS, *The Population of India and Pakistan*, Princeton 1951, pp. 127–8.

2. ERIC LAMPARD. *Urban-Rural Conflict in the United States, 1870–1920: An Ecological Perspective on Industrialisation*, a paper read at the University of Michigan (May 1959). (mimeographed.)

3. All data in this and the preceding paragraph are from BOSE. *Op. cit.*, pp. 217–218.

4. See A. F. WEBER. *The Growth of Cities in the Nineteenth Century*, New York (1899), *passim*.

5. Estimates of recent migration to the large cities of India have been published in S. N. AGARWALA. A Method for Estimating Decade Internal Migration in Cities from Indian Census Data, *Indian Economic Review*, **4**, No. 1 (February, 1958), 59–76; a comprehensive study of rural-urban migrations in later-nineteenth-century Europe is found in P. MEURIOT. *Les agglomérations urbaines dans l'Europe contemporaine*, Paris (1897), pp. 309–32.

6. See MEURIOT. *Op. cit.*, pp. 285–7.

7. The increasing population pressure on agricultural resources in India is the main theme of the Report of SHRI R. A. GOPALASWAMI, I.C.A., the census commissioner of the last census; see *Census of India, 1951*, I, Part I-A, pp. 138–50, and Part I-B, Appendixes I and V. For a later analysis see *Report on India's Food Crisis and Steps to Meet It*, Delhi 1959, pp. 9–20, by the Agricultural Production Team of the Ford Foundation.

8. See BERT F. HOSELITZ. Population Pressure, Industrialisation and Social Mobility, *Population Studies*, XI, No. 2 (November, 1957), p. 126. This paper is also reprinted in BERT F. HOSELITZ. *Sociological Aspects of Economic Growth*, Glencoe, Ill. (1960).

9. See MAX WEBER. *The City*, trans. and ed. Don Martindale and Gertrude Neuwirth, Glencoe Ill. (1958), chap. ii.

10. For a publication which graphically represents some planned urban growth in mediaeval cities see F. L. GANSHOF. *Étude sur le développement des villes entre Loire et Rhin au moyen âge*, Brussels (1943), especially the Appendix (maps).

11. For some examples of this see the sections on Neighborhood Relations, and An Indian 'Ghetto', in A. BOPEGAMAGE. *Delhi: A Study in Urban Sociology*, Bombay (1957), pp. 93–109.

11 Some Residents of Upper Nankin Street, Singapore

BARRINGTON KAYE

UPPER Nankin Street is in the heart of Singapore's 'Chinatown'. Bounded on the north by New Bridge Road and on the south by South Bridge Road, it is one of a grid of streets evidently laid out shortly after 1835[1]. It is about one-eighth of a mile long, and is bounded both ends by busy one-way streets carrying a good deal of the cross-city traffic, which give it an isolation of its own. Apart from two vacant lots, on one of which a shack has been built, and the back of a Chinese temple opening into Upper Hokkien Street, it consists entirely of two- and three-storey shophouses, built back-to-back to similar rows in the parallel streets: Upper Chin Chew Street on the west, and Upper Hokkien Street on the east. There is no means of communication between these back-to-back houses, and this tends to train social interest towards the street itself. In the street there is a great deal of activity most of the day: people coming from and going to work; itinerant hawkers selling cooked foods and other commodities; the activity stemming from the shops, some of which are in fact workshops, or small factories; children playing on the stairs and on the pavements; people gossiping; and so forth.

It is difficult today to visualise the plan of these shophouses before alterations. It would seem that on the ground floor the space behind the shop was used as a kitchen, and possibly as a dining-room. The first and second floors were probably both divided into two rooms, one at the front and one having windows on to an air well. T'ien shows the plans of a shophouse in Padungan Road, Kuching, before and after alterations[2], but he does not give the source of these data, and as 'the original plan' of the first floor includes two cubicles, it may be doubted whether this was in fact how it was designed.

Whatever their original layout, there is no doubt that the picture they present today is vastly different. With very few exceptions,

For References to this chapter, see page 199. The text published here is a contraction, with abbreviations, of Chapters 3 and 12 of the original.

every floor has been subdivided by interior partitions, very often of a makeshift and temporary nature, into a maze of cubicles. The plan of a typical first floor is given below in Fig. 11.1.

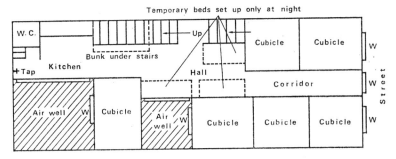

Fig. 11.1   Typical first-floor plan of a shophouse.

On the ground floor, cubicles have been built in behind the shops; on the top floor, they have been built up into the attic. Where there is no room for a cubicle, then bunk-spaces have been constructed, and are let out to single persons. In the resulting conditions people are born, spend their lives, and die. . .

CASE-STUDIES

Wong Kwok Tong

Schedule data. Wong Kwok Tong lives with his two unmarried sons. He is 66 years old; his sons are 26 and 24. He has occupied the cubicle for about 20 years; he left his previous residence because it was too small. He was born in Kwangtung Province, and came to Singapore at the age of 22.

He occupies a back room on the first floor, lit by two windows, one of which looks on to the backs of houses, the other into an air well. The partitions of the room go right up to the ceiling. The room measures 9 ft × 7 ft (2·7 × 2·1 m), and is furnished with a double bed, sideboard and table. Wong Kwok Tong and one of his sons sleep on the bed; the other son sleeps on the floor. There is no electric light, and the room is lit by oil lamps at night.

Interview. Wong Kwok Tong went to school at the age of 7, and studied for about 1½ years. The school hours were from 7 a.m. to 6 p.m. He has a very high opinion of the old-fashioned schools, and believes that one year of study in China is equivalent to several years of study in Singapore.

Between the ages of 8 and 12, he helped to farm. When he was 13, he went to Canton, where he worked in a general store for 4 years. Then he went to Hong Kong, doing the same kind of job. At the age of nineteen, he returned to his own village to get married. After marriage, he went back to Canton to work for 6 months. The shop in which he worked went bankrupt as a result of bad business. Then he came to Singapore, leaving his wife with his mother and his paternal grandmother.

After 6 long years in Singapore working as shop assistant in a general store, he managed to save enough money to go back to China to see his mother and grandmother. He returned, bringing his wife and the eldest son who was then about 6 years old. This son is now in the Federation.* His wife gave birth to five children in Singapore. His second son died. The third son is married now and lives on the same floor, but does not share eating arrangements with him. The fourth and fifth sons are staying with him. The sixth child was a daughter. She is now staying with a relative. His wife died during the Japanese occupation.

During pre-war days he went back to China with the family about three times to see his mother and grandmother. Each time they stayed in China for about 2 to 3 months. Both mother and grandmother are now no longer living.

Singapore people are complex. In China you hardly ever meet people like Hokkien, Teochew, or Hainanese. Everybody around you speaks the same dialect as yourself. Singapore people are heartless ('have thin love'); Chinese people remember kindness for a thousand years.

Wong Ah Sam

Schedule data. Wong Ah Sam lives in an attic cubicle with her husband and two children; a daughter aged 5 years, and a son aged 4 years. She herself is 37 years old: her husband is 38.

Her husband, a Cantonese, was born in Indonesia, where he went to Chinese Middle School. He came to Singapore in 1936 at the age of 19, and took a job under a building contractor, fitting drainpipes into houses under construction. He has done the same

* Malaya (Ed.)

kind of job ever since, taking casual employment where he can. He is not able to find enough work to keep him fully occupied.

She herself is a Cantonese, born in Singapore, and did not go to school. They were married 12 years ago in a Registry Office, and they arranged their own marriage without the help of relatives.

The cubicle which they inhabit is approached by a ladder at an angle of almost 90 degrees. The room measures 12 ft × 10½ ft (3·6 × 3·2 m), and is windowless. As it is an attic-cubicle, there is only room to stand in the centre of the floor; at the sides the rafters come down to within 4 feet (1·2 m) of the floor. Apart from boxes and chairs, the cubicle is furnished with a double bed (5 ft × 6 ft, 1·5 × 1·8 m) and a sideboard. Her husband sleeps on the bed; she herself sleeps on the floor with the children.

Interview. When she was a child she lived with her parents and her grandmother who looked after her. She never went to school, but played all day long. When she was 12 years old, her family shifted to her father's shop, where she began to learn the trade of box-making. Her mother was her father's second wife (the first having died childless), and she bore him two daughters: Wong Ah Sam and her elder sister. Her father had a third wife, who was childless. As the first wife had died, Wong Ah Sam's mother was principal wife. When the third wife died, Wong Ah Sam's mother sent back to China for a fourth wife, to come and help in the business and look after the grandmother, but she herself died before this fourth wife arrived. When the fourth wife came, she turned out to be an imbecile, unable to take care of herself. She also brought her own mother. She became pregnant, but before the child was born, Wong Ah Sam's father died. As it was, the new baby also died shortly after birth.

Meanwhile, Wong Ah Sam's elder sister had married and gone to live with her husband, so she was left to run the business, and look after her aged grandmother, and her imbecile 'fourth mother' and her mother. She married her sub-tenant, the present husband, who helped her run the business. Unfortunately their shop was bombed by allied planes during the war, and so they lost it. During the Japanese occupation her grandmother and her fourth mother died. (She did not say what happened to the latter's mother.)

She is so used to the present housing conditions in Upper Nankin Street that she does not think she would be very much happier if she were given a better place to live in. She once was admitted to the Middle Road Hospital for 2 weeks, and a nurse there asked her where she preferred to stay. She had replied that although the hospital was a better place, being airy and clean, yet she preferred to live in Upper Nankin Street.

She does not mind very much about the housing conditions, but money is very hard to earn. With regular employment, life would be easier. . . .

Lee Ah Mok

Schedule data. Lee Ah Mok is 26 years old. She lives with her husband (31 years), and her five children aged 6, 5 and 4 years, 18 months, and 2 months respectively.

Her husband was born in Kwangtung Province, China, and first came to Singapore at the age of fifteen. He attended the village school for 4 years beforehand. He is a tinker, and specialises in repairing leaking oil-drums. He travels round the oil-factories in Singapore, taking on odd jobs of this kind. He has done this type of work for 7 years.

The Lee family occupy a front room on the first floor, with a window on to Upper Nankin Street. The room, of which the partitions reach right up to the ceiling, measures 7 ft × 10 ft (2·1 × 3·0 m), and is furnished with a double bed and two sideboards. This leaves an area of footspace about 6 ft × 5 ft (1·8 × 1·5 m), on which all five children have to play. The parents and baby sleep on the bed; the remaining four children sleep on the floor. There is no electric main, and the room is lit by battery.

Interview. Lee Ah Mok was born in Singapore, but brought up in the Federation. Her father was a building contractor. When she was 1 year old, her father got a contract in Kuala Lumpur, and the whole family (paternal grandmother, mother, father, and herself) moved there. She played with her brothers and sisters during childhood, and did not go to school until she was about 10 or 11 years old. Her grandmother had always said it was unnecessary to send girls to school as they had to get married, and once they were married they belonged to other people, so why bother to educate them? She went to school for about 1 year or so, until her father lost his contract business.

As there was nothing her father could do there, the whole family came back to Singapore. At the age of 13 or 14, she went out to work as a resin sorter. She used to cry a lot as she could not agree with her fellow workers. At night she always thought of the good old childhood days, when her father had the contract business. Then she had lived in the lap of luxury. Her family had occupied a four-roomed bungalow, and they had had servants to work for them. Now she had to go out to work.

She had been in this occupation for a few months when war broke out and the Japanese came to Singapore. She then worked in the General Hospital. Her work ranged from carrying corpses to mixing medicines. She did this sort of work throughout the Japanese occupation.

When the British came back she lost her job. She then worked in a rubber factory as a rubber grader. She did not stop work until 3 months after her marriage. She has five children now; none of them is of school age. The elder boy will be 7 next year. She is rather worried about how to get him into an English school. She also remarked that she is rather worried about the future of the children as her husband earns just enough to keep the family. In future, when the children are older, a larger income will be needed. The present living conditions are not too bad, however.

Lam Ah Thai

Schedule data. Lam Ah Thai is 43 years old. She lives with her husband, aged 47, and their seven sons, whose ages range from 16 years to 18 months.

Her husband was born in Kwangtung Province, where he went to the village school. He came to Singapore at the age of 17, and has not since returned. He is a bricklayer, a trade he has followed since he first arrived.

The three eldest sons go to a Chinese primary school; two of them have part-time employment, one as a building labourer, the other doing odd jobs in a printer's shop.

The Lam family occupy a cubicle without windows on the second floor. The internal measurements are 8 ft × 7 ft (2·4 × 2·1 m), and it is furnished with a double bed and a sideboard. The mother and the two youngest children sleep on the bed; the father and the remaining five sons on the floor. (At the House Condition Survey interview, one of the sons complained that it was very hot at night, being forced to sleep so close together.) There is no electricity, and oil lamps are used.

Interview. Lam Ah Thai was born in the Saam Shui district of

Kwangtung Province. She never went to school, but helped her mother to take care of the younger siblings. Sometimes she went to cut yam leaves to feed the pigs and at times she gathered wood for fuel. When she was about 14 years old, she followed a *Sui Kah** to Singapore. She worked in a rubber factory for 8 years, afterwards returning to China to get married. Her husband was a carpenter.

She came to Singapore again soon after marriage. Her husband worked as a labourer; she carried earth. Sometimes she worked in a rubber factory, sometimes in a resin factory. She stopped work recently only because there was nobody to look after the family.

Singapore is a better place to live in. If one has money, one can purchase anything one likes, whereas in China one has to work extremely hard in order to get a full meal.

She has no opinion about the living conditions. She believes that people everywhere are the same; if you are good and kind to them they will treat you likewise.

Her children stay on the 5-feet (1·5 m) way, or roam about the street most of the day. They come back only to have their bath, to eat, and to sleep. The cubicle is far too small for her family. . . .

Yip Sam Mui

Schedule data. Yip Sam Mui, an old woman of 62, lives with her 32-year-old son, who works as a smelter in an engineering shop. They have no cubicle, but occupy two bunk-spaces in a first-floor corridor. She has occupied her bunk-space for 24 years.

Interview. Yip Sam Mui was born in Kwangtung Province. She cannot remember what she did in China. She was given to her father's younger sister when small, and came with her to Singapore at the age of 5. Between the ages of 5 and 12, she returned to China several times. When she was 13 years old she returned to China to get married. Her husband was a furniture-maker, working in Canton, and he came to see her only a few times a year. She stayed in the village and did farming.

When she was 21 years old, she came to Singapore with her husband and three brothers-in-law, as their home and rice-field were destroyed by flood. Her husband worked as a furniture-repairer, and she worked in a resin factory.

---

* A man whose main livelihood was derived from buying goods in China to sell in Singapore, but who also undertook, for a small commission, to look after emigrants on the boat. (Ed.).

She gave birth to eight children in Singapore; six of them died, some during infancy, others at an older age. (She would not disclose the sex of the dead children, as she said that Cantonese people do not like to mention dead children.) The son who is staying with her is the eldest of all her children. The other remaining child is a girl who accompanied her father to China 24 years ago. Her husband went back to China for good as he had lost his eyesight, and she did not think it was advisable for him to remain in Singapore as he could not earn a living. He died 11 years ago in China. Her daughter is married, and still alive in China.

She worked in the resin factory right up to the war. During the Japanese occupation, she became an earth-carrying labourer. Later, she worked in the army cleaning rifles. She has stopped work since the British came back.

People in China were very shy, especially the womenfolk. During her young days womenfolk did not have any idea what their husbands looked like, as the only time they lifted up their heads and looked at them was when their children had grown up, unlike Singapore people who are so daring as to walk hand-in-hand in public. To see such things makes her feel embarrassed. . . .

Leong Chee Chiew

Schedule data. Leong Chee Chiew, a man of 49, lives with his wife and their three children in a front cubicle on the first floor. Their daughter is 14 years old; their two sons are 8 and 4.

Leong Chee Chiew's wife was born in Saam Shui district of Kwangtung Province, and first came to Singapore at the age of 23.

The cubicle, which they have occupied for fourteen years, has a window on to Upper Nankin Street. It measures 9 ft × 8 ft (2·7 × 2·4 m), and is furnished with a double bed, a sideboard, and a shelf. Attached to the end of the bed is a board, supported by chains to the ceiling. Leong Chee Chiew, who suffers from tuberculosis, sleeps on this board; his wife and two of the children sleep on the bed. His daughter sleeps on the floor.

Interview. Leong Chee Chiew was also born in Saam Shui. He was the third son in the family. He stopped school when he was 13 years old, and went to work in his parents' rice field.

He was engaged at the age of 8 and got married at the age of 15. He carried on farming till he was 27 years old. He found life was very hard in China and wanted a change. Therefore he came to

Singapore. He did not bring his wife and daughter as he intended to go back after a few years. Once in Singapore, however, he changed his plan, and decided not to go back to China. He asked his wife and daughter to join him, but his wife refused because she was the only child of her mother, whom she was reluctant to leave. Therefore he married another wife. Now they have two sons and one daughter (excluding his daughter in China).

When he first arrived he was an odd-job labourer. Later he picked up the trade of carpenter, and was a carpenter until 1951. He was forced to leave this trade as he was suffering from tuberculosis. He is still under treatment in Tan Tock Seng Hospital. Social Welfare has cut off his tuberculosis allowance. He now gets $60 per month for unemployment allowance.

Upper Nankin Street is far too overcrowded. As far as he knows there are 20 people in the street suffering from tuberculosis. He finds the fire-proof dust from the safe-making shop opposite most annoying, as they put it on the roadside to dry, and it blows up into the room.

Conditions in Singapore would be better if the import tax were not so high.

He does not find any difference between the people of Singapore and of China. Singapore is a very much better place to live in than China. . . .

SOURCE: *Upper Nankin Street, Singapore*, Oxford University Press, Singapore 1960.

REFERENCES

1. A map, dated between 1835 and 1838, is given in BUCKLEY. *Op. cit.*, i, facing p. 320. Nankin Street is given on this map, together with an indication that part of Upper Nankin Street was already laid out. Braddell observed to the Housing Committee in 1918: 'It is possible that Upper Macao Street, Upper Hokkien Street, Upper Nankin Street, Upper Chin Chew Street, and Upper Cross Street were also made quite soon after the first layout shown in red ink, date 1830 to 1835. They are natural and easy extensions of the original layout and would be likely to occur quite early.' *Proceedings and Report of the Commission on Housing*, op. cit., C24.
2. JU-KANG T'IEN (1949). *Report of a Survey of Overcrowding in Kuching, Sarawak*, typescript; copy on file at the Secretariat, Kuching.

12 Squatter Life in Salvador

NAN PENDRELL

AT TWENTY, Vicos is largely responsible for supporting no fewer than thirteen people in addition to himself. He said that he earns 50 000 cruzeiros (about US $25.00) monthly for sweeping up and tending bar at a nearby café. The manager seems to be fond of Vicos, who he feels typifies those poor back-country *pretos* (blacks) who are responsive to Communist propaganda because they are childlike and innocent of urban ways. The *Senhor* was of the opinion that at least some of the *invasores* were Communists or had been egged on by Communist agitators; and he found this notion sufficiently stimulating to stand on a chair and wave his arms in imitation of a 'Communist agitator exhorting the masses to take the land that was really theirs'. He was quite serious about this, but as he sat down again, he sighed: 'After all, what else can they do? All Brazil is underdeveloped, and Bahia is the worst State of all.' The contrast between Vicos' family's way of life and that of Martin and his family is quite stark, though both are squatters in the same invasion.*

Vicos' two aunts, Betty and Sofia, had come to Salvador from Sitio six years ago, and he had followed shortly thereafter. Betty's husband (they had not had either a civil or religious marriage) deserted her and their nine-year old daughter, and was now living in the invasion with another woman. He sometimes visits them, but 'he never has any money for us'. Betty occasionally works in a Salvador hotel as a cook's helper, but has not worked for several months because she has been ill. Sofia's husband Romano, to whom she was married in a civil ceremony, is presently 'doing well'. He is employed as a bricklayer on a large house that a Salvador lawyer is building in one of the invasion's main thoroughfares. For a six-day work week, Romano is paid the going wage of 50 000 cruzeiros monthly and has been working for three months, but he too is now ill and thinks he will soon have to stop working. He has not saved any money because a

* Other parts of Pendrell's study demonstrate that Martin and his family are much wealthier. (Ed.).

part of his wages goes to repay a loan to Sofia's uncle, who lives in the invasion of Massaranduba in the Alagados and 'doesn't work very much'.

The oldest of their nine children is fourteen, the youngest are two-year old twins, and the other six range from four to twelve. All were born at home, Betty serving as midwife. Typical of the Brazilian poor, none of them has ever gone to a clinic or seen a doctor. Except on feast days, for which the two women sew children's underwear, shirts, pants, and dresses with great concentration (they had brought a manual sewing machine from Sitio), all but the eldest children are always naked. For these holiday occasions, all the money that can be amassed is spent on yard goods, bought at one of the local shops. Sofia and Betty and the older girls have two changes of cotton blouses and skirts, and each has a pair of plastic sandals, but usually they go bare-foot. Of this joint family of four adults and ten minors, only Vicos and Romano regularly wear shoes. Vicos' wardrobe of outer clothing consists of three white cotton shirts and two pairs of cotton pants, and a zippered cotton jacket that Romano greatly admires, for all he has to wear are the jeans he works in and two extra shirts and trousers.

The two families occupy adjoining two-room *barracas*, and at night the children are distributed between both. They sleep on the earthen floors while the adults sleep on wood platforms piled with thatch. Only Vicos has a 'private room' in Betty's *barraca*; an enclosure separated from the front room by a curtain made of tar paper. Several times a month the women and children fill the gasoline cans they use for fetching water from a stream or a public tap, with sand collected from the dunes. This sand is swept onto the floor, and it makes for a certain temporary cleanliness, but when it rains, the floors indoors are only slightly less muddy than the road outside; consequently the entire family is usually *com gripe* (down with a cold).

The diet may be guessed from the children's distended bellies and everted navels: *farinha* (manioc meal) and *feijão* (beans). Occasionally Vicos brings home bits of left-over meat, or fish, or cheese from the café, and sometimes he walks four kilometers to buy some fresh fish from the *pescadores*. Oranges went up in price from forty to a hundred cruzeiros each during a single month in the winter of 1965, and the only fruit this family eats is a rare *mamão* (papaw) or bananas when Vicos can manage to get them at the café.

They 'do not remember' how they happened to come directly to the invasion from Sitio, but 'perhaps a friend' had told them they could find a place to live here. They had already built the two *barracas* when a general razing was ordered, but these had not been burned down, probably because the destruction of houses started at the other end of the settlement, and the police did not get as far as their shacks. They had no idea why the demolition was stopped but imagined the reason was that too many *ricos* had protested against it. They had never paid any taxes and had 'never been bothered' by the *Prefeitura*.

The two thatch *barracas* are low and always dank; there are no windows and light and air enter only through the front doorway opening and through open spaces in the thatch roof and walls. The family clothing is suspended on wire clothes hangers and strings on the walls, and in each *barraca* there are a table and several chairs, rather than the crates which are used for tables and chairs in many other *barracas*. Betty even has a 'china closet' in which she keeps both families' dishes; there are no table utensils, and food is eaten with the fingers, which appeared to embarrass Vicos when I was present.

Baths are taken in a small stream or in the sea because it is pleasurable, and in order to save the water which the women and children fetch from long distances The cooking is done on a hearth of bricks in back of each shack, and when there is not enough of the expensive kerosene that is used mainly for lighting the lamp, twigs and brush are gathered for this purpose All waste is thrown directly out on the street, where pigs, dogs, and chickens scrabble about in it Toilet needs are attended to in the dunes and, except in winter, in the sea; the smaller children relieve themselves in the street.

Vicos and Romano cannot afford to buy materials with which to improve the *barracas*. They think it is the city's job and not theirs to clean up the gutted road in front of the dwellings and also to build a bridge across the ditch they have to cross when coming into and leaving the invasion. 'Aren't you afraid that one of the children will fall off this plank and drown in the ditch?' I asked Vicos. 'Yes, I am.' 'Then why don't you and your friends put up a better bridge? There's plenty of wood around here.' It is Vicos' apparently unshakable conviction that this is 'the *Prefeitura's* business, and not ours'. It is as likely that many of the *barraca* dwellers sense that improving the place may invite too much interest and spark further attempts by public authorities to evict them.

As does practically every other male adult here, Vicos and Romano each have a transistor radio, which they carefully wrap in a plastic bag when it is not in use; i.e., when they go to bed, and they are *au courant* with the daily news and especially with the latest happenings in *futebol*.

When he was alone with me, Vicos expressed a good deal of bitterness about *ricos* and about the café management. He observed that recently several Salvador 'big shots' had been taking luncheon at the café and that regular meetings seemed to go on; he suspected that they were plotting another attempt to evict. This was why a newspaper was now publishing articles about 'new invasions' in the café area. On the day this newspaper stated that overnight four new houses had been built in the section enclosed by café boundary markers, Vicos pointed the place out to me. Except for one lathe-and-plaster dwelling which had been under construction for several days, there was nothing there but brush and sand.

Vicos had 'a feeling' that someone would come along soon to buy the two *barracas*, and his family will get out, but if this does not happen, they will 'fight' to keep the shacks. It stands to reason that the *ricos* would not be building all these costly new houses if they were not perfectly sure that nothing would happen to *them*. The *ricos* are experienced in the *jeito*, nobody can beat them, and if the *ricos* stay, 'so will we, at least until we sell the *barracas*'. It would be nice to hold on to the *barracas* 'until the *Prefeitura* begins the *urbanização* everyone is talking about, decause then we can get more money for them'.

Vicos does not know where they will go if they actually sell the shacks, but certainly they will not go back to Sitio. After all, life is better here. They would like to live nearer the city centre if they sell the *barracas*, especially because then they will be able to send the children to school, but how long will the money last if they have to rent a place large enough for all of them? They can hardly expect to get more than 1 000 000 cruzeiros (u.s. $500.00) for the two shacks. Perhaps it would be best if they go to Isabela, where there are two invasions and there is still room for more people, or they might stay here and build better houses out near the *mata*.

The café manager may greatly underestimate Vicos'—and by extension perhaps many of the *barraca* dwellers'—grasp of 'urban ways'.

SOURCE: 'Squatting in Salvador: An Exploratory Study', unpublished Ph.D. Thesis, Columbia University, 1968, pp. 128–35.

13 Attitudes Towards Spontaneous Settlement in Third World Cities

D. J. DWYER

THE rapidity with which urbanisation is now proceeding in the Third World and the enormity of the problems this process is producing have to date been very little recognised in terms of research effort either within the Third World itself or within the economically advanced nations. This is surprising in view of the startling nature of even the most basic and easily accessible facts. Turner has, for instance, pointed out that within the lifetime of many of its present inhabitants the population of Lima will increase one thousand per cent[1]. This is one simple measure of the magnitude of urbanisation processes now well under way in the Third World and indeed rapidly accelerating. In 1940 Lima was a city of 600 000 people: it is expected that on present trends Lima's population will have grown to six million by 1990. Calcutta is already approaching seven millions and will at least double in population within the next twenty-five years. With urban growth rates generally between 3 and 10 per cent, Third World cities, in terms of their built environment and especially in housing provision, can be said not simply to be bursting but more accurately to have burst already at the seams. Substantial and growing numbers of people are living within or on the edges of such cities in what may be called spontaneous settlements. These, at least initially, consist of dwellings of extremely flimsy construction, lacking in basic urban services such as a safe water supply and sewers and without the benefit of legal land tenure. They are often known by a variety of local names expressive of their origin, for example *gecekondu* in Turkey, which acknowledges the fact that in this case the structures for legal reasons have to be erected overnight. Such settlements are usually referred to in English as squatter settlements, a term which, it is worth noting, automatically carries with it prejudicial legal connotations.

For References to this chapter, see pages 217–18.

Spontaneous settlement has become a major urban form throughout the Third World during the last thirty years; and in the future it will undoubtedly grow further in relative importance. In 1961, 320 000 or 23 per cent of Manila's population were living in *barongbarongs* or spontaneous settlements; Djakarta had 750 000 people or 25 per cent of its population in such settlements in the same year; there were 580 000 spontaneous settlers in Hong Kong (17 per cent of the total population) in 1964 and such persons comprised 200 000 of Delhi's population, or 13 per cent of the total the same year[2]. Already one-third of the population of Mexico City lives in *colonias proletarias*, nearly one-half of Ankara's population in *gecekondu* and one-fifth of the population of Caracas in *ranchos*[3]. And undoubtedly this situation will soon become much worse. Turner has estimated that, by 1990, 4·5 millions out of Lima's anticipated population of six millions will be living in *barriadas*. He has also pointed out that growth rates of such settlements are now reaching 12 per cent annually in several countries, for example Mexico, Turkey, the Philippines and Peru, or in many cases double those of city growth rates as a whole[4]. The present study examines official attitudes towards such problems, with special reference to eastern Asia and Latin America; outlines certain findings of the meagre current volume of research carried out on spontaneous settlement to date; and finally offers some general comments on the possible trend both of future planning policy and of planning research in relation to this aspect of the housing problem.

OFFICIAL ATTITUDES

In general the best that can be said for most official policies towards problems of spontaneous settlement in the Third World is that they are characterised by a neglect that is usually benign, but exceptionally may not be, according to local circumstances at any particular time. In 1963, for example, after years of indifference and a change of mayor in Manila City (one of the eight local government bodies comprising the metropolitan area), a legal decision was secured by the authorities to the effect that, in order to secure an abatement of public nuisance, squatters could be required to vacate their premises[5]. This decision, based upon a provision in the city charter, circumvented a previous court injunction against the eviction of squatters which had prevented action. Following the failure of the squatters to vacate their premises voluntarily, the authorities undertook a large scale eviction within the walls of Intramuros, the original core and fortress part of the city, which had been devastated during the Second World War and subsequently covered by squatter shacks. Within three weeks almost 3000 shacks were demolished in the area and some 11 000 squatters moved to Sapang Palay, a small municipality of about 600 persons in Bulacan Province, some 16 miles (26 km) from Manila, an area where practically no social or transport provision, let alone employment provision, had been made for them. 'There seemed to be no planning at all in the allocation of sites for squatters' new homes', commented the *Manila Chronicle*. 'They were just dumped anywhere around the community and left alone to themselves to build *barong-barongs*'[6]. To be fair, however, it must be added that after the transfer a variety of social agencies, official and unofficial, rallied to the aid of the squatters.

A representative of the national government claimed that the action of the Manila City authorities had taken it by surprise, though this may well have been intentional on the part of the national government because of a running conflict with City authorities as to whether squatters were primarily a local or a national responsibility. The operation also engendered considerable antagonism between the City of Manila and certain of the other local government units comprising the metropolitan area because the latter feared invasion by displaced squatters.

Generally, however, energetic squatter policies of this or, it is to be hoped, a more constructive nature are not characteristic of urban authorities in the Third World. Most are largely inactive, and there are several reasons for this. Many authorities, it seems, regard themselves as politically powerless to affect the course of events once spontaneous settlements have become established. Such settlers are acknowledged to be effectively organised, if only for the purposes of seizing land and subsequently preserving and improving their position. There are often well-formed links of mutual benefit between settler groups and local politicians; and there may even be a national association to protect the interests of such groups, as in Peru. The political interest-group factor thus plays a large part in most urban planning calculations for spontaneous settlement. But even where this is minimal, action is difficult for a variety of reasons. It is, for instance, almost impossible to formulate coherent development strategies of any kind for most Third World metropolitan areas because of their subdivision into local government units. This is not, of course, a problem peculiar to the Third World. It has not been solved even in many cities of the economically-advanced nations but, in general, the Third World is at a much more primitive stage in grappling with the problem. Manila is split into eight, usually mutually-antagonistic, local government units. Caracas has spread from the original Federal District eastwards along its valley into the Sucre District of Miranda State and two separate planning offices share concern for its problems. The Calcutta Metropolitan Planning Organisation has no mandate for areas outside West Bengal, yet in regional terms, and especially in respect of in-migration, it is clear that Calcutta's problems hinge upon developments in the four-state area of eastern India comprised by West Bengal, Bihar, Assam and Orissa.

A further inhibiting factor is the amount of finance generally available for housing improvement. National development planning, which until very recent years has been dominated by economists to the almost total exclusion of other social scientists, has set very little store by housing provision. Capital investment in housing has generally been regarded as largely unproductive, and in circumstances in which there are chronic shortages of capital even for obviously directly productive developments such as irrigation, roads and education, developing countries are characterised by extremely low rates of investment in housing. Expressed as a proportion of the gross national product, housing investment in the ECAFE countries, for example, has been below the 2 per cent level in recent years, whereas the countries of Western Europe have averaged an almost 5 per cent investment in housing. Furthermore, even within the limitations of national planning in this respect, it is true to say that few cities have organised local financial arrangements in such a way as to maximise housing development. A feature of most Third World cities is the existence of relatively large tracts of unoccupied or under-utilised urban land obviously being held for speculative purposes. In the inflationary conditions that have characterised many Third World countries, urban land has proved one of the best investments, and often high rates of return have been possible for speculators through failure to levy and collect realistic property taxes in such a manner as to penalise the holding of idle land. Moreover, high rates of tax delinquency are common: 50–60 per cent in Naga City in the Philippines, for example[7]. Where landowning interests predominate in both national and local politics there are few grounds for expecting such situations to be fundamentally reversed.

Moreover, physical planning has too often become simply one of the many playthings of politics in the Third World. This is true in at least two important senses. One is that in many cases physical planning organisations form part of the general system of dispensation of patronage by successful politicians so common in developing countries. This largely accounts for the rapidity with which planning organisations are closed down and new ones founded or, where this does not happen, the regularity with which senior staff are replaced in many agencies. In the Philippines, for example, an Urban Planning Commission was created in 1946 to prepare general plans for the zoning and subdivision of urban areas[8]. With the inauguration of a new national administration, the commission was supplemented in 1947 with a Real Property Board to deal with problems involving real estate in connection with the planning of Manila. Neither body had any practical effect. A Capital City Planning Commission was created in 1948 and charged with the preparation and execution of a master plan for a new national capital at Quezon City. The plan was completed in 1949 but has not yet been translated into reality. With a change of government in 1949, the Capital City Planning Commission, the Real Property Board and the Urban Planning Commission were abolished and their powers transferred to an agency within the Office of the President known as the National Planning Commission. A master plan for Manila was completed by this Commission in 1954. The Municipal Board of Manila conducted public hearings on the plan but as late as 1963 had failed to enact new zoning ordinances for the city. Meanwhile the Local Autonomy Law of 1959 empowered local authority boards and city councils to adopt their own zoning regulations and, though the National Planning Commission might be consulted, it reserved the final decision for the local authorities to make. Such a case history could be multiplied at least twentyfold from cities elsewhere in the Third World.

In the second sense in which physical planning has become the plaything of politics in many developing countries lies much of the explanation of its almost total dedication to what might be called 'paper planning'. Most Third World cities now have their master plans but these are largely static land-use exercises, influenced to an undue degree by the planning experience of the more developed nations of the West, and especially by British practice; indeed it has by no means been uncommon for the preparation of such plans to be contracted out to consultants from Western nations and even completed in part in the West by persons who possess but the briefest acquaintanceship with the communities whose futures the plans concern. As a result they are often excessively rigid and antiseptic in concept. Most fail to give due weight to the growing significance of spontaneous settlement within the urban form or, where they do, tend to look forward to a millenium when all squatter huts will be eliminated and replaced by regularly laid out minimum-standard housing in the image of the Western city, without specifying the immediate rungs on this particular ladder to urban heaven. In particular analysis of the financial aspects of such strategies is usually conspicuous by its absence. To make this criticism is not, however, to belittle the ability of the planners involved. Because of the patronage relationship of urban planning to politics in many developing countries, and particularly because of the dominance of landowning interests in politics, the prospects of decisive action in favour of the community as a whole on any significant scale are generally bleak. Yet, paradoxically, there is a political need to delineate an image, the blue-print for the rosy urban future which is, it seems, always just about to be born: hence 'paper planning', which is idealistic in concept and never likely of execution. Spontaneous settlement in these circumstances, being unplanned, unpretentious and apparently chaotic, is usually either totally neglected in the delineation of the image of the future or else condemned.

SOME CURRENT RESEARCH

Comparatively little work has been carried out so far on the Third World city and, in relative terms, even less upon housing problems and the spread of spontaneous settlements. Nevertheless, even from the few studies published to date considerable discrepancies in evaluation of spontaneous settlement are apparent. At one end of the scale, reflecting a common attitude but one which now is being increasingly challenged, stands Lerner, who has written in scathing terms of '... "tin can cities" that infest metropolitan centres of every developing country from Cairo to Manila', and has seen their inhabitants as '. . . "displaced persons", the DPs, of the developmental process as it now typically occurs in most of the world, a human flotsam and jetsam that has been displaced from agricultural life without being incorporated into modern industrial life'[9]. Very near the other end stands Turner, who consistently emphasises the positive aspects of the role of spontaneous settlements in contributing towards the solution of the immense problem of urban shelter[10].

Turner's views deserve examination in some detail because they have been developed in a number of papers; furthermore, they are action-oriented and they directly concern housing problems within the overall context of the physical planning of the Third World city, the topic of this chapter. Throughout his writings, Turner contrasts the self-built home in the spontaneous settlement with what he calls the 'instant development' procedure, that is the officially-provided, minimum-standard housing project[11]. He is strongly in favour of the former, indeed he would go so far as to claim that '. . . orthodox modern housing policy—the direct construction of dwellings units with public funds—inhibits rather than stimulates the investment of popular savings, skills, and initiative', in the sense that '. . . government policy should be based upon the provision of the elements of environmental security—appropriate locations, tenancies, and investment opportunities—rather than on the direct construction of new buildings'[12]. Turner consistently stresses the need of squatters for security of tenure; he sees this as their most fundamental requirement; and he links aspirations to tenure with what he has called the 'creative' nature of home building, the need for an 'anchor of hope' and 'the stimulation of social development through the cultivation and strengthening of the family'[13], though nowhere does he define these terms more precisely; and he also fails to consider in any depth possible linkages between housing condition, individual motivation and the stimulation of higher rates of economic growth on a national scale.

As an architect, Turner usually demonstrates a much firmer grasp of the physical aspects of spontaneous settlement. He makes what may prove to be a highly significant distinction between 'improving' or 'consolidating' squatters—those with blue-collar jobs who have come to the spontaneous settlement via inner city tenement areas and show a high degree of dedication to the physical improvement of their dwellings—and those who belong to the very poor of the city or else are recent migrants from the countryside. Through selected case studies, he particularly stresses the enormous progressive improvements readily observable in the form both of individual dwellings and of whole settlements (for example, Cuevas in Lima[14]) when the bulk of the community is composed of squatters of the 'improving' type. This is the strongest of all his arguments. His major prescription for the solutions of housing problems in Third World cities is, therefore, the directed development of spontaneous settlement linked essentially with security of tenure. He sees the latter as essential to the progressive improvement of both the individual dwelling and physical facilities for the community as a whole.

On the other hand, there are certain significant difficulties in such possible programmes, some of which Turner himself acknowledges. One of the largest lies in the poor design and layout both of individual settlements and of communities when constructed almost wholly by unskilled and often ignorant workers who, if not direct migrants, may be only a very few years removed from rural hinterlands. At the level of the individual dwelling unit there is usually a marked tendency to reproduce known forms, either those of houses of the poor in the countryside or those of the urban slum near the city centre. At the community level, whilst there are instances, some of which Turner quotes, of spontaneous settlements which have either begun or quickly assumed regular layouts, and where the settlers themselves have voluntarily left space free for the later installation of community facilities, there are also many, especially in eastern Asia, in which densities characteristic of such settlements are far too high and building patterns too chaotic to permit of their easy rationalisation. Official programmes based upon the creation of new areas for spontaneous settlement in these circumstances might face formidable control problems.

Moreover, whilst there are certain problems of high density associated with spontaneous settlement in some areas, the low density character of much spontaneous settlement elsewhere presents formidable problems of another kind. Turner writes of the typical *barriada* family of Lima building two-storey houses with 1200 square feet (1110 square metres) on each floor, and he stated that when the squatter invasion of the Cuevas area took place the majority of the individual building plots marked out were 8 by 16·5 metres[15]. He recounts a case history in which the subject complains of his newly allocated government house with its 12 by 18 feet (3·7 m × 5·5 m) floor area because in his old squatter shack 'twenty people could sit inside and be comfortable'[16]; and he quotes with approval Patrick Geddes' early prescription for the happiness of the Indian poor: 'I have to remind all concerned that the essential need of a house and family is *room* and that the essential improvement of a house and family is *more room*'[17]. 'Observations of what ordinary families in urbanising countries do, when they are free to act as they will', writes Turner, 'show that they prefer to live in large unfinished houses—or even large shacks—rather than in small finished ones'[18]. This is, of course, quite true as far as it goes. It is entirely reasonable on an individual level if only the individual family and not the community as a whole is to be considered, but it does immediately raise the major issues of the ultimate form of the city and what can be afforded by basically poor societies in terms of urban land and the extension of services.

Turner tends to minimise these important aspects of the problem. He omits the cost and alternative use aspects of land throughout his writings; he contends that, 'Initially sewers and even water mains are unessential' (a statement which probably has as little validity for a desert city, such as Lima, as for a city built in a swamp, such as Calcutta); and as for transport he writes merely that, 'An efficient bus service requires very little capital and, in any case, is usually a commercial proposition'[19]. Perhaps of most vital importance, however, is the overall view he holds of the form of the city. This is never clear. The fostering of spontaneous settlement will, it seems, inevitably imply in a majority of cases a widely-spread city of relatively low density with such settlements on the periphery, and while this may have merit as a possible solution to the housing problem in certain circumstances, inherent difficulties of transport services, of the extension of roads, water supply, lighting and sewerage, of industrial location and of the journey to work must also be recognised. Turner himself quotes the case of Arequipa, Peru, which in 1960 had a regularly built-up area of 900 hectares and an additional built-up area of *barriadas* covering 1100 hectares, the average gross density in the *barriadas* being only 22 per hectare[20].

Lastly, Turner's strongest argument, the self-improving nature of spontaneous settlement, also requires considerable qualification. Though this is a marked feature of certain Latin American situations and has rightly attracted attention as one of the most forceful examples of the creative forces latent in the urban poor of the Third World, it must be recognised that self-improvement is not character-istic of a large number of squatter cases. It is, for example, possible to set against the self-improving experience of the several parts of the Lima *barriadas* quoted by Turner the generally static experience of the *bustees* of Calcutta, and most east Asian squatter areas seem to conform more to the Calcutta pattern in this respect rather than to that of the 'improving' parts of the Lima *barriadas*. Turner tends to relate improving activities to the level of family income[21], but in reality the situation is much more complex than this. Selective in-migration of working-age males who leave their families behind in the countryside is obviously a highly important factor in the case of Calcutta, as is the fact that many of the *bustees* are in reality rooming-houses owned by a principal tenant or an absentee landlord. The form of tenure is also important in the case of many of the squatter 'yards' of Kingston, Jamaica. Although family occupation is more normal in the Kingston case, there too the relationship is often that of sub-tenants to principal tenant or landlord rather than a pattern of owner-occupation. Again, prospects for eventual tenure also play a role of importance in many cases. Where control is firm (for example in Hong Kong, where extensions to squatter structures may be demolished by the authorities and the materials confiscated), it is usually not worth trying to improve a structure whatever the family income.

CONCLUSION

Even allowing the criticisms and qualifications made above, there is still considerable force in Turner's argument: the criticisms serve rather to reveal the complexity of the problem. The basic fact, which Turner rightly emphasises and which must be faced, is that urban housing problems in the Third World have now reached such for-midable dimensions, and are likely to become so much more serious, that they are not capable of solution within the forseeable future solely by Western-style methods, even given greatly improved capital inputs into housing and the possibility (which is doubtful in many cases even with the capital) of developing conventional con-struction capacities markedly larger than those at present in existence in most Third World countries. The economic and social forces at work in shaping the residential pattern of the contemporary Third

World city[22] must in these circumstances be further evaluated. Physical planning must seek to turn such forces to advantage, for attempts to create wholly Western-style cities are likely to be doomed to failure.

Yet it is relevant at this point to look at the example of Hong Kong, for during the last fifteen years the Hong Kong government has housed one million squatters in multi-storey dwellings and has sought to eliminate the squatter hut through the construction of massive resettlement estates and the strict control of new squatting. Space does not permit an explanation of these programmes in detail[23] but some brief comments bearing on the previous discussion may be made. The first is that Hong Kong's achievement of rates of economic growth which have probably been unparalleled in any other part of the developing world during the last two decades[24] has made relatively high capital inputs into urban housing that much easier to achieve. It is also worth noting that as Hong Kong is virtually a city state there is an important element of uniqueness about it compared with most other Third World urban situations, not so much in respect of in-migration (for between one and two million refugees have been received from Mainland China since the late 1940s) but more because of the degree of attention within the total planning effort that can be paid to the urban areas in the absence of sizeable rural hinterlands. The political situation of Hong Kong must be mentioned. Political activity is minimal—the only real choices are between remaining under British control or reverting to China—and the colony is run in a competent manner by career civil servants rather than by politicians with half an eye on the next election.

Despite these elements of uniqueness, there are, nevertheless, important lessons to be learned from Hong Kong[25]. It has been the Hong Kong experience, and especially in the early 1950s before the resettlement schemes were begun, that uncontrolled spontaneous settlement can quickly paralyse a city in terms of overall planned physical development for higher rates of economic growth, especially in the pre-empting of sites that may eventually be required for non-residential purposes, in the extension of infrastructure facilities, and in the blocking of access to sites on the urban periphery immediately beyond the squatter settlements. The faster the planned physical development proceeds, therefore, the more necessary it becomes to relocate larger and larger numbers of squatters. This will inevitably become the experience of many Third World cities even if they eventually adopt large-scale solutions to future problems of spontaneous settlement along the planning lines advocated by Turner, if only because of the degree of importance which such settlements have already assumed in the urban fabric in quite unplanned fashion. The best means to persuade settlers to move from areas that must be cleared will need to be thought out carefully in each particular case. Such strategic clearances may prove politically very difficult but it will be vital that they be accomplished. Equally vital will be the exercise of control over the location of future spontaneous settlement. It must be recognised that at present such control is virtually non-existent in many cities and that in such circumstances no overall city planning can be effective. If the award of tenure is to form a major part of policy, as Turner advocates, then it must be selective, that is applicable only in approved areas and coupled with strong measures to discourage squatting elsewhere. Strict squatter control has formed a major part of urban policies in Hong Kong in recent years and the methods employed would possibly repay study by planning agencies elsewhere. Despite such policies, the relationship of the official Resettlement Department to the squatters has remained generally good. This has possibly been due to the considerable care which is devoted to explaining the necessity for clearances to the people concerned, to the general climate of firmness which is now well-established and widely recognised within Hong Kong, to the relative absence of politicians and also, of course, to the fact that the government is in a position to offer to all those moved alternative permanent accommodation which, though built to minimum space standards, is available at a rent the poor can afford.

With regard to space standards in government resettlement projects in Hong Kong (until recently 24 square feet [2·2 square metres] per person), the fact that there is as yet no evidence that the high densities involved have led to the kinds of breakdown that sociological theory would postulate is of great potential significance. Some Third World housing agencies are known by the writer to be working on the formulation of minimum tolerable housing standards for their own particular cultural contexts. This is an extremely important field of research because the general tendency so far has been for permitted residential building standards to be too high in the context of the realities of the economic situation of the vast majority of the urban inhabitants of developing countries. Several hundreds of thousands of people in Hong Kong have already proved widely-accepted previous conclusions in this field to be wrong. This aspect of Hong Kong's housing achievement, amongst others of potential significance, as yet, however, has neither been very widely recognised nor subjected to detailed research investigation.

A further major point of relevance in the Hong Kong situation lies in the form of the city that has been produced. A basic difficulty with massive solutions to housing problems along Turner's lines is that it is exceedingly difficult to reconcile them to anything but cities that are relatively low in population density by Third World standards. There is an inherent contradiction between such city forms and the economic status of the vast majority of the urban inhabitants of the Third World in the sense that such inhabitants cannot afford to pay for much transport. In contrast, largely because of official housing policies, a very compact, high-density urban area has been created in Hong Kong. This has greatly simplified problems of the journey to work and the extension of services; and it will probably also mean success for the mass-transport rail system which is planned.

To point to this contrast, and to make the other allusions to the Hong Kong situation above, is not, of course, necessarily to advocate the transferability of Hong Kong urban policies elsewhere. The above paragraphs merely serve to emphasise further the difficulty of the housing problems in the Third World, especially in the complex relationship with other vital aspects of city development, to say nothing of the interconnection with problems of regional planning and of rural development as such. In the future, it seems, an increasing proportion of planning agencies in Third World cities will be forced to recognise the inevitable and to begin actively to consider the necessity for planned spontaneous settlements. Resistance to such policies is, nevertheless, likely to occur, for example from interests intent upon preserving a Western city image for political and nationalistic reasons. Therefore high-density but, it is to be hoped, true minimum-standard housing projects along Hong Kong lines are likely to grow in importance also. There may be cases in which a mixture of the two approaches may be thought most appropriate. What is certain is that we are only as yet at the beginning of vast processes of urban development which will undoubtedly transform the Third World during the next three or four decades and that both in research and in the application of the present body of planning knowledge we are woefully equipped to meet this challenge. The importance of the thinking of those who now advocate housing solutions based upon spontaneous settlement lies not in the fact that in the present state of knowledge they provide complete answers but rather in the new channels for further research inquiry such thinking has opened up. At the same time, given the fact that certain important housing agencies (for example in Hong Kong, Singapore, Rio de Janeiro and Caracas) still accept, and will probably continue to accept, the possibility of at least limited solutions through high-density, multi-storied housing, the evaluation of existing experience in this respect, particularly in Hong Kong, which is the foremost example, must also be given high priority in planning research.

SOURCE: D. J. Dwyer (ed.), *The City as a Centre of Change in Asia*, Hong Kong University Press, 1972, pp. 166–78.

REFERENCES

1. JOHN F. C. TURNER. Uncontrolled Urban Settlement: Problems and Policies, Working Paper No. 11, Inter-Regional Seminar on Development Policies and Planning in Relation to Urbanisation. University of Pittsburgh (1966). Reprinted in Breese, Gerald (ed.), *The City in Newly Developing Countries*, Englewood Cliffs (1969), pp. 507–34; reference on p. 523.
2. D. J. DWYER. The Problem of In-Migration and Squatter Settlement in Asian Cities: Two Case Studies, Manila and Victoria-Kowloon. *Asian Studies*, 2 (1964), pp. 145–69; estimates from p. 153.
3. TURNER, in Breese. *Op. cit.*, p. 507.
4. JOHN F. C. TURNER. Barriers and Channels for Housing Development in Modernising Countries. *J. Am. Inst. Planners*, 33 (1967), 167–81; reference on p. 168.
5. See DWYER. *Op. cit.*, pp. 145–6.
6. *Manila Chronicle*, December 9, 1963.
7. J. H. ROMANI and THOMAS M. LADD. *A Survey of Local Government in the Philippines*, Manila (1954), p. 105.
8. DWYER. *Op. cit.*, pp. 168–9.
9. DANIEL LERNER. Comparative Analysis of Processes of Modernisation, in Miner Horace (ed.). *The City in Modern Africa*, London (1967), pp. 21–38; reference on p. 24.
10. See the following papers by TURNER: *op. cit.*, 1966; *op cit.*, 1967; The squatter settlement: an architecture that works. *Architectural Design*, 38 (1968), 355–60; and Housing priorities, settlement patterns, and urban development in modernising countries. *J. Am. Inst. Planners*, 34 (1968),

354–63. Also JOHN F. C. TURNER with ROLF GOETZE, Environmental security and housing input. *Ekistics*, **23** (1967), 123–82.

11. TURNER and GOETZE. *Op. cit.*, p. 123.

12. *Ibid.*

13. TURNER. The Squatter Settlement. *Op. cit.*, p. 357, and Barriers and Channels. *Op. cit.*, p. 177.

14. TURNER. Barriers and Channels. *Op. cit.*, pp. 169–72.

15. *Ibid.*, p. 171.

16. TURNER. Housing Priorities. *Op. cit.*, p. 356.

17. TURNER. Barriers and Channels. *Op. cit.*, p. 167.

18. *Ibid.*

19. *Ibid.*, p. 178.

20. TURNER. *Op. cit* (1966), p. 524.

21. *Ibid.*, pp. 515–56.

22. D. J. DWYER. The city in the developing world and the example of South East Asia. An inaugural lecture from the Chair of Geography, University of Hong Kong, *Supplement to the Gazette*, **15** (1968), No. 6.

23. D. J. DWYER. Problems of urbanisation: the example of Hong Kong, in *Land Use and Resources: Studies in Applied Geography*, Institute of British Geographers, Special Publication No. 1, London (1968), pp. 169–85; and Urban squatters: the relevance of the Hong Kong experience. *Asian Survey*, **10** (1970), 607–31.

24. D. J. DWYER. Size as a factor in economic growth: some reflections on the case of Hong Kong. *Tijdsch. econ. soc. Geogr.*, **56** (1965), 186–92.

25. D. J. DWYER (ed.). *Asian Urbanisation: a Hong Kong Casebook*, Hong Kong University Press (1971).

14 Planning the Development of Bangkok

LARRY STERNSTEIN

PLAINLY, the city is the centre of change, the element essential to progress, the prime mover in development, and deleterious, even distressing, concomitant effects are secondary though awfully immediate[1]. Clearly, the growth of the urban population of the world has accelerated remarkably in recent decades, and is now proceeding at an unprecedented rate. The so-called developing countries, among them most Asian countries, are claiming a rapidly increasing share in this urban population while retaining large rural majorities. Certainly, the enormous growth in the populations of the great cities of Asia owes much to a considerable, if not overwhelming, influx of migrants from the rural areas and, as certainly, there is a considerable feedback from these centres to the countryside. Obviously, then, the Asian city—as any city—must be regarded as an integral part of the scheme of national development: in planning, an urban-rural dichotomy is unrealistic.

What is needed, it seems, is a national urban development policy that is manifested in planning directed by a strategy of national development that, in turn, recognises the pivotal role of the city. Presupposing the concerted activity of all administrations concerned, a national urban development policy would guide planning so as to provide a coherent system of centres and the necessary infrastructure, and would need appropriate legislation, proper allocation of resources—financial, technological, human—and a long-term phased strategy for its implementation. Thailand is not among those few countries blessed with a national urban development policy and such a policy is not being considered; though, in common with most countries, Thailand possesses a national economic and social development plan[2] and, of course, it is in the cities and towns that many of the developments scheduled are to be effected. A national urban development policy is not now being considered

For References to this chapter, see pages 234–36. The References in this version have been reorganised.

because, in part, less than 15 per cent of the population can be regarded as 'urban'[3], more than half the total population resident in the nation's municipalities is in the city of Bangkok,* which is thirty times as large as the next largest centre; and recent increases in the proportion of the population that may be classified as urban reflect little else than the growth of the capital.† But the central government is well aware of the pivotal role of the nation's urban centres and of the need to arrange these in a coherent system; in fact, the present network of centres is remarkably coherent and has developed from a conscious effort to maintain effective control over as large an area as possible from a single centre, Bangkok[4]. Again, the significance of the region in co-ordinating the activities of various administrations and linking national policy to local planning is duly appreciated; further, since regional development is directed from Bangkok, there is little tendency for regional authorities to be semi-autonomous. (This is not to imply that there is a single regional system. In fact, the number of different regionalisations of the kingdom is nearly as many as the number of agencies involved.)

It may be argued that centralisation is excessive; that the nation's provincial centres have been subordinated so totally to the capital as to be denied a truly vital development; that, basically, the central government distinguishes two sub-national units, the capital city and the rest; and that this precludes consideration of a national urban development policy. It may be argued also, however, that centralisation is insufficient, for while the central government controls local affairs to a remarkable extent, agencies of government are virtually independent from each other, responsibilities are not clearly resolved and activities are woefully unco-ordinated.

In Bangkok, City Hall does not have jurisdiction over all municipal activities or, indeed, throughout the area within the municipal boundary. For example, the Police Department (to which is attached the Fire Department), the Metropolitan Water Works Authority and the Metropolitan Electricity Authority are semi-independent

---

* Here, the city of Bangkok includes the transfluvial municipalities of Bangkok and Thon Buri.

† In 1947 the population in the 117 municipalities totalled 1·73 millions, or 9·7 per cent of the population of the kingdom. The city of Bangkok included 0·78 million, or 45 per cent of the population of the municipalities. At the end of 1967 the population of 120 municipalities totalled 4·67 millions, or 14·6 per cent of the population of the kingdom. Bangkok included 2·69 millions, or 57 per cent of the population in the municipalities.

agencies under the Ministry of the Interior; and the Telephone Organisation is a semi-independent agency under the Ministry of Communications. A number of the larger canals and major roads traversing the city are maintained by the Irrigation and Highways departments respectively, and these agencies are under the Ministry of National Development. All railway installations, including extensive facilities for railway personnel that occupy considerable acreage, are controlled by the State Railways, and the large area that is the Port of Bangkok is under the sole jurisdiction of the Port Authority of Thailand. Both these latter agencies are semi-independent and under the Ministry of Communications. Large tracts of land are Crown Property and the Ministry of Defence maintains a considerable military establishment in the heart of the city. Housing estates are planned and executed by any number of government departments and subdivision is controlled by the Department of Lands. Industrial estates are planned by the Ministry of Industry; most hospitals are erected by the Ministry of Public Health; and most schools above primary level are the property of the Ministry of Education. City Hall is clearly not in control of the city. In itself, the independence of the numerous agencies responsible for development in Bangkok is a cause for concern. That the plans and projects of these agencies are unco-ordinated is the cause of an uncontrolled development that robs efficiency from those very activities for which the city exists. And the great and rapid growth of Bangkok in recent years has made the penalty heavy and so painfully obvious as to prompt attempts to co-ordinate metropolitan development, but as yet these have had no success[5].

The different agencies involved in the development of the city cite current budgetary procedure as the major obstacle to co-ordination of their activities. Though there is some variation in the budgetary process to accommodate different legal relations to the State, the budget is little more than a list of authorised annual expenditures by each agency for specific projects determined by their separate priorities. That this system frustrates orderly development is clear, but to introduce progressive budgeting techniques—performance (programme) budgeting or planning-programming budgeting or even rather simple regional capital budgeting—is a particularly tricky task. It is complicated by the different character of the agencies involved and the need for a corps of superior, well-trained personnel not now available, not to mention the need for a refashioning of the administrative hierarchy. Admittedly, there is much that can be done to improve present budgetary procedures—and these improvements should be made—but failing a supreme co-ordinating body charged with the responsibility for improving the condition of the city and powered by control over the allocation of funds, growth will continue to be unbalanced.

Just as importantly, planning legislation must be enacted to provide for the co-ordination of the many agencies involved in developing the city. At present there is no legislation that recognises comprehensive planning as a necessary and continuous function, or that embodies provision for the implementation of plans over a reasonable period of time[6]. While as much as possible should be undertaken under existing 'action' legislation, and new laws should be considered most carefully, explicit planning legislation must be enacted if development is to be governed[7]. Vital to a directed urban development is control over the use of land, and while the creation of a central land bank is not now possible, existing legislation for controlling use, for condemnation and for acquisition of land is inadequate. It is true that traditional controls over the use of urban land, such as zoning ordinances, building codes and subdivisioning regulations, may tend to a negative approach to development, but such controls are necessary if development is to proceed according to plan. The fault is not that the traditional controls are restrictive but that, all too often, land policy is restricted to the traditional controls. As important as the enacting and enforcing of controls over the use of urban land, is legislation providing for the ready acquisition of land for public use and the taxing of landowners to discourage speculation.

The reason that traditional methods have been altered only slightly and that changes have been introduced only gradually is an inability to effect real and rapid progress without disrupting development. That the traditional methods are not able to promote urban efficiency under conditions of rapid growth is clear; that progressive methods have been devised to cope with the situation is known and the working of these methods is appreciated by those directing the nation's affairs. Nowhere is there any complacence. But everywhere there is a want of trained personnel able to promote and to carry out the necessary fundamental changes, to formulate and implement plans, to provide effective and efficient management and co-ordinated administration, and to cope with technical matters. In time this limitation will be mitigated, but at present the number of able people is insufficient for a sustained development.

It has been suggested that the central problem in developing countries at present is the severely limited number of competent high-level administrators and executives and that the need is for training that focuses on co-ordination in administration and decision-making in planning (with such aids as game theory) rather than on professional or technical competence. In fact, it appears that many developing countries have embarrassing numbers of professional planners, though many have received training abroad at schools of engineering or architecture where emphasis is on techniques of design and physical layout. For Thailand the issue is doubtful. Certainly competent top-level administrators are few (as anywhere) but professionals and technicians are fewer. But for a limited capability to implement them, any number of reasonable plans might be formulated. It appears that technical training, including the learning of certain techniques under actual working conditions, is most important at present. Again, a relatively large number of Thais hold advanced academic degrees from foreign institutions but very few have had the practical experience essential to the adaptation and implementation of the principles learned. Obviously training is necessary at all levels and for all types of personnel. If development is to be sustained a team of able people must interact.

In the absence of adequate numbers of professional and technical people it is not surprising that there is available for Bangkok only a meagre store of that information necessary to a planned development. And, though interest in the collection and analysis of such data has quickened in recent years, there is not yet a full realisation of the vital importance of maintaining a progressive body of accurate, meaningful, comprehensive, readily available information[8]. Certainly, data are collected and analysed, but largely for specific purposes and after the decision is made to engage in some project. Also, since the agency undertaking a particular project conducts the necessary surveys, data are apt to be inconsistent and non-statistical. Such data are of limited use to related agencies when, on occasion, they are made available.

Recently, an electronic data processing centre was established at the National Statistical Office—an Office in existence little more than a decade[9] but as yet this has resulted more in improving processing than in developing the concept of an information system, or heightening an appreciation of the value of continuous data collection and analysis, or introducing new ways into the decision-making process. Of course, as its name suggests, the National Statistical Office is concerned primarily with national censuses and surveys, and most of the data collected either are not pertinent to or are too general for urban planning. Still, a beginning has been made and, doubtless, a metropolitan data centre—a clearing house handling all necessary urban information—will be established in time. Meanwhile, development in Bangkok proceeds on the basis of rather little knowledge.

Lacking data, the working of Bangkok is inadequately understood and, consequently, there is a penchant for dealing with symptoms rather than with causes of urban growth. This leads to a preoccupation with solving problems rather than with planning for development, as in most cities, be they in the developing or the developed world.

As elsewhere, for example, the roadway system is ever-proliferating, and ever more complex schemes of traffic management are introduced to solve the traffic problem that is ascribed to a burgeoning vehicular population.* But neither the most ambitious programme of public works nor the most efficient management will solve the traffic problem if a considerable, and ever-increasing, proportion of the population must move over considerable and ever-increasing distances in pursuing normal daily activities. The traffic problem will be 'solved' only if technical, legal and organisational measures are coupled with a programme seeking to relieve this travelling. Recent developments have unfortunately compelled greater movement and are encouraging the traffic problem: actively (since 1960), through so-called slum clearance projects that razed entire downtown residential areas to erect instead such necessities as hospitals, office blocks and the new National Library, and forced most residents to the suburbs (in fact, the limited numbers of homes specially provided for those uprooted by the clearings were erected in the suburbs); and passively, in assuming the non-residential Central Business District to be inevitable and even desirable[10].

A recent survey of the labour force in the Bangkok and Thon Buri

---

* In 1947 only 3000 cars, 100 taxis, 200 buses, 1300 trucks and 700 motorcycles were registered in Bangkok; in 1968 more than 100 000 cars, 10 000 taxis, 4000 buses, 40 000 trucks and 60 000 motorcycles were registered, as well as 8000 motorised tricycle taxis.

municipalities indicated that somewhat more than 15 per cent were government employees, a high proportion, but of course Bangkok is a capital city[11]. Some four-fifths of all government employees work at the main offices of the central and local administrations and, with a few exceptions, these offices are located in the inner built-up area.* As government offices proliferate and the number of government employees multiplies (recent growth has been remarkable), the inner built-up area has come increasingly to resemble a homeless Western-type Central Business District[12]. Most government employees funnel into the area at one swoop in the morning only to spread abroad all at once in the late afternoon. And though Bangkok is without a system of mass transit, this movement actually is being encouraged by the different units of government, on the one hand by over-building long established sites in the inner and innermost built-up area, on the other by setting aside large tracts of land in the suburbs for employees' housing. A programme could be envisaged which would include schemes to site whole administrative departments amid a large number of the employees, in well-appointed largely self-contained suburban complexes and, more importantly, would provide housing and the necessary adjuncts, in the inner and inner-most built-up areas, for a reasonable proportion of the great majority of government workers who would continue to be employed at present sites. The information necessary for such planning must come from periodic surveys eliciting the data necessary to identify the dynamic factors determining the growth of the city.

Unfortunately, even foreign experts, engaged to conduct feasibility studies or to draw up plans for some proposed facility or other, devote much of their too limited time in the field to gathering simple information they might reasonably expect to be given at the outset. This is not to excuse contractees from the obligation to determine the practicability of a proposed study prior to acceptance, but it is an extravagance to engage an expert to do the work of an intelligent clerk.

Late in 1960, following almost three years of study, *The Greater Bangkok Plan 2533 (A.D. 1990)* was submitted to the Thai Government by American consultants[13]. Though the consultants believed a

---

* The innermost 1.4 square kilometres between the Lot Canal and the Chao Phraya River contain little else but the Grand Palace, several large ministries, several large monasteries, the Thammasat and Fine Arts Universities, the National Museum, the National Archives, the National Theatre and the Phra Mën Ground.

comprehensive plan to be concerned with the physical environment of a city or region, *The Greater Bangkok Plan 2533* may be considered the first attempt at a comprehensive urban plan in Thailand and the first plan seeking to provide a rational, consistent framework wherein specific physical plans could be developed. At the same time the consultants were 'to develop general, practical plans, including programmes for their implementation' for a number of facilities and 'to institutionalise planning as a continuing . . . process in the . . . Metropolitan Area' (p. ix).

On arrival, the consultants found no adequate map of the city. A base map of the area was then produced from aerial photos. Compiling information gathered from the many and various agencies involved and from field surveys, first-ever maps were made of such fundamentals as administrative divisions in the Metropolitan Area, population distribution, land use, land assessments, traffic characteristics and the location of various facilities such as schools and markets. Obviously, a considerable time was devoted to providing the bare necessities of planning; further, Thai personnel were employed extensively and had to be trained prior to assuming even petty responsibilities. But it appears that a considerably greater period of time ought to have been devoted to the compilation and analysis of basic data, for the result is neither complete nor critical. In particular, it seems strange that the available population data were not carefully assessed[14]. More importantly, most of the information acquired is static and descriptive of the leavings of past growth rather than indicative of trends in development. Since the worth of a comprehensive plan is obviously in its use as a guide to directing anticipated developments most profitably, this is most unfortunate.

Not surprisingly, then, the Plan itself is essentially a land-use plan. Blocks of different uses are separated by access ways and designed to produce a pleasant mosaic-like structure able to accommodate comfortably four and a half million people, attendant facilities and anticipated industrial growth to 1990[15]. The Plan is thus apparently the very model of that type of planning eschewed in the so-called new planning philosophy that insists on strategic measures and provision of the necessary fiscal, legal and administrative infrastructure[16]. But, in fact, *The Greater Bangkok Plan 2533* includes a budgetary document indicating the costs involved in providing necessary facilities, translates the land-use plan into a series of projects strategically phased over time, discusses the need for fiscal, legal and administrative change to enable implementation of the Plan, and makes perfectly clear that a comprehensive plan is a guide—a means to an end, not an end in itself. The 'old' planning philosophy is not less aware of the nature of comprehensive planning than is the 'new' planning philosophy, but where the 'old' produced a comprehensive plan regardless, the 'new'—painfully aware of the failure of comprehensive planning introduced directly into the developing countries—seeks first to provide the necessary planning milieu by gradually turning the *ad hoc* project-by-project approach into an integrated programme. This difference is fundamental and the merit of the new philosophy is evident.

Thai authorities refer to *The Greater Bangkok Plan 2533* in bolstering arguments for specific developments included in it when these crop up in the traditional project-by-project approach and ignore it when the project is not included in the Plan. Neither the Plan nor any of its parts received official approval. The value of the land-use plan is, however, appreciated. While the project-by-project approach is actively pursued by each agency involved in developing the city, each agency wants a guide to overall growth. A land-use plan rooted in actual use, duly cognisant of all projects contemplated by the many and various agencies responsible, and merely filled out through a clear and simple extrapolation, is a satisfying tactical device in working towards integrated, comprehensive planning.

The Report on the First Revision of the Plan for the Metropolitan Area[17], as is suggested by the title, attempts to confirm *The Greater Bangkok Plan 2533* in the very changed condition of the metropolitan area at present and, by implication, in future. In the main, parameters critical to the invention of a comprehensive plan have been revised, though certain not unreasonable suggestions in *The Greater Bangkok Plan 2533* are reiterated as are, disconcertingly, certain sadder features. Essentially, revision of *The Greater Bangkok Plan 2533* stems from a very great difference in the population anticipated in the metropolitan area in 1990: 6·5 million in the *First Revised Metropolitan Plan* as against 4·5 million in *The Greater Bangkok Plan 2533*. This considerable difference derives from the fact that the authors of *The Greater Bangkok Plan 2533* envisaged the government limiting growth to 4·5 million in 1990 in the belief that, failing this, population densities would increase and a huge financial outlay would be necessary to provide the public facilities

required. Wisely, the authors of the *First Revised Metropolitan Plan*
doubt the practicability of attempting to limit numbers in the
metropolitan area to 4·5 million. The *First Revised Metropolitan
Plan* argues that the population in 1990 will be 6·5 million and that
government must find the wherewithal to provide the necessary
facilities. The approach suggests a healthy pragmatism, but nevertheless, the estimate of 6·5 million people in 1990 is strewn with those
questionable assumptions common to the prediction of population
levels. Unfortunately, the *First Revised Metropolitan Plan*, as had
its lineal ancestor *The Greater Bangkok Plan 2533*, appeared immediately before the results of a national census. This is the more
unhappy since the lack of accurate, readily usable data is officially
bemoaned and the gathering of such information is urged on
agencies of government as being indispensable to planning.

The two plans appear to include approximately equal areas but to
differ in general configuration (Figs. 14.1 and 14.2). *The Greater
Bangkok Plan 2533* includes 780 square kilometres and the *First
Revised Metropolitan Plan* only 732 square kilometres. But none of
the area of the *Revised Plan* is zoned for agricultural use as compared
with more than two-fifths of the area in *The Greater Bangkok Plan
2533*. It may seem reasonable to exclude fringing cultivated lands
from a plan of metropolitan land-use, but this suggests an 'empty'
countryside into which the city may sprawl if necessary when, in
fact, the countryside is already well populated. A first aim of city
planning must be to contain this sprawl, since the integral metropolitan area comprises the city and the country surrounding. This
interdependence should be clear on the land-use plan.

Despite embracing both the haphazard growth of the past decade
and ungoverned developments scheduled, the disposition of the
various land uses in the *First Revised Metropolitan Plan* is more
coherent than that in *The Greater Bangkok Plan 2533*. The removal
of what intricacy there is in *The Greater Bangkok Plan 2533* gains
credibility for the *First Revised Metropolitan Plan*; certainly it
appears more a guide than a goal. This is not to imply that the
First Revised Metropolitan Plan profers no specific suggestions.
Several novel ideas are brought into the plan. For example a national
park is proposed immediately south of the Port of Bangkok on a
piece of land surrounded almost completely by the Chao Phraya
River. Here, the river is not bridged and the island-like area is yet
rural, but the next five years will probably see the land built-up and

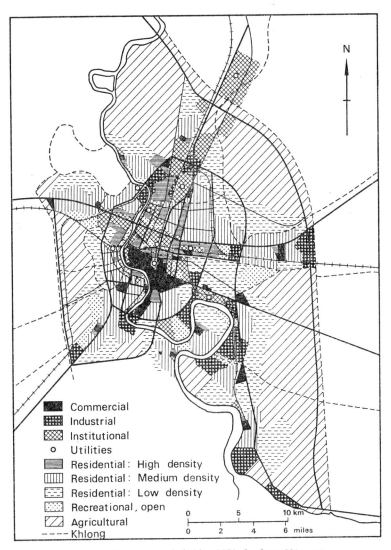

N

| Commercial |
| Industrial |
| Institutional |
| ○ Utilities |
| Residential: High density |
| Residential: Medium density |
| Residential: Low density |
| Recreational, open |
| Agricultural |
| ---- Khlong |

0   5   10 km

0   2   4   6 miles

Fig. 14.1   Greater Bangkok Plan 2533: land use 1990 A.D.

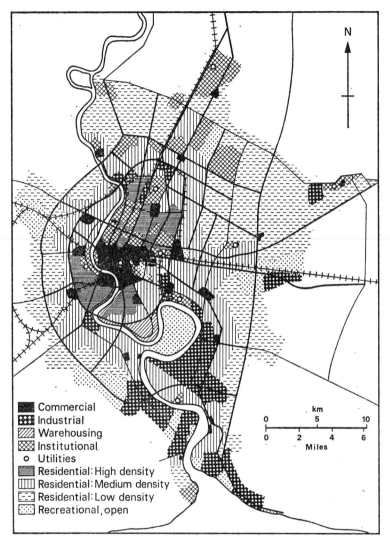

N

	Commercial			
	Industrial			
	Warehousing			
	Institutional			
o	Utilities			
	Residential:High density			
	Residential:Medium density			
	Residential:Low density			
	Recreational, open			

km
0   5   10
0   2   4   6
Miles

Fig. 14.2   First Revised Metropolitan Plan: land use 1990 A.D.

government is urged to seize the opportunity to preserve it. The uniqueness of this site was not noticed in *The Greater Bangkok Plan 2533* and the area was scheduled for residential use in most part.

It is also proposed that a large block of 'empty' land in the northeastern part of the city be purchased by government and that new offices and extensions to existing offices be located there. In *The Greater Bangkok Plan 2533* a new government area was proposed on the Thon Buri side of the Krung Thon Bridge and extension of the existing government area was also urged. The authors of the *First Revised Metropolitan Plan* argue that to extend the area now used by government is virtually impossible since this is in the heart of the city where land values are very high and surrounding properties are in private hands. The argument is true only in part, for the existing national administrative centre could be expanded if the military moved from a number of spacious encampments in the heart of the city. The military is unlikely to move at present, however, and so the possibility is not mentioned. Allowing this as politic, still the existing seat of government might be expanded in other ways, particularly upward. Almost as obviously, it might also be extended along processional Ratchadamnoen Klang Boulevard, which is now faced on both sides by squat, dismal, woefully inadequate and decrepit structures housing a mixed bag of activities. Ratchadamnoen Klang Boulevard could be faced by efficient and attractive high-rise office buildings, interconnected and with ample off-street parking, and backed by attractive high-rise apartment blocks housing a good number of those employed in the offices adjacent. Shopping and recreational facilities are already to hand and could be readily augmented[18]. Finding the finance for this would be no more difficult than for a similar scheme elsewhere, perhaps less so. The reason for rejecting the Thon Buri site for government proposed in *The Greater Bangkok Plan 2533* is not stated in the *First Revised Metropolitan Plan* but the area has passed into different use, mostly residential, during the intervening decade. The *First Revised Metropolitan Plan* sees Thon Buri more as a residential area than does the first plan and this is consistent with present use, but is the encouraging of a dormitory-like Thon Buri wise in the face of increasing congestion on the ways over the river?

The *First Revised Metropolitan Plan* proposes a much more elaborate system of communications, particularly with regard to land transportation. The roadway system described in it (for which nothing less is claimed than that it will solve present traffic problems and prevent these recurring in future or at least for the next forty years or more) comprises three circumferential roads, a large number of radial and cross-town roads, many lesser major roads and several new bridges across the Chao Phraya River, as well as a riverside drive actually overhanging its eastern edge so as to mini- mise costs incurred in expropriating land and demolishing buildings. The need for this riverside drive may be doubted since the plan includes a number of proposals that would thin traffic in the area. Well aware of the uncertainty of implementing such a grandiose scheme, even in part, an alternate way to 'solve' the traffic problem 'immediately' is proffered: two elevated roads with limited access, one above main canals for much of its length, the other above a major avenue. A monorail system that has been mooted previously would seem a better immediate solution but no mention is made of it. It is warned that 'immediate solution' will require a huge financial outlay. Doubtless, the cost will be high but no higher and conceivably lower than the cost of providing a comparable portion of the proposed ground-level system. The elevated roadways scheme may find favour, but it is unlikely to solve the traffic problem. A proliferation of roadway, in itself, has not answered the traffic problem anywhere. In any event, the *system* of roadways necessary will take more than a few years to build. At the present pace of roadway construction, even a half century would be a foolhardy schedule.

In concept and in execution a third plan for Bangkok, *The Greater Bangkok Plan 2543*[19], published in 1969, is not different from *The Greater Bangkok Plan 2533* or from the *First Revised Metropolitan Plan*. Like the latter it attempts revision of the first plan in order to incorporate present and scheduled uses of land different from those set out a decade before and to allow for the greater population anticipated, 6·5 million in the year 2000. As in *The Greater Bangkok Plan 2533* a restriction of population in the metropolitan area is envisaged, for the author foresees an insupportable 13·62 million in the year 2000 if growth is uncontrolled. To accommodate 6·5 millions, *The Greater Bangkok Plan 2543* includes 975 square kilo- metres, a quarter again as much area as in *The Greater Bangkok Plan 2533* and earmarks land somewhat more generously for industry, government and other institutions, commerce and public utilities, decidedly less so for residential use, and more or less equally for recreation and for agriculture. *The Greater Bangkok Plan 2543* lies between *The Greater Bangkok Plan 2533* and the *First Revised Metropolitan Plan* in land use allocations, in the area in non-agricultural use and in configuration, but the use of land is set out more particularly than in the former and the system of road and railways is more elaborate than in the latter.

The *First Revised Metropolitan Plan* was published in 1971 by the Department of Town and Country Planning in the Ministry of Interior. *The Greater Bangkok Plan 2543* was published in 1969 by the City Planning Division in the Municipality of Krung Thep, one of two municipalities making up the city of Bangkok. The Department of Town and Country Planning was established in 1961 and assumed the responsibility for overall planning in the metropolitan area and in up-country centres as well. The City Planning Division was to plan only special projects that were consistent with the comprehensive plan set out by the Department of Town and Country Planning. In producing its own overall plan, the City Planning Division has pleaded the urgency of the situation and has got a generally sympathetic hearing, except at the Department of Town and Country Planning where *The Greater Bangkok Plan 2543* is ignored, officially. In fact, the Department of Town and Country Planning was established in order to avoid the criminal waste o severely limited time, money and manpower represented by separate yet similar plans for the metropolitan area. Effective planning stems from critical discussion and the airing of different views and must be encouraged, but the use of near-identical means to gain near-identical ends by two agencies of government each of which is aware of but does not acknowledge the activities of the other is irresponsible. In the circumstances, however, the Department of Town and Country Planning should acknowledge the *de facto Greater Bangkok Plan 2543*, credit that which is good and incorporate as much of it as is possible into the *de jure* plan.

The *First Revised Metropolitan Plan* and, more especially *The Greater Bangkok Plan 2543* carry over from *The Greater Bangkok Plan 2533* a too conservative approach to the planning of the metropolitan area and each proposes a schedule that will allow in future only a city of the Western fashion. I think it fair to insist that the great lesson to be learned from the city of the 'developed' world is what not to do in the city of the 'developing' world and that to grasp the opportunity for planning Bangkok needs people in authority who are aware of what is going on in the many and varied fields pertinent to urban development and who know Bangkok. There are few such people and their scarcity is all the more serious because all the many and varied ills of a remarkable and chaotic development appear equally urgent and hopelessly entangled. Forced to do something, authority turns blindly to the experts, but the experts are not more than able technicians. In consequence, the planning of the metropolitan area is too much a mimicry of happenings elsewhere, inevitably in arrear of thinking and not dedicated, particularly, to discovering what is happening in Bangkok. Unique Bangkok, most primate of cities—embodiment of the distinct and splendid Thai ethos—is rapidly becoming any mean 'modern' city of some gen erations past and the planners seem intent on endorsing this.

Neither the *First Revised Metropolitan Plan* nor *The Greater Bangkok Plan 2543* yet has official approval; in time, perhaps, revised plans will be approved. Planning legislation is being considered; in time, planning legislation may be enacted. The first administrative step towards co-ordinated metropolitan-wide development has been taken; in time, metropolitan-wide development may be undertaken. Meanwhile, indiscriminate growth continues and will reduce the advantages that might be gained from integrated planned development for some time to come.

SOURCE: This chapter is an amalgamation of 'Planning the Future of Bangkok', previously published in Dwyer, D. J. (ed.), *The City as a Centre of Change in Asia*, Hong Kong University Press, Hong Kong (1972), pp. 243–54, and parts of 'Bangkok 2000' which was previously published in Ho, R. and Chapman, E. C. (eds.), *Studies of Contemporary Thailand*, Department of Human Geography, Australian National University, Canberra 1973. The author has revised the text for this volume.

REFERENCES

1. I would hesitate to consider the degraded human environment characteristic of large portions of the city as necessary or inevitable, and I do not minimise the immediate plight of large numbers of the inhabitants of some of the great cities of the world and particularly of Asia; indeed, it has been remarked that perhaps the only difference between the situation of large portions of the population of some large cities and that of the victims of a natural

disaster is that no campaigns are mounted to come to the rescue of the former.

2. The First National Economic Development Plan (1961–66) has been followed by the Second National Economic and Social Development Plan (1967–71).

3. The Population Census of 1970 will consider as 'urban' residents of municipalities and of *sukhaphiban* (sanitary districts) with at least 10 000 inhabitants. This is too generous a definition since *sukhaphiban* are overwhelmingly rural and, in fact, many municipalities include a large number of agriculturalists. Here, only those resident in the 120 municipalities are considered 'urban'.

4. See LARRY STERNSTEIN (1966). Contemplating a Hierarchy of Centres in Thailand. *Pacific Viewpoint*, Vol. 7, pp. 229–35; The distribution of Thai centres at mid-nineteenth century. *J. Southeast Asian History*, 7 (1966), 66–72; An historical atlas of Thailand. *J. Siam Society*, 52 (1964), 1–20.

5. A Greater Bangkok Metropolitan Area administration is being considered. The choice has narrowed to two schemes: in one (favoured by academicians), three elected representatives from each of several Metropolitan districts would elect a Lord Mayor who would work with an appointed Governor; in the other (favoured by government officials), three elected representatives from each of several Metropolitan districts would elect a Lord Mayor who would work with a Metropolitan Board including representatives from the various ministries and an appointed Governor. The area to be included is not yet finalised but would include the trans-river municipalities of Bangkok and Thon Buri as well as Nonthaburi to the north and Samut Prakan to the south.

6. A City and Town Planning Act was passed in 1952, but a Royal Decree is necessary to activate it in any particular place. In reality, the Act is concerned with construction and reconstruction rather than with planning and places a heavy financial burden on the particular municipality concerned. The Act has not been applied in Bangkok and only in a very few instances up-country.

7. Note must also be taken, however, of the number of the 'developing' countries which have laws but do not use them. See, for example, A. A. SOLOW. Tools and Techniques for Implementation of Urban Planning. *Urbanization in Developing Countries*, International Union of Local Authorities, The Hague (1968), p. 117.

8. See LARRY STERNSTEIN. Municipality of Bangkok: a Critique of Population Data and a Proposed Reorientation of the Registration & Statistics Division. *Greater Bangkok Metropolitan Area Population Studies, Number 1*, Municipality of Bangkok, December 1968.

9. Mom Chao Athiphon Phong Kasem Si, former Director of the National Statistical Office, provides a brief, informative history in 'The Chronicle of Statistics in Thailand to my Knowledge and Memory, in *National Statistical Office, Office of the Prime Minister*, published on the occasion of the inaugural ceremony of the National Statistical Office, September 1956, pp. 11–31 (in Thai).

10. This is an unfortunate consequence of what may be termed 'mimic-planning' —planning based squarely on happenings elsewhere and inevitably lagging behind current thinking. New York and London, renowned for the efficiency of their mass-transit systems, now acknowledge the need to turn the 'single purpose, eight hours a day, five days a week, commercial centre to a full-time, well-balanced commercial, residential and sight-seeing area where

people live, work and play . . .', and in each of these cities huge developments are now underway. In New York, for example, the Battery Park City Corporation Authority, created in 1968, is to develop Battery Park City on 104 acres (42 hectares) in lower Manhattan as a waterfront residential and commercial community at a cost of some 1·1 billion dollars. See 'Battery Park City to cost $1·1 billion', *Metropolitan Area Digest*, **11** (November–December 1968), The Graduate School of Public Affairs, State University of New York, p. 6.

11. See National Statistical Office, *Preliminary Report of the Labour Force Survey: Bangkok-Thon Buri Municipal Areas 1966–7*, Bangkok, 1968. The first *Report of the Labour Force Survey; Bangkok-Thon Buri Municipal Areas 1965–6*, National Statistical Office, Office of the Prime Minister, Bangkok 1967, indicated also that somewhat more than 15 per cent of all employed were employed by government.

12. This is not to imply, of course, that extension of government offices alone is bringing this change; a substantial portion of the area between the Ong Ang Canal and the Chao Phraya River has been occupied by or reserved for government and religious use since the very founding of the capital.

13. *The Greater Bangkok Plan 2533 (A.D. 1990)* is the final report on the Bangkok-Thon Buri City Planning Project undertaken jointly by the Thai Government, represented by the Ministry of Interior, and the International Co-operation Administration, represented by the United States Operations Mission to Thailand. Litchfield, Whiting, Bowne & Associates, Architects and Engineers, of New York City and Adams, Howard and Greeley of Cambridge, Massachusetts, were consultants. The contract was entered upon in December 1957 and, following some expansion in scope, terminated in August 1960.

14. See Sternstein (1968), *op. cit.* The Population Census of 1960, the first by the Central (now National) Statistical Office, is the most informative yet taken, many characteristics of the population becoming known for the first time. None of the data elicited were used in preparing *The Greater Bangkok Plan 2533*. Apparently, advance returns for the Metropolitan Area were not requested or could not be supplied in time since the contract between the Thai Government and its consultants terminated in August 1960.

15. Indeed, the consultants thought of the future land-use pattern presented as the Plan. See *The Greater Bangkok Plan 2533*, Litchfield, Whiting, Bowne and Associates and Adams, Howard and Greeley, Bangkok, August 2503 (1960), pp. 68–70.

16. Further, under the 'new' planning philosophy a 'Plan' is not prepared. See, for example, A. Waterson *et al.*, *Development Planning, Lessons in Experience*, Baltimore (1965). J. Friedmann, Planning as Innovation: the Chilean Case. *J. Am. Inst. Planners*, **32** (1966), 194–204; and Calcutta Metropolitan Planning Organisation, *Basic Development Plan, Calcutta Metropolitan District, 1966–1986*, Calcutta (1966).

17. Department of Town and Country Planning. *Report on the First Revision of the Plan for the Metropolitan Area*, Bangkok (1971) (in Thai).

18. See Larry Sternstein. Greater Bangkok Metropolitan Area: Population Growth and Movement 1956–1960 and Research for Planning, the Traffic Problem. *Greater Bangkok Metropolitan Area Population Studies; Number 2*, Office of the Municipal Adviser, Municipality of Bangkok (1969).

19. A. Chancharoensook. *Memorandum Describing Activities Under the Responsibility for Planning and Proffering Advice Concerning the Future of Bangkok* or *The Greater Bangkok Plan 2543*, Bangkok (1969) (in Thai).

15 New Cities in Venezuela

ALAN TURNER and
JONATHAN SMULIAN

THE planning and building of new centres of urban growth should be thought of as one element of a comprehensive national strategy to contain expansion, and to provide housing and job opportunities in a regional framework. They must be closely allied to programmes of urban renewal and revitalisation in the older cities. In the United States the sporadic and poorly distributed development of new towns by the private sector will only absorb a very small fraction of population growth and it is this aspect which has motivated the severest critics of American new towns.

To be effective there must be a national and regional policy of locating new towns or cities in those places where spatial relationships with existing centres of population will work to their mutual advantage. In Britain for example, 29 new towns have been designated since 1947 and 800 000 people are living in the first 22[1]. They have been extremely successful in social and economic terms and are entirely due to a national policy initiated by central government. In America, on the other hand, there is no policy and 'new towns' are almost entirely privately inspired. 'As critics like Marshal Kaplan have pointed out the new town label has been placed wrongly on hundreds of large but ordinary subdivisions giving rise to misleading statements about the number of new towns here'[2]. Consequently there are many calls for a national policy such as that by the National Committee on Urban Growth Policy calling for '100 new communities averaging 100 000 population each and 10 new communities of at least 1 000 000'[3]. The point has now been taken by leading legislators, and bills which will help to implement a policy are before Congress.

If there is a case for new towns in highly developed countries with good regional structure, to what extent can a policy contribute to the effective growth of regional centres in a developing country?

For References to this chapter, see page 253. This is an abbreviated version of the original article.

It is the authors' intention to demonstrate the gradual emergence of a Venezuelan programme based on relatively ad hoc decisions to build three new cities. The first of these, Ciudad Guayana, is already well known[4]; the second and third, Tuy Medio and El Tablazo, are less so.

The country has no 'new towns' policy as such. No legislation exists governing the design or implementation of new towns and there are only limited tools for acquisition of land on a large scale in the public interest. Any corporation controlling large scale development would require a special act of Congress to establish its powers and fiscal resources. Thus the three new cities planned in Venezuela are very much an adjunct of other development decisions taken at national level or are planned as the partial expression of unresolved regional and sub-regional policies. Ciudad Guayana was envisaged in 1960 as a means of establishing ordered development for a population which had already settled in the area as a result of the granting of major resource development concessions and massive government investments which commenced 10 years prior to the city's conception. The idea of a new city in the Tuy Medio was conceived in 1957 as the first of a number of satellite cities to be located in the Caracas sub-region with the purpose of acting as a brake to population migration into the capital city and as a reception area for overflow population and industry. El Tablazo, 10 km (6 miles) from the regional capital of Maracaibo across the Lake was proposed in 1967 as a reception city for the wave of urban population which it was considered would be attracted to the area by the Government's decision to build a major capital-intensive petro-chemical plant.

THE NATIONAL CONTEXT

Venezuela is a country of great contrasts, both natural and man-made. The north of the country, along the Caribbean, varies between arid plains, fertile valleys and mountainous regions and supports almost the entire population. The southern part, south of the cattle-rearing Llanos, is largely impenetrable jungle supporting no more than a handful of Indians. In the towns the contrast between rich and poor is apparent to even a casual visitor; the ever present 'ranchos' or shacks on the hillsides are a constant reminder of this. And yet Venezuela is by no means a poor country—the per capita income is about $1000 (£417), which is high by Latin American standards. Unfortunately, the national wealth is unevenly distributed and the great majority of people are still very poor.

The production of petroleum accounts for about 20 per cent of the GNP and oil has been the sole reason for Venezuela's wealth. The oil industry is, however, notoriously capital intensive and is becoming more so, with the consequence that fewer and fewer people are able to share directly in the country's most valuable resource. It is a common sight in the State of Zulia (the site of one of the new

Table 15.1   Population Forecasts (thousands)

Forecasting authority	1970	1980	1990	2000
Instituto Nacional de Obras Sanitorias, 1962	10 163	13 658	18 177	23 957
Ministerio de Fomento, 1963	10 399	14 283	19 574	26 267
Ministerior de Obras Publicas	10 486	15 524	—	—

Source: MOP Oficina Ministerial del Transporte Estudios de Poblacion.

cities) to see an automatic oil pump slowly sucking wealth out of the soil, surrounded by the shacks of desperately poor people for whom the industry will never provide employment.

The rate of population growth is high and this compounds the problem; in 1961 the population of the country was 7 524 000 and of this total 33 per cent were aged 0–9 and 21 per cent were aged 10–19. In other words more than half the population was under 19. This high proportion of young people coupled with improving medical services is responsible for a very rapid growth rate as the various forecasts in Table 15.1 show.

In round figures the population of 10 million today is going to double by 1990, and the sheer physical task of housing and creating job opportunities for this new population is going to require effort and imagination on a huge scale. It would be simplistic to think that housing will ever be 'provided' for the whole population. The normal market method of building for sale or rent will not for the foreseeable future have any meaning at all for the 44 per cent of families in the country as a whole who earn less than Bs 500 a month (£50). The cost of housing bears no relation to the ability of these families to pay, and they will no doubt continue to build their own 'improvised' housing. It will be shown later that future housing policies must accept this and make the labours of this large section of the community an integral part of the programme[5].

In common with other Latin American countries Venezuela is experiencing a very high rate of urbanisation, and the flow of migrants to the cities shows little sign of slowing down. At present about 67 per cent of the population live in cities and towns compared with 70 per cent for the USA, 80 per cent for Britain and 36 per cent for Brazil[6]. Migratory trends have been predominantly towards the prosperous central region, the Valencia-Maracay Basin and Caracas itself, with the result that about 600 000 of the 2 000 000 people who live in Caracas are estimated to live in improvised housing. The imbalance in the regional structure of the country is probably the key to the problem. Although Venezuela is approaching the level of urbanisation of developed societies such as Western Europe or the United States, it is still dominated by the capital and the surrounding central region to an extent that would be unworkable in those countries. This aspect of regionalism in the development of a country's economy has been extremely well analysed by John Friedmann in his excellent book on regional planning policy[7]. Friedmann puts forward the thesis that the importance of regionalism varies over the period of national development. He says that a regional planning policy is inappropriate in a pre-industrial society, is critical in a transitional society and that in a post-industrial society, such as the United States, there is a 'shift in focus'[8] to urban renewal and metropolitan planning.

Venezuela is essentially a transitional society and the dominance of Caracas in relation to regional capitals makes an overwhelming case for regional development plans. 'Venezuela may in some ways be considered the perfect prototype for a study of regional policy. The spatial structure of the economy has a classical simplicity. Until recently, it was moulded chiefly in the image of the centre-periphery model. Political power, wealth and population were heavily concentrated upon Caracas while the periphery, excepting the oil regions, deteriorated out of mind of Venezuela's central decision makers'[9]. The government of Venezuela has been trying to redress this regional imbalance and the proposals for the new cities are evidence of this.

Ciudad Guayana is sited at the confluence of the rivers Orinoco and Caroni in the mineral rich Guayana region. The new city is a part of one of the world's most important regional development plans which was created in 1959 by President Betancourt who recognised the potential of the region and formed the Corporacion Venezolana de Guayana to develop it. The Corporation engaged the assistance of the Joint Centre for Urban Studies of the Massachusetts Institute of Technology and Harvard University, and the new city is now well into the stages of implementation. Its ultimate population is expected to be 300 000 to 400 000. It is not a purpose of this article to add to what has been written about Guayana; however, its importance as the first of the current Venezuelan new cities is paramount.

The second proposal, made by the Ministerio de Obras Publicas, was for a new city of 400 000 accompanied by induced expansion of three existing towns in the Tuy Valley south of Caracas[10]. The third new city, El Tablazo, also proposed by the Ministerio, is to be located across the lake from Maracaibo in the oil-producing region of Zulia[11].

The pattern produced by these proposals is shown in Fig. 15.1 and takes the form of three major new nodes of development spaced evenly (about 563 km [350 miles] apart) across the north of the country. Ciudad Guayana is a new resource frontier and will attract migration; Tuy Medio and El Tablazo are located at the foci of major apparent migratory movements, as recorded by Friedmann[12].

THE REGIONAL BACKGROUNDS OF TUY MEDIO AND EL TABLAZO

The regional backgrounds of the two proposed cities are very different. Caracas is still the dominant centre of Venezuela. It is the centre of industry, information and government. Its population of 2 000 000 is expected to be 4 500 000 by 1990. The city itself is situated in a long narrow valley measuring about 15 by 5 km (9 by 3 miles), situated 880 metres (2900 feet) above sea level. It is connected to the Litoral or north coast by a four-lane toll road which winds majestically through the mountains down to the port of La Guira, and the airport of Maiquetia. This is the one and only lifeline connecting the capital directly to the nearest outlets to foreign trade. To the west, along the fertile valleys of Valencia and Maracay, important sites for industrial location form a crescent

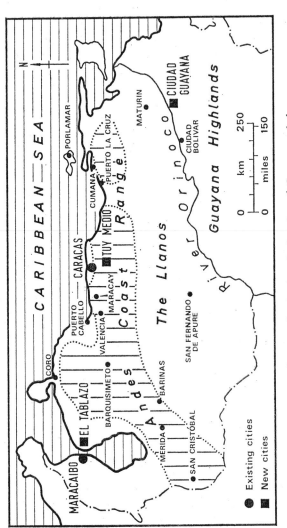

Fig. 15.1 Map of Venezuela showing the location of Caracas and the new towns of El Tablazo, Tuy Medio and Ciudad Guayana.

which ends with the port of Puerto Cabello. The modern and beautiful toll road which has been built from Caracas to Valencia passes through the western part of the Tuy Valley and thus has connected it into the sphere of influence of industrial expansion. To the east lie more mountains and the smaller valley of Guatire-Guarenas. The Venezuelan government has proposals to extend the Valencia highway through the Tuy Valley eastwards to the Guayana region. This will place the Tuy Medio at what might be called the national crossroads, and will make it an extremely important centre for new urbanisation.

The reasons for developing a new city in the central region can be stated as follows:

(1) to relieve pressure on Caracas;

(2) to provide a counter magnet for migration;

(3) to provide a more even distribution of population in the central region;

(4) to provide sites for industrial development which can no longer be found in Caracas;

(5) by providing new centres of development for industry, to satisfy a large percentage of the increasing demand for consumer goods in a growing economy;

(6) to reduce the reliance on heavy industry in the country as a whole.

In other words, the main reason for development of the Tuy Medio is to take some of the heat off Caracas caused by the very rapidly increasing population of Venezuela which over the next 20 years will produce very intense demands for housing and employment, particularly in the central region.

A measure of the problem is given by the forecast of the Ministerio de Obras Publicas for a population of about 9 000 000 people in the Caracas-Valencia sub-region in 1990, and about 4 500 000 people in Caracas. The number of economically active people is expected to increase from 886 000 in 1961 to about 2 500 000 in 1980. That is to say there will be an extra 1 500 000 people seeking work in the next ten years in the Caracas-Valencia sub-region. The conclusion reached has been that it will be necessary to locate approximately half a million people in the Tuy Medio by the year 1990, in addition o the future population of the Valencia-Maracay basin, the Litoral, the Guatire-Guarenas valley and Caracas itself.

Land in the Caracas Valley is becoming increasingly scarce, especially for industrial use. The strategy, therefore, is to try to attract population both from Caracas itself and also migrating population from other parts of the country, to relocate in the new growth area in the Tuy valley. Employment will be mainly in manufacturing industries and in public and private services. The major market will be Caracas.

The context of the new city at El Tablazo is very different. It is situated in the state of Zulia on the opposite bank of the lake from the city of Maracaibo. Maracaibo has a population of about 600 000 people, which is expected to grow to 1 000 000 by 1990. Traditionally the region has been dependent on the oil industry which, as has been pointed out, is extremely capital intensive. . . .

The region has a high rate of unemployment (in 1961, only 22·7 per cent of the population of Zulia was classified as remuneratively occupied) and a large increase in population is forecast, from about 1 080 000 in 1968 to 2 000 000 in 1990. The Venezuelan government, therefore, took the decision to establish a new petro-chemical industry at El Tablazo which, with its related secondary industries, would provide a major new source of employment. This was to be the economic base of the new city. However, it soon became obvious to the consultants that the petro-chemical industry would only support a small town of about 25 000 people, and that even allowing for secondary industries using basic petro-chemical products the increasing demand for work in the sub-region would not be met. A study of economic factors, demographic trends and migration suggested that the optimum size for a new city at El Tablazo would be about 300 000. This would be big enough to compete with Maracaibo as a place for higher paid workers to live; one of the problems of a small town across the lake from the regional capital was that it would almost certainly be inhabited only by the workers who could not afford to live elsewhere. The goal, therefore, was to avoid the image of the one-industry one-class town, by attracting a wide range of industries not necessarily directly related to petro-chemicals.

REGIONAL INTERACTION

Although the two new cities are some 560 km (350 miles) distant and their economic bases are quite different, they really form two poles of a single national strategy; that of absorbing in-migration to the central region and of reducing out-migration from the western states. Population forecasts for the Maracaibo region, after allowing for reasonable growth in the smaller towns, show an excess of 32 000 people who may migrate to Maracaibo in search of work, producing a city of 1 320 000.

Alternatively a large part of this population may migrate towards Caracas, increasing the problems of the central region. The adopted strategy of establishing a large new city at El Tablazo is intended to attract a great deal of the predicted population increase and to help prevent massive migration from Zulia to the Caracas region. However, some west–east migration must be anticipated as must further natural growth of the Caracas region and the new city at Tuy Medio is intended to absorb this growth. The two new cities are therefore components of a national system rather than unrelated growth points.

PLANNING PROPOSALS

The major conceptual framework for the two new cities may be summarised as follows:

1. *A clear statement of goals*

This immediately raises the question of whose goals; the government's? The planners? The community's? Ideally the answer should be an amalgam of all three but in Venezuela at the present time there is no mechanism for community involvement. Even if there were, there is no simple way to define who 'the community' is, especially when designing a new town. Should the 12 000 people in Altagracia speak for the eventual 300 000, many of whom are living in dispersed parts of Zulia, and most of whom are not even born? Will the experience and life style of the people in Altagracia enable them to speak for what will be a more sophisticated population?

In the event, the goals that were adopted were proposed by the planners as their view of a reasonable basis for structuring a new town in Venezuela. Implicit in the goals was the need to organise the incoming migrants so that as a real community developed, it would have an increasing share in the process of deciding its own future. The goals, therefore, were interim in nature and will need constant review and re-evaluation in the light of future social change.

2. *Flexibility in the physical plan*

To achieve the greatest degree of potential for change, land use plans were developed which dispersed major traffic generators fairly evenly over the whole town. At the same time a uniform coverage of primary roads in the form of a grid ensured that these dispersed generators would have fairly even accessibility. The grid in Tuy Medio was about 1·5 kilometres square and at El Tablazo about 1 kilometre square. The interstices of the grid became the 'cells' of the plan which would have their own identity. The difference in size relates largely to different assumptions about bus routes. At Tuy Medio the buses were routed through the cells on the secondary roads; 'bus-only links' gave them a built-in advantage over private cars. At El Tablazo the buses were routed on the primary roads and the smaller grid size gave acceptable walking distances. Each cell would have a mixture of land uses although some would be predominantly residential and some predominantly industrial.

In this way changes in land use could take place over time without destroying the validity of the primary road-network; huge tidal flows would be avoided.

The flexibility achieved is naturally limited and there are fixed elements such as the main roads and certain major land uses. The planning goal was to achieve a scale of fixity in which some areas would be 'hard' and some 'soft'. In the Venezuelan context, where development control is limited and most low cost housing is improvised by the families who live in it, it is important to distinguish in this way. At El Tablazo, in order to provide a simply administered development system, it was proposed that there should be a band adjacent to the primary roads where there would be tight control; this band would be used largely for higher-density housing and non-residential uses. The 'soft-centre' of the cell would be less strictly controlled, densities would be lower and large areas would be set aside for improvised housing.

3. *Acceptance of the 'rancho' as a major component of the total housing programme*

Forty-four per cent of families in the country earn less than 500 Bolivares (£50) a month. The national housing agency, Banco Obrero, has not so far attempted to provide low cost housing suited to these families' needs. In other words about 4 000 000 people must find shelter without any help from government housing institutions and these people are in the lowest income group. The statistics are somewhat unreliable and the definition of 'sub-standard housing' varies, but in 1950 it was estimated that although three-quarters of the houses in Venezuela were owner-occupied, more than half had mud floors and less than a third had running water[13].

'Rancho' building is a vital part of Venezuelan life. A simple structure composed largely of scrap materials will suffice in the early years of a family's life in the city. As time goes by the original shack is replaced on the same site by a much more sophisticated dwelling having clay or concrete block walls, tiled roof and glazing. It may have electricity and running water but seldom, if ever, main drainage.

In Caracas it is common to hear people say, 'The ranchos must be removed—we must tear them down and build new housing in their place'. Even if this were possible from an economic point of view it is probably not socially desirable. Anthropologists have shown that there is a strong sense of community in the *barrio* and it has become evident that the physical task of building their own houses gives the residents a greater stability than might be expected in mass housing projects[14]. Furthermore the vast (if amateur) labour supply of 'do-it-yourselfers' becomes in effect a component part of the building industry. To ignore this in a new city would be completely unrealistic but to accept it means setting relatively low standards of environment, at least in the early years, and it means discarding preconceived notions of what large parts of the city are going to look like.

Several policies were defined in the planning proposals which would enable land to be parcelled out to new immigrants and yet leave open certain options for the future. For instance, it was thought to be essential that main drainage and sewerage lines should be installed before land parcels were made available.* Assuming that the buildings would change but the parcels would remain (that is, better houses in the same parcels) the housing density would remain constant and the service installations would not become overloaded. However, it was suggested that certain sites might be chosen for large scale housing developments to be carried out within a few years, and that in these cases the services could be installed for the

---

* This was not the case in Ciudad Guayana, where large housing areas have developed without main services.

later project and used below capacity by squatters until such time as the permanent housing could be made available.

4. *The need for new institutional forms to implement large scale developments*

It has become apparent in the last two decades that intervening in the urban development process is so complex that the existing structure of local government cannot cope with the task.

It follows that large scale planned developments cannot take place in the absence of new powerful organisations with all the necessary expertise to see the job through. In Venezuela there are two possible existing agencies: the Ministry of Public Works and the local authorities. The Ministry is responsible for planning over the whole country and it is understaffed and overloaded; the local authorities are so weak that they could not conceivably do the work. It was considered to be absolutely essential to create new and powerful development corporations for both the Tuy Medio and El Tablazo, with offices in the development areas and a full complement of trained professionals.

5. *The need to ensure a balance of public and private investment*

Misconceptions about the nature of new towns are widespread. In the United States there is a view that the British new towns are 'government new towns' and, therefore, irrelevant to the American situation. The assumption is that they are funded entirely from tax money, while the American new towns are entirely the result of private investment. The truth is that there is a considerable element of private investment in the British new towns in the commercial and industrial areas and this is now beginning to apply to housing. It is also certain that the American new towns are not going to supply housing for the lower income groups without federal programmes to help pay the bill. The same thing is true in Venezuela; it will be impossible to build balanced new towns unless the load of investment is carried by both the public and private sectors. One of the first jobs of the new development corporations will be to initiate massive public relations campaigns which will encourage private industry to locate in the new towns.

These general principles formed a basis for the planning of the cities in the Tuy Medio and El Tablazo, but the different physical and economic conditions produced plans having distinct qualities. . .

NEW CITY, TUY MEDIO

The rate of migration into the central region of the country is increasing and Caracas is receiving population at approximately 80 000 persons per year.

As early as 1956, forward-looking government planners, working without the legal or administrative control mechanisms to contain this deluge, proposed as a partial remedy the construction of a new city in the valley of the Tuy Medio. This valley, some 45 minutes by road to south of the capital, is skirted by the main national motorway linking Caracas with the west of the country. It is a low lying valley, some 300 metres (984 feet) above sea level, in contrast to Caracas at 880 metres (2900 feet) above sea level, and historically has been an agricultural area served by six small market towns. The valley is separated from Caracas to the north by the mountains on the coastal range.

The government, apart from expropriating some 6900 hectares (17 000 acres) in 1957, between the small towns of Santa Teresa and Santa Lucia in the eastern extremity of the valley, shelved plans for a new city until 1967, when interest was again aroused in the idea of finding land to relocate congested Caracas industrial installations and alleviate the vast population pressures engulfing the capital.

At a sub-regional scale, five alternative development strategies were assessed. These ranged from the extreme of encouraging large expansion of the existing towns to take a valley population of 500 000 persons in 1990, with no new city; to a new city to take all the estimated population allied to a policy restricting growth in existing towns.

After assessing the various strategic alternatives a plan was devised by which industry and population would be attracted to a new city in the initial stages. This would allow a period for the existing towns to have major improvements carried out to their substandard services infrastructure which would in turn stimulate limited growth. The target populations for 1990 are shown in Table 15.2.

An earlier project to continue the main national highway through the valley to link the east of the country with Caracas and the west, was revived and relocated to form the southern limit of the city. Thus the city would be sited at the very fulcrum of Venezuela's national road network with easy access to all the major ports and markets.

The total valley population for 1990 of half a million was estimated on the basis of demographic projections and migrational tendencies into the Central Region. Caracas itself was expected to grow to 4·5 million inhabitants by 1990[15]. The employment structure of the new city was predicted in relation to the number of jobs needed to support such a population and the type of light industry which, it was considered, would wish to locate in the Tuy to take advantage of its proximity to the main consumer market, available cheap land

Table 15.2   The Target Populations for 1990

Town	Population
New City at Santa Teresa	417 000
Ocumare	86 000
Charallave	48 000
Cua	33 000
Remainder of valley	11 000
Total	595 000

and the possibility of establishing a stable labour force by providing new housing close to the sources of employment. In order to reduce pressure on the capital, the city was designed to be as self-sufficient as possible; to provide a wide range of work opportunities and a choice of housing types and locations. It was considered that given these new facilities and inducements in terms of social, recreational, and educational services, which would become gradually more difficult to use in Caracas itself, commuting between the two cities could be cut to a minimum.

The city, sited in two parallel valleys, was designed to grow out from Santa Teresa and Santa Lucia in order to use existing roads as development spurs and make the most economic use of existing services.

The structure of the city was determined by a primary road network in the form of a 1·5 kilometre grid fitted on to an undulating site. Within the cells created by the grid, a residential population of some 25 000 persons was divided into units of 5000–6000 persons.

The primary network has limited access and is designed to facilitate cross-town movement; a secondary road system carrying public transport feeds into and across the main cells, serving local centres and residential population.

The central business district of the city is sited on the ridge which separates the two valleys. The centre can be seen from virtually the whole area of the city and should act as a focus to development. It will begin on a district-centre scale between 5 and 10 years after construction of the city commences. Its service potential is reinforced by three new district centres, each located to service some 80 000 persons. The redeveloped centres of Santa Teresa and Santa Lucia serve as additional district centres. Figure 15.2 shows the development for 1990.

In order to create the greatest possible flexibility and to safeguard against the formation of large one-income areas within the city, development sites for specific groups have been kept as small as possible. This is particularly important as it is estimated that of the incoming population—a growth rate of 20 000 a year is predicted— some 20 per cent will be able to afford housing built by the private sector, 60 per cent will be served by public agencies and the remainder will have to be settled in reception areas, where plots will be available for improvised housing.

A number of policies including progressive improvement and self-help schemes have been suggested in the plan. It is certain that great numbers of immigrants in the lowest income brackets will have to be incorporated in the new city. Social development plans are being prepared and the administrative structure to support these plans is being designed.

A development corporation based on the British new town's type of agency was suggested under the quinquennial fiscal control of the Ministry of Public Works. It was considered a fundamental strategic consideration that a planning team should be set up on the site at the earliest opportunity to show confidence in the project.

To date the government has made no move to set up a development corporation or expropriate the additional area needed to build the city. However, industries are already locating close to Santa Teresa. Under existing laws, it is only by negotiation that these industries, already creating 400 new jobs, can be located so as to fit into the proposed plan. In order to use every possible existing development agency, plans are being prepared to use new services

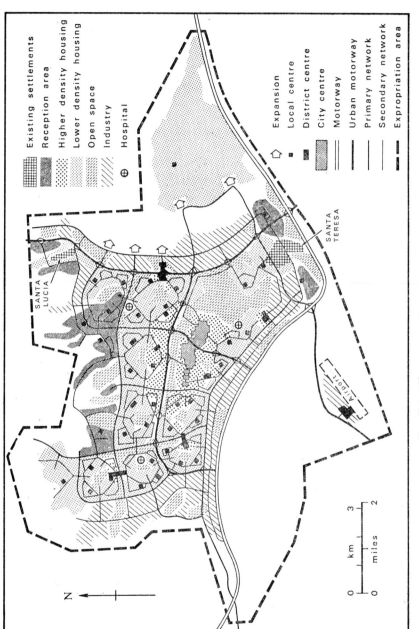

Legend:

Existing settlements
Reception area
Higher density housing
Lower density housing
Open space
Industry
Hospital

Expansion
Local centre
District centre
City centre
Motorway
Urban motorway
Primary network
Secondary network
Expropriation area

SANTA LUCIA

SANTA TERESA

N

0   1   2   3   km
0   1   2 miles

Fig. 15.2 The new city of Santa Teresa in 1990.

infrastructure which already has a financial allocation in the 1970 budget. Construction agencies such as the Workers' Bank and the Rural Housing Agency are being persuaded to locate new development along these service lines. It is hoped that the development will gradually gather sufficient impetus to attract major fiscal allocations and government support.

SOURCE: *Town Planning Review*, **42**, 1971, pp. 3–18.

REFERENCES

1. F. J. OSBORN and A. WHITTICK (1969). *The New Towns: The Answers to Megalopolis*, Leonard Hill, London pp. 139–416.
2. *J. Am. Inst. Planners*, November (1967), p. 40.
3. *The New City*, Urban America Inc. (1969), p. 172.
4. LLOYD RODWIN. Ciudad Guayana: a new city. *Scient. Am.* (September, 1965).
5. The general problem of improvised housing in Latin America has been well covered by JOHN TURNER and WILLIAM MANGIN. In particular: Squatter Settlements, by William Mangin, *Scient. Am.* (October 1967); and Barriadas, by William Mangin and John Turner in *Progr. Arch.* (May 1968).
6. EMRYS JONES. *Towns and Cities*, Oxford University Press, London (1966), chap. 2.
7. JOHN FRIEDMANN. *Regional Development Policy: A Case Study of Venezuela.* MIT Press, Cambridge, Mass.
8. *Ibid.*, p. 7.
9. *Ibid.*, p. 123.
10. Llewelyn-Davies Weeks Forestier-Walker & Bor, planning consultants, Nathaniel Lichfield & Associates, economic consultants, in association with the Ministerio de Obras Publicas, *Planning Proposals for the Tuy Medio, Venezuela* (March 1968).
11. Llewelyn-Davies Weeks Forestier-Walker & Bor, Nathaniel Lichfield & Associates, in association with the Ministerio de Obras Publicas. *El Tablazo New City: Development Proposals for a new city at El Tablazo, Estado Zulia,* February 1969.
12. J. FRIEDMANN. *Op. cit.* map 7.
13. EDWIN LIUEWEN. *Venezuela*, Oxford University Press, London (1965), p. 14.
14. LIZA PEATTIE. *The view from the Barrio.* University of Michigan Press.
15. ANTHONY PENFOLD. Caracas. Urban Growth and Transportation. *Tn Plann. Rev.*, **42** (April 1970), p. 103.